Dad,

With all of my heart [I give you?] this gift of love. I pray [that God?] will teach us both the truth from His word so we can grow in our faith and trust in Jesus. I know I've learned so much about sincerity and integraty by the way you have lived your life. You have set a power ful example in those areas for me.

Dad, I love you so much and I ask God that as you read this book from day to day that you and I to- gether can learn to trust and believe for miracles. We need them. Amen and Amen.

Happy Birthday!

Love,
your son,
Mitch

DAILY BLESSING

DAILY BLESSING

A Guide to Seed-Faith Living

ORAL ROBERTS

FLEMING H. REVELL COMPANY
OLD TAPPAN, NEW JERSEY

Library of Congress Cataloging in Publication Data

Roberts, Oral.
 Daily blessing.

 Selections from the Daily blessing magazine.
 Includes index.
 1. Devotional calendars—Methodist Church.
I. Title.
BV4811.R62   242'.2   78-12233
ISBN 0-8007-0962-4

CONTENTS

PREFACE

The day God healed me of tuberculosis He called me to take His healing power to my generation. Only a boy of seventeen at the time, I had no idea what He meant. But in 1947 God began to show me. He gave me a vision of people as He sees them. I saw that everyone is sick in some way . . . that everyone hurts either spiritually, mentally, or physically. And it was when I caught this vision of a sick and needy humanity that this ministry of healing began.

One of the means God has given me to take God's healing power to those who are hurting is *Daily Blessing* magazine. Since 1959 this pocket-size quarterly magazine has been touching the lives of people, uplifting them when they are down, inspiring them when they are faced with problems, giving them hope when they are near despair.

I've based these devotionals on the fundamental principles of this ministry—that God is a good God, that each of us is unique and irreplaceable to Him, and that He wants us to get all our needs met through giving and receiving, or what I call the three miracle keys of seed-faith living—

- Looking to God as the Source of our total supply
- Giving of ourselves and all that we have as seeds of faith
- Expecting many miracles from His mighty hand.

I've chosen some of the very best of *Daily Blessing* for this book. I can think of no better way to start the day than by reading a fresh uplifting thought based on God's Word. I pray and believe that as you read and study these daily messages your whole life will be healed, enriched, and blessed.

ORAL ROBERTS

DAILY BLESSING

JANUARY

January 1

From A to Z

Christ is the heart and theme of the Bible. From Genesis to Revelation, the message revolves around the person and work of Jesus Christ. All things reveal Him and point to Him.

From before creation Christ was, and into the eternal ages He is. The Bible says, "In the beginning was the Word, and the Word was with God, and the Word was God. And the Word was made flesh, and dwelt among us" (John 1:1, 14).

Jesus said, "I am Alpha and Omega, the beginning and the ending" (Revelation 1:8). The alphabet is the cornerstone of all literature. The numberless volumes in the libraries of the world are composed of a varying combination of its twenty-six letters. *Alpha* is the first letter in the Greek alphabet and *omega* is the last. Jesus chose these two symbols to describe Himself. Had He been speaking in English, He would have said, "I am the A and the Z." Or, "I am the alphabet."

What the alphabet is to literature, Christ is to all of life. He is its essence, its structure, and its composition. Jesus is called the Word of God because He is the full thought or expression of the mind of God. We know and understand the Father through Christ. He conveys the truth of God to us, just as the alphabet is the vehicle for bringing the thought of the author to the reader.

Christ permeates the Word of God with His presence. He springs forth from every page to meet every man in the form of his need. He knows your life from A to Z. He is acquainted with all your needs.

As I behold the wonders of Christ in God's Word, the sheer beauty and harmony of the Man fill my eyes with tears and I cry, "O Lord, that I might be like You!" I know this will be your feeling also as you become acquainted with Him through His Word.

11

January 2

A Leap of Faith

While filming a television special on top of Grandfather Mountain in the Blue Ridge Mountains of North Carolina, we saw young people flying hang gliders. The gliders were frames covered with nylon, with a harness underneath in which the fliers strapped themselves, and levers used to maneuver. I watched in awe as they leaped off the top of that 6,000-foot mountain and glided across the valley.

I asked some of them how they had faith to trust themselves to that nylon glider, how they could leap into space not knowing how they'd land. It looked frightening to me.

Each of the gliders had an answer, but one young man's really struck me. He said, "Well, I'll tell you how I have faith to do it. I watched other gliders. I saw them glide—and I believed if they could do it, I could."

I said, "You mean you had faith in their faith that it was possible?"

"Yeah," he said, "that's one way to put it. As I watched them leap off and land at a precise spot, as I saw the maneuverability of the gliders and the ability and courage of the people flying them, I began to live it, until it became an experience with me before I ever tried it."

"Well, weren't you scared the first time?"

He said, "A little, but once I was buckled in and I leaped off, I was okay. It was an exhilarating experience."

As we talked, it struck me that learning how to fly a glider is like learning how to trust God. It's all right to start by having faith in somebody else's faith, but then you have to live that experience in your heart until *you* do it.

Before you can have the joy and thrill of living a life of faith in God, you have to come to the point of taking that first leap of faith, that total surrender of your life to God, when you say: *I commit everything to You, Lord, trusting You to help me. And I know You will!* (Psalm 37:5 PARAPHRASED).

January 3

I Ran Out of Life

The secret of life is in EXPECTING MIRACLES. At one time I couldn't believe Jesus lives, let alone *does* anything. I lived as if He didn't exist. I had faith, but I didn't put it into Jesus Christ. I put it in myself—taking my life into my own hands and doing things my way.

The Bible was like a blur to me, its words meaningless. It didn't enter my mind to turn my life over to God, to have faith in Him as my personal Lord and Savior, or to use my faith as a seed I plant.

As for expecting miracles, I felt I could make my own. I made some. At least they appeared to be. I did a lot of things that excited me.

Then one day I ran out of life. Like a car out of gas, I couldn't go any further. *Life had stalled for me.* With bleeding lungs and hemorrhaging almost daily, where was my own power to make miracles? to control my life? to do it all myself?

That's when I woke up on the *inside*. I understood for the first time that *no man can ever make his own miracle.* Somewhere, sometime, he must come to the end of himself and establish a relationship with God. Out of this powerful new understanding, I repented of my sins and received Jesus Christ as my Lord and Savior.

A transformation began in me, vibrations of Christ's presence surged through me, *and I turned on to miracles.* A miracle of healing opened my lungs and loosed my stammering tongue. LIFE flowed up within my inner being. It never runs dry. It's there all the time. Day and night. Every minute. The only failures I've had have come because of my shortcomings—my failure to keep God as my Source, or to give first, or to expect a miracle.

Jesus said, "I am come that [you] might have LIFE, and . . . have it more ABUNDANTLY" (John 10:10). The miracle you need today is LIVING and EXISTING in the man Christ Jesus. Turn on to *His* life and power through faith. Know that He can do anything. After all, He is God! And when God speaks, it is so!

January 4

Seed of Benefit

> . . . *God turned into good what* [*was*] *meant for evil* . . . .
>
> Genesis 50:20 LB

Soon after my conversion and healing, I began preaching. My father, E. M. Roberts, was a well-known and powerful evangelist in those days. He and I would take turns preaching. The only trouble was, I couldn't preach as well as my father. And soon the pastors found it out. In one revival the pastor came to my father and said, "I just can't have this boy preaching again. Promise me that you will preach the rest of the meeting."

The next night, just before I was to preach, my father whispered, "Oral, I'd better take the service tonight." After a couple of services, I began to catch on. When this happened again and again, I decided to try the ministry on my own. Out of my rejection by this pastor, I was "kicked out of the nest" into my own ministry. It was one of the best things that ever happened to me.

I held a small meeting, and several people came to Christ. Soon I was being showered with invitations to hold meetings. This incident taught me a great spiritual lesson: *In every failure there is the seed of equivalent benefit that is as good as the one you lost, if you will look for it and apply it.*

January 5

"I See a Little Blue Spot!"

> *Happy is he that hath the God of Jacob for his help, whose hope is in the Lord his God.*
>
> Psalm 146:5

An accountant at Oral Roberts University is known for his irrepressible optimism. He has developed the very important habit of making his relationship with Christ constantly joyful and positive. For instance, when the weather is at its dreariest and other people see only the clouds, he looks for the patches of blue sky. With puddles everywhere, he'll point upward and say, "I see a little blue spot!"

And that is typical of his approach to life. No matter what the obvious situation is, he persists in being hopeful and cheerful, for he knows that there are "blue skies" somewhere close—and he looks for them.

This is not a Pollyanna attitude. It is an optimism based on a solid trust in the Lord. Genuine optimism is based on the faithfulness of God and stems from knowing that He is present and powerful in every situation.

January 6

"I Wish We Couldn't Feel"
by EVELYN ROBERTS

Let all those who take refuge and put their trust in You rejoice . . . because You make a covering over them and defend them.

Psalm 5:11 AMPLIFIED

One day a woman was telling me about the persecution and criticism she was suffering from her family. She said, "Evelyn, I wish I could get to the place where I didn't care what people say. But I feel so deeply that I get hurt."

I said, "You remind me of my granddaughter Brenda. She dropped a toy on her foot, and it hurt. She looked up through her tears and said, 'I wish we couldn't feel.' "

But we are human and we do feel. What Brenda wanted, of course, is what we all want—to be insensitive to life's hurts but to keep our capacity to enjoy pleasant feelings. This is an unrealistic dream, for much of the molding of our lives is done through avenues that wound us. But the economy of God is such that no hurt is wasted if we give it to Him to use for His glory. And nothing can harm you, because God's covering is between you and that which hurts you.

January 7

"All I Need Is on Deposit in Heaven"

God's riches are laid end to end across heaven, waiting to be given to you!

In the early days of this ministry, I applied for a building loan from a bank that had already made one building loan to us. We had paid off the first loan on time and had a good relationship with the bank. But, to my surprise, this time the banker refused. He said, "Mr. Roberts, you are a sincere young man. We believe you are doing a good work. But you are in religious work. From a business standpoint, we have no guarantee that you can repay us."

One day I was asking God to make this banker open up to us. As I did, I felt a check in my spirit. I remembered Philippians 4:19. I thought, "This banker is not God. He doesn't control all the money I need. God does. However, God's riches are in heaven. And that's a mighty long way off."

That's when it hit me! God didn't say He would supply my needs *with* His riches in heaven but *according* to His riches in heaven *by Christ Jesus*. That means here in the now. God was telling me that all I need is on deposit in heaven, but payable in the coin of the realm down here through Christ, if I would look to Him as my Source.

My inner man was now standing up instead of lying down. When I thought of the banker, I no longer disliked him, for he was only doing his job according to standard banking rules. I prayed for God to bless him for the first loan he had made, which helped me get started. Then I found myself praying for GOD to supply this loan I needed.

A few days later I saw God perform a miracle by causing the banker to change his mind. (*See* Proverbs 21:1.) I was the same man. My assets hadn't changed. But I was no longer looking to the bank. I was looking to the Source that never fails: GOD. And God gave me a miracle supply.

When I saw the banker a few weeks later, he smiled and said, "Reverend Roberts, I should have my head examined. I just don't know what possessed me to make this loan."

I smiled back and said, "I know."

January 8

The Bible Relates to You *Now*

The word of God is quick, and powerful . . . and is a discerner of the thoughts and intents of the heart.

Hebrews 4:12

One day a member of my staff said, "Brother Roberts, it amazes me how in your sermons you can adapt the Bible to any problem or situation of our day."

Maybe this is because I condition my mind to relate what I read in the Bible to the *now*. For example, I didn't live thousands of years ago, when the Bible was written. I know, however, that man has the same nature he has always had. And, despite different methods of living, his problems and needs are still the same. Even though I live in an age and generation entirely different outwardly from the times the Bible was written, as I read God's Word I feel in the deepest part of my being that God is talking to Oral Roberts. I am aware that God is! Always was—is—and ever shall be!

The Word comes alive to you when you realize that, through it, God is speaking to you personally. He is inviting you to enter into the experiences of the people in the Bible and to relate them to your own problems for comfort, peace, strength, guidance, enlightenment—all this and more.

January 9

God's Will Is Good

Don't let the world around you squeeze you into its own mould, but let God remould your minds from within, so that you may prove in practice that the Plan of God for you is good . . . .

Romans 12:2 PHILLIPS

Probably the biggest single question—and the source of more agony in Christians' personal lives—is the question concerning the will of God. How can I be sure what God's will is?

First, you can be sure that God's will for you is good, because God is a good God. That truth is basic in all the Bible. The idea that God is some kind of celestial killjoy intent upon making everyone miserable is a slur on God's character!

Listen to this Scripture: "He that spared not his own Son, but delivered him up for us all, how shall he not with him also freely give us all things?" (Romans 8:32). This is a good God, giving to His children—all things. Oswald J. Hoffman once said, "Having given us the package, will God not also give us the ribbon?" If God has given us the best He has, will He not give us those lesser bests that come day after day into our lives?

God's will for you is good. You can be sure of it, because God is a good God.

January 10

The Art of Listening
by RICHARD ROBERTS

There is . . . A time to be quiet . . . .
Ecclesiastes 3:1, 7 LB

A minister tells about a parishioner who frequently called him on the telephone to tell him about her problems. He says that as soon as he'd say hello, she'd start talking, and she'd chatter on and on, never letting him say a word. When she'd finish, she'd just hang up. Nothing irritated him more, and he began to dread her calls.

But one day it occurred to him that the way the woman talked to him was exactly the way he often talked to God. He'd tell God all the things he had to say, never stopping to listen to what God had to say in return.

I've found this true in my own prayer life. If I go on and on about my problems, I'm not really taking the time to listen to what God is saying.

The older I get, the more I recognize my need of taking time to be quiet so that I can hear what God is saying to me. As my dad, Oral Roberts, says: *Prayer is not an audition; it's a two-way conversation.*

January 11

Breakthrough From Heaven

In January 1977, a new fresh word from the Lord came to me. It exploded inside me one day while I was praying. And ever since, it's been burning in my soul, as the Prophet Jeremiah said, "as a burning fire shut up in my bones."

The word is *breakthrough*. Breakthrough from heaven for you and your loved ones!

For weeks, nearly every time I opened the Bible to read, the word *breakthrough* leaped at me. I was reading in John 5 about the lame man who lay by the pool of Bethesda waiting for a miracle of healing. For years nothing happened. Then one day Jesus of Nazareth walked up to him and said, "Rise, take up thy bed, and walk" (verse 8). Immediately the man stood up and was healed completely. It was *his moment of breakthrough* after years of frustration and hopelessness.

You may have been waiting a long time for your breakthrough. You may have thought it would never come. But God has impressed me to tell you that *your moment of breakthrough is coming.* It's on its way. Jesus of Nazareth is passing your way!

Believe that in your heart and say it over and over: *My breakthrough from heaven is on its way!*

January 12

Pray Your Way Through

I've been reading in 1 Kings 17 how Israel backslid and how a great drought came. For forty-two months there was not a drop of rain. Can you imagine having no rain for a year, for two years, or for three and a half years?

The earth was cracked and parched.
Famine was in the land.
People and cattle alike were dying.
And a man prayed—Elijah prayed.

He prayed to heaven for God to give a breakthrough, and suddenly he leaped up and shouted, "There is a sound of abundance of rain" (1 Kings 18:41).

And it rained. My, how it rained! It's been said that it poured so hard, it made Noah's flood look like a morning dew. It broke the drought. And out of that came a spiritual awakening. Israel came back to God. *It was a breakthrough.*

What is the breakthrough you need in your life? Is it reconciliation for a broken relationship? Is it healing for your body or mind? Is it money for unpaid bills? Whatever it is, you can pray your way through to breakthrough!

January 13

A Crack in the Shell

If the Son liberates you . . . then you are really . . . free.
John 8:36 AMPLIFIED

When the word *breakthrough* exploded inside me, God gave me a vision—a vision of a little baby chick closed up in its shell, alive but unborn. I saw the egg move slightly; something inside it wanted out. I saw a crack in the egg and a little foot stick out. Then I saw a bigger crack and a little head poke through. In a few seconds the eggshell broke wide open, and the baby chick hopped out into a new life, into an entirely different kind of life than it had inside the shell.

That is a vision of you, which God has given me. I see you as a baby chick inside a shell. I see the movement as you struggle to break out of that shell. I hear the cry of your heart. I sense the frustration, the fear that sweeps in. I sense the uptightness, the worry over loved ones. I sense the spirit of defeat that makes you wonder, "How am I ever going to get out of this thing I'm in?" But I see the shell cracking. I see part of you reaching out. And I know your time has come.

You're about to break through into a whole new life that is totally different from any you have ever had. A life of freedom to grow, to expand, to really live!

January 14

You Have to Be Anointed

The anointing which ye have received of him abideth in you.
1 John 2:27

I think one of the greatest dangers a Christian faces is trying to do God's work in his own strength and power, rather than depending on the Holy Spirit to anoint and empower him.

Early in my ministry I made a vow to God: *I would never try to preach or pray for people without the anointing of the Holy Spirit upon me.*

I have kept that vow. I remember a crusade I had in Philadelphia. One night I was in prayer just before I was to leave my hotel room to go to the meeting. But I didn't feel God's anointing coming upon me. It was within minutes of the time I was to preach. Finally, I said, "God, I won't leave this room. If I go without the anointing of the Holy Spirit, I can't face those people who have terrible needs."

When I said that, I felt the Spirit coming up through my body, my spirit, and my mind. I jumped up and said to the man who was driving me to the service, "I'm ready to go." When I walked into the auditorium that night, I didn't have to tell the people that I was anointed. They knew the anointing was there. If I've learned any lesson in life, it is that you can't do God's work within your own power. You have to be anointed by the Spirit of God.

January 15

Something Wonderful Happens

Many people have trouble just believing in miracles, much less that a miracle can happen to them personally. This is not surprising, for I fully believe it is intellectually impossible to believe in miracles unless the Holy Spirit enlightens your spirit and understanding. That is one reason God has given us His Holy Spirit: ". . . that we may know the things that are freely given to us of God" (1 Corinthians 2:12).

You see, when you are baptized in the Holy Spirit, He unites with your spirit, producing a new language pattern by which you can (*if you will*) speak directly to God. The Spirit prays through you, from the deepest levels of your being—and does it according to God's will for you (Romans 8:26, 27).

Now the most beautiful and effective part of this is that, as you pray in the Spirit, something wonderful happens to your understanding. There comes flooding into your mind a knowledge you never had before—an ability to grasp and to do much more of God's will and purpose in your life. Your intuitiveness is sharply increased, your understanding of the impossible is enlightened, and you begin to feel, from deep within, that a miracle from God *can* actually happen to you!

January 16

There's Healing in a Touch

They shall lay hands on the sick, and they shall recover.
Mark 16:18

Recently a minister friend of mine said, "Oral, I believe there's something in the touch of a person in prayer that affects your healing. When I go to the hospital to visit people, I always pray with them. And often, I'll see their hand reach out from under a blanket or a sheet. People want to touch hands when they pray."

Doctors say the most sensitive part of our body is the skin. When some part of it is touched, it feels good. You know how it is when you cuddle a little baby. It snuggles right up to you. In the Bible, people brought their children to Jesus just so He would touch them (Luke 18:15). Even then, they recognized there's more to the touch than we can see. For when we touch one another, it isn't just our hands touching—it's our hearts.

Do you know someone who is suffering, either physically or mentally? Are you suffering yourself? Touch somebody. Join hands and pray one for another. The healing power of Christ can come not only through God's delivery systems of medicine or prayer, or a combination of these, but it can also come through the loving touch of a person who cares.

January 17
Perfect Meeting Place

And you, that were sometime alienated and enemies . . .
hath he reconciled.

Colossians 1:21

Once a father and son became very angry with each other. The boy stalked out of the house and vowed never to return. The months rolled into years. One day the mother became ill and was dying. She begged her husband to send for their long-lost son. When the boy returned home, he didn't even glance at his father, but fell across his mother's bed and cried, "Mother, please don't die! Don't leave us!"

The mother looked at the father and son, and she saw the enmity between them. With feeble strength, she took hold of their hands. In a desperate burst of strength she pulled them together across her dying body. She breathed a sigh and was gone. The father and son looked at each other and began to weep. Broken by mutual sorrow, they were reconciled because of the death of the one they loved.

When Christ cried, "It is finished," He reached up with the right hand of His divine nature and took hold of the hand of an offended God. With the other hand He took hold of the hand of offending sinners. With the last strength He had, He pulled God down and man up and reconciled them at His cross. Since that time, the Cross has been the most perfect meeting place between God and man.

January 18

Seed-Faith

The kingdom of heaven is like to a grain of mustard seed, which a man took, and sowed in his field: Which indeed is the least of all seeds: but when it is grown, it is the greatest among herbs, and becometh a tree, so that the birds of the air come and lodge in the branches thereof.

Matthew 13:31, 32

The idea of *seed-faith* was born in my heart one day when I saw that everything God does starts with a seed planted. I was facing a staggering need as I drove down the highway in the Pacific Northwest. Passing through the area where Delicious apples are raised, I saw refrigerated rail cars being loaded to carry them to markets throughout America. Everywhere I looked, nature was in production. Seed had been planted, the soil cultivated, and now the mighty reproductive forces had produced the harvest. It was a striking sight.

Suddenly I saw that, on the practical level of human need, God has made it possible for a person to conceive, to believe, and to get right results. The vision was all around me: the harvest in the fields bursting forth from the tiny seeds planted months before and carefully tended. The inevitable result was a harvest!

It came to me with an impact that Jesus is the *seed* God planted. Jesus is God's covenant of blessing for every man. Through Him we can make a seed-faith covenant with God, based on our faith in Jesus. Each time we have a need, we can make our faith an act—a seed we plant. The seed is our giving something of ourselves, as God has given His Son. Through our *seed-faith* we can expect God to reproduce and multiply it to meet our needs.

January 19

Your Total Source

I really began to understand that God is my Source when I became desperate with my needs and had no one to turn to. God had to become my Source of *total* supply, or I was finished. It was when He spoke to my heart to return to the church of my youth.

After much prayer and soul-searching, I obeyed God and was graciously received.

The Scripture God gave me for this move was: *A great door . . . is opened unto me, and there are many adversaries* (1 Corinthians 16:9). A great door opened for my ministry of healing, but there was much opposition. Our finances decreased almost 50 percent, and I had to go to the bank and borrow money to pay our personnel.

One day I had it out with God: Was He God to me, or was He not? The Lord focused my attention on Philippians 4:19: "My God shall supply all your need according to his riches in glory by Christ Jesus." Then it hit me—God is my Source of total supply. God. God. God. Before, I had seen God as my Source, but I had seen my partners and my ministry as sources, too. Now, I saw that God uses many different instruments, but He alone is *the* Source.

This is the first miracle key of seed-faith. Say it: *God is my total Source of supply*.

January 20

Seeding for Your Miracle

When you study Jesus' Sermon on the Mount, you see that giving is the heart of all He taught. He said, "Give, and it shall be given unto you; good measure, pressed down, and shaken together, and running over . . ." (Luke 6:38). He put emphasis on what we *do* and *do first*—such as forgiving first, hungering and thirsting after righteousness first, seeking the kingdom of God first, and giving first.

Jesus said, "If ye have faith as a grain of mustard seed, ye shall say unto this mountain, Remove hence to yonder place; and it shall remove; and nothing shall be impossible unto you" (Matthew 17:20). While Jesus was saying if we could have even a little faith, it would grow until it would be big enough to move our mountains of need, there is much more! Faith is a seed you plant to get a desired result. Faith is what causes you to sow seed—to give and to believe the seed will be multiplied back in a return far greater than your giving.

When you have a need, if you can have the courage to seed for your miracle—which is giving something of yourself first—it will give you power to speak to your mountain of need, to command it to be met in full, and nothing will be impossible to you! This is what I call *seeding for your miracle—the second miracle key of seed-faith.*

January 21

Expect a Miracle

The third miracle key of seed-faith is: Expect a miracle (see Mark 11:24). Now, expecting a miracle is absolutely essential. Just as you look to God for your supply and give to God as seed you plant, so you expect to receive a miracle from God.

This is a key point on which many people fail in their seed-faith covenant with God. One man said to me, "Mr. Roberts, I didn't think I was supposed to expect anything back from God."

I said, "Why would a farmer sow seed if he didn't expect the miracle of a harvest?"

Every farmer I know goes to the field regularly, to see how much the seed has grown and how soon he is to send his trucks in to gather the harvest. If he didn't expect a return, he wouldn't check the fields. And if he didn't check the fields, the harvest could be there and he wouldn't know it. Thus it would be wasted.

When you do your part and release your faith, God will send the miracle. This is why you must expect it—so you will recognize it when God sends it and reach forth and receive it from His hand. Expectancy is a marvelous thing. It makes you look forward to every new day as the most important day in your life. It creates a joy and a challenge in your new way of giving as a way of life.

January 22

Red-Letter Day

Though our outward man perish, yet the inward man is renewed day by day.

2 Corinthians 4:16

Christianity is more than a moment of acceptance of Christ in the past. It is a *daily* surrendering of our life to Jesus Christ. When we fail to have a current relationship with Christ, we become like the man who drew a red circle around January 22 on his calendar. "That was the day I was saved," he said proudly.

Soon the man got a big marking pen and enlarged the mark around the date. Before long the date became so significant to him that he bought a little trowel, some cement, and a few bricks and built a wall around it. Of course, by now his testimony had become hollow and empty. Eventually the date was so important that he decided to build a castle around it. The castle looked so good that he made up his mind to go live in it. The last we see of this man, he is sitting inside the castle all alone, saying, "That was a great experience I had with the Lord." But Christ had ceased to be his personal Savior and had become a professional God.

The beauty of our walk with God is that there are no periods, just commas. Christianity is a continual revelation of our lovely Lord and Savior.

January 23

Drilling for Faith

I grew up in Pontotoc County, Oklahoma, among the oil fields. When they struck oil in our part of the state, men drilled down deep into the earth and the oil came gushing upward. When I think about the Scripture, "Faith cometh by hearing, and hearing by the word of God" (Romans 10:17), I think of oil coming up out of the ground. The oil had been there for centuries, lying undiscovered and unused.

In the same way, faith is in your heart (*see* Romans 12:3). That faith may never have been tapped. You may have never even known it was there. Yet your faith is so powerful that once it is released, you come into the fullness of all that God has planned for your life.

People sometimes say, "I have all the faith in the world." That's the trouble—they still have it. Faith doesn't need to be in you. It needs to come *out* of you. *For faith to be effective, you have to release it!* Faith *cometh*—it comes out of you as you hear the Word of God preached. The minister is the driller, and the Word is the tool he uses to drill into your heart to bring forth that magnificent fighting force that God calls your faith.

This is the victory that overcometh the world, even our faith.
1 John 5:4

January 24

A Life Pattern of Good

When something bad happens to you, it's just human nature to feel that your whole life is ruined, that nothing will ever go right again. That's why it's important to think of life *not* in terms of one isolated experience, but as a whole.

This idea is illustrated by comparing life to a ship. Although a ship is made to sail, not all of its parts will float by themselves. If you put the engine on the water, for instance, it immediately sinks, and so do the propeller, the compass, and many other parts. But when they are all properly and securely put together, the ship sails above the turbulent waters.

Romans 8:28 says, "We know that all things work together for good to them that love God." God wants us to remember that He is greater than anything that happens to us—that He is a good God, that He is working for our good, and that He can change even the bad things into good.

In your life you will experience some sadness, some disappointment, some trouble. Everyone does! But God weaves all your experiences—good and bad—into a life pattern of good for you.

January 25

A Heartfelt Prayer
by RICHARD ROBERTS

One day my wife, Patti, was driving the car while our five-year-old daughter, Juli, was riding on the armrest that pulls down in the middle of the back seat. That's her favorite spot to ride, because she can see out all the windows.

Patti was telling her about the drought we were having. "Juli, we need rain," she said. "The grass needs a drink. The flowers need a drink. The bushes are leaning over because they are thirsty. The ground is parched." She said, "Juli, why don't we ask Jesus to send rain?"

Juli just listened. But a couple of minutes later, when Patti was looking in the rearview mirror, she saw two little arms suddenly shoot into the air and heard Juli call out, "O Lord, God, Jesus Christ, send the rain! No thunder! No lightning! Just rain!"

Sure enough, it rained that night. There was no thunder. No lightning. Just rain!

> *The earnest (heartfelt, continued) prayer of a righteous man makes tremendous power available . . . . Elijah was a human being with a nature such as we have . . . and he prayed . . . and the heavens supplied rain and the land produced its crops.*
>
> James 5:16–18 AMPLIFIED

January 26

Who Am I?

by REBECCA ROBERTS NASH

For almost everyone, achieving an identity is a difficult thing. I know it was for me. For years I never felt I was anyone in my own right. When I was young, I was known as Oral Roberts' daughter. When I married, I became known as Marshall Nash's wife. Then when we had children, I became known as their mother. Now— would you believe it—I'm Richard Roberts' sister!

It took me years to feel I had worth as a person. And there were many times I failed to do things I knew I should have done, simply because I lacked the self-confidence to do them.

The Bible says, "Your own completeness is only realized in him [Jesus]," and God "hath made us accepted in the beloved [Jesus]" (Colossians 2:10 PHILLIPS; Ephesians 1:6). That means it is only in Jesus Christ and His love that we find who we really are and what we are intended to be. And God's love is not earned. It is a gift. He accepts us as we are—with all our human limitations!

God accepted me as a person of worth and value. My problem was that I was not accepting myself. Learning this great truth helped me to come to the realization that there were worthwhile values in me. Honesty, integrity, fairness—things I had been taught as a child. And what I am is different from what any other person is. That makes me unique!

Gradually I began to like myself. I stopped trying to copy others and started being me. It became easier to face my shortcomings as well as to give myself credit for commendable traits. Being natural came more easily. Believing in myself helped me to learn to believe in others and to see the good in them.

It is a great moment when we realize that we do not have to earn God's love or be a different person. His gift of love means that we are free to be ourselves—and to like it! He declares us worthy. When we look at ourselves in the mirror we can say, "I am worth something. I am a child of the living God."

This is the first of several devotionals written by my daughter Rebecca during the last three years of her life. She and her husband, Marshall Nash, went home to be with the Lord on February 11, 1977, as a result of an airplane crash—*O. R.*

January 27

God Lived in Our House

. . . I have called you by name; you are mine.
Isaiah 43:1 LB

My parents always had family prayer. They had a habit of ending their prayer by bringing each of us children by name to God. "O Lord," they prayed, "bless Elmer, bless Jewel, bless Vaden, bless Oral."

I became so accustomed to it that once, when they forgot to call my name, I blurted out, "Mamma! Papa! You forgot to call my name. You didn't ask the Lord to bless me!" They laughed and bowed their heads again to say specifically, "God, this is our son Oral. Bless him, Lord, and be with him."

My parents talked with God in familiar terms. And I grew up believing that God lived in our house—that He was a member of our family—and that He knew me. God's nearness and personal awareness of me has been very meaningful in my spiritual experience.

God is not shrouded in a mist of indefiniteness; He's not some far-off being a million miles away. God is closer to you than your breath, more familiar with you than your family. You can merely *whisper* His name and know that He hears—or send Him a *thought* and know that He is aware. This marvelous relationship with God is yours to enjoy!

January 28

"The President, My Father"

I . . . will be a Father unto you, and ye shall be my sons and daughters, saith the Lord Almighty.
                                                    2 Corinthians 6:17, 18

Little Tad Lincoln, who had apparently been in a fist fight and come out the loser, ran into the White House crying, "I want to see my father." Several members of the cabinet, who were waiting to see the President, began teasing him affectionately. "You wish to see *the President of the United States?*" one asked.

"I want to see *my father*," little Tad insisted.

Another member jested, "You want to go into the presence of *the head of our nation?*"

"I want to see *my father*."

Still another official continued the joke. "Let's take this boy in to see *the commander-in-chief of our armed forces*," he said.

"I want to see *my father*."

Everything they said about the President was true—but to Tad Lincoln the truth was not titles. It was flesh and blood—*his father*. If he could only get to his dad, who would put his arms around him and pull him up close, things would be different.

God has many titles and names—the Great I Am, the Lord of Hosts, the Prince of Peace, God Almighty—but when we are in need, He is first and foremost *our Father*.

January 29

Dirty Socks
by EVELYN ROBERTS

When I was a little girl I wanted to be a missionary so much! I'd hear friends who had received calls to be missionaries cry because God called them to go so far away from home, and I'd think, *O dear Lord, call me. I'll never tell You any place is too far*. It wouldn't have made any difference to me where God sent me. I would have gone. But the Lord wouldn't call me to be a missionary. Later on I told my husband, "Oral, I guess God knew you needed someone to wash your socks, and that was me."

I feel like I have a part in all of Oral's ministry. When students leave Oral Roberts University, going to all parts of the world, I feel that I'm getting to be a missionary through them. And when they win people to God, I take part of the credit because I like to think they are going in my place.

Your place in God's work may be outwardly important or down-right unglamorous at times. But whatever you are doing, whenever you are where God wants you, doing your part in His plan, your work is important—even if it's washing dirty socks. It's God's work!

Whatever your task, work heartily, as serving the Lord and not men.

Colossians 3:23 RSV

January 30

When Nobody Notices

Have you ever gone out of your way to help someone, but nobody seemed to notice? This is what happened to a little boy who had been in an automobile accident and was left crippled. One day he was invited to a swimming party at the home of a friend. The other little boys were swimming and laughing and jumping in the water. But this boy could only watch.

After a while all the others went indoors to get some refreshments, except him and one boy in the pool. That boy suddenly got cramps in his legs and went under. The crippled boy began to yell, "He's drowning! Quick! Someone come! He's drowning!" The boys rushed out, jumped into the pool, and saved the boy's life. And the little crippled boy, smiling and crying, said, "We saved him! We saved him, didn't we?"

One of the boys said, "What do you mean *we* saved him? You can't swim. The other boys and I went in and got him out." But the little boy just kept smiling, because in his heart he knew "we" saved him.

That little thing you do that nobody seems to notice may be the big thing upon which eternity turns. Remember the widow's mite! (*See* Mark 12:41–44.) When she dropped her penny into the offering box, nobody noticed—no one, that is, except Jesus. Jesus always notices!

Is God deaf and blind—he who makes ears and eyes? . . . He knows everything—doesn't he also know what you are doing?

Psalm 94:9, 10 LB

January 31

"Who Is Jesus?"

Once Jesus asked His disciples, "Who do *men* say that I am?" Then He personalized it and asked, "But who do *you* say that I am?"

There followed that beautiful confession by Peter, without qualification, without hesitation; *"Thou art the Christ, the Son of the Living God*—that's who You are!"

Jesus became very animated, for He was looking for that answer. And He said, "Peter, in light of your confession of who I am, I am going to make a confession of who you are. You've identified Me; now I shall identify you. *Thou art Peter, and upon this rock I will build my church"* (*see* Matthew 16:13–18).

In the original Greek this meant that Peter was a fragment, a small part of a much greater whole. It was as if Jesus were saying, "Peter, you are going to be a significant part of a magnificent whole."

The question of our age is: "Who am I?" And the way to answer that question is by first answering the question: *Who is Jesus?* When we acknowledge Him to be our Savior and Lord, then we come into an understanding of who we are and what we are meant to become—a significant part of God's magnificent whole!

FEBRUARY

February 1

Are You Listening?

Oh that one would hear me!
Job 31:35

A family was sitting at dinner one evening when all of a sudden the little four-year-old son stood up in his chair and shouted, "Pass the butter!"

"Get down out of that chair and go to your room," his mother said. "You're not going to have any dinner until you can learn some manners."

"But—but, Mother," the boy pleaded.

"No 'buts' about it. Go to your room."

Later the father called the family into the living room. "You didn't know it, but I made a recording of our conversation at dinner tonight," he said. "I want us to listen to ourselves as we really are." When he turned on the recorder, they all heard themselves talking at the same time. Amid the chatter a wee little voice said, "Please pass the butter." Later, a little louder, "Would somebody *please* pass the butter?" And finally, ***"Pass the butter!"***

Many of the problems and misunderstandings in our relationships could be avoided if we would just listen to one another. It would be good to stop once in a while and ask ourselves: "Am I listening?"

February 2

Those Dots and Dashes

When the Morse code was first invented, an employment agency posted an ad for a telegraph operator. The anteroom of the agency was filled with applicants when a young man came in. Just as he sat

33

down, he heard dots and dashes. Immediately he jumped up and disappeared through the door. Soon he came back and said, "You can all leave now. I've got the job."

"What do you mean you've got the job?" the others said. "We've been waiting here all morning."

"Didn't you hear those dots and dashes?" he asked. "They were saying, *Are you listening? Can you read me? If you can, come on in. You've got the job.* I understand the dots and dashes, and I was listening—so I got the job."

A great truth the Bible holds out is that God speaks to us. The problem is, we don't always have a listening heart. How do you cultivate the art of listening to God? By simply beginning to understand that God is in the now and that He is concerned about you as a human being.

And then by saying with a sincere and open heart: *"Speak, Lord; for thy servant heareth"* (1 Samuel 3:9).

February 3

"I Have to Obey God"
by RICHARD ROBERTS

Obey my voice, and I will be your God, and ye shall be my people.

Jeremiah 7:23

I recall how back in the middle fifties our family would drive down Lewis Avenue in Tulsa, Oklahoma. My dad would stop the car and get out and point to a pasture with a big white house, a silo, and some horses. And he'd say, "God has told me to build Him a university, and someday, with His help, I'm going to build it right here on this pasture."

Being only seven or eight years old, I didn't understand. In fact, even though Oral Roberts University is now standing on that pasture, I still don't know that I completely understand. And I don't know that I ever will. But I don't think that's the question. I think that whether or not we understand what God is telling us to do, we have to obey.

Something I've heard my dad say so many times is what my grandmother—his mother—used to say: "Oral, one thing you always have to do is obey God!" And I'm finding that true in my own life.

I have to obey God.

And I challenge you to obey God. Whatever He is asking you to do, do it. This is the secret of having God's power in you.

February 4

I'm So Glad I Listened
by REBECCA ROBERTS NASH

He hath said, I will never leave thee, nor forsake thee.
Hebrews 13:5

I was sitting in a car agency waiting for my car to be serviced when an elderly man, who was also waiting, began to talk to me. My first instinct was not to talk to him, because I don't make a habit of talking to strangers. You know, the atmosphere is such today that a woman has to be extremely careful. And also, like many others, I'm usually wrapped up in my own problems and thoughts and just don't bother to talk to most people. But the more this old gentleman talked, the more interested I became, and before I knew it, he was telling me his life story.

He told how he had lost his first wife to cancer when he was a very young man—how the depression of the thirties and his wife's illness just about wiped him out financially—and how he had such a hard time getting over her death and he didn't remarry for ten years. He said he then remarried and raised a family and was able to rebuild his finances, but his second wife had died just recently.

"How do you feel about being alone?" I asked.

He looked at me for a minute and then smiled. "I'm not alone," he said. "Now there's a story behind that. Anyone who believes in God is never alone. I'm seventy-six years old and my life is nearly over. But I've always believed in a God who promises eternal life. But more than that, He promises to be with me through everything. I wouldn't have made it if I hadn't believed that. No," he mused, "I'm not alone."

What he said didn't really sink in until I was driving home about an hour later. He had made a very powerful statement: *Anyone who believes in God is never alone.*

That shook me, because thoughts of being left a widow sometimes cross my mind. I have a good friend my own age who was left a widow just last year, and her situation had been on my mind. But here was a man who had lost the nearest and dearest person to him not just once, but twice. And he still had such an unshakable faith in God's loving presence and care that he could share it with me. I'm so glad I listened!

February 5

You Don't Have to Understand

If thou canst believe, all things are possible to him that believeth.

Mark 9:23

God is a miracle-working God. And for Him to work a miracle in your life it is not necessary to understand *how* He will do it. God responds to our faith, not our knowledge.

A man once said to me, "Oral, how does God perform miracles?"

I answered, "I don't know *how* He does; I only know that He does." Then I asked him this question: "How does God make a black cow that eats green grass to give white milk that makes yellow butter?"

He said, "I don't know, but it doesn't make any difference, just so I get the milk and butter."

"Right," I said. "Now apply that same thinking to God's performing miracles."

Jesus said, "All things are possible to him that *believeth*." He didn't say that all things are possible if we understand—but if we have faith. God has put it in your heart (Romans 12:3). And God has made Himself the object of your faith. Believing is an inner knowing, an inner certainty that when you bring your problem to God, He will work it out. When you start to believe, God moves into action!

February 6

New Understanding of "Reverence"

Let them reverence your great and holy name.
Psalm 99:3 LB

Jesus had a deep feeling about the name of God. He never used it irreverently. He honored the name of the Father, and He taught us in the Lord's Prayer to reverence the name of God.

When I was in Moscow, Russia, a number of years ago, I had an experience that gave me a new understanding of reverence. Every day I saw a long line of people—perhaps two miles long—lined up to visit the tomb of Lenin in Red Square. The people walked by on either side of the coffin to see the body of this man, and no one was allowed to stop. The soldiers standing guard kept the lines moving.

I decided to go one day. I caught just a glimpse of the dead Lenin as I walked by. His right hand upon his chest was not open into a hand, but closed into a fist, which to me is indicative of the violence with which his life was associated.

But the thing that stood out most to me was the reverence these many Communists gave to their long dead leader. I mean they reverenced him.

Lenin died with his fist clenched in hatred. Jesus died with His hand open in love and healing to every human being.

How much more should we reverence His name!

February 7

Give Off the Top

Elijah said unto her . . . make me . . . a little cake first . . . and after make for thee.

1 Kings 17:13

When my brother Vaden and I were growing up, we'd milk the cows and then Mamma would let the milk set so the cream would rise. Oh, that cream was so good! We'd sneak in to try to get a taste of it, but Mamma would say, "Now, Oral, you and Vaden get away from there. I'm saving the cream." Later, when the cream had risen to the top, she'd skim it off, and that's what she'd use to make butter.

To me, this illustrates how God teaches us to give—first—off the top. Why? Because that's where the cream is. And the cream is the richest and best part. If you give of what's left over, you're giving off the bottom—the skimmed milk.

You see, the important thing is this: What you give God is what He multiplies back. If you give God the skimmed milk, that's what is multiplied back to you. Wouldn't you rather give God the cream—your best—and have the cream multiplied back? When you realize that your giving is a seed that you sow, and you know that you've given the cream off the top—and that's exactly what

God is going to multiply back to you—you can get pretty excited about giving!

Read 1 Kings 17:8–16.

February 8

A Great Scripture

Ye are complete in [Christ].
Colossians 2:10

In the summer of 1968 I was the guest of the late Prime Minister of Israel, David Ben-Gurion. He had retired and was living south of Beersheba in the desert, writing his memoirs. During my visit I said, "Mr. Prime Minister, what would you say is the greatest Scripture in the Bible?"

He said, "Reverend Roberts, I believe the greatest Scripture is where God says, 'Let us make man . . . and God created man' " (Genesis 1:26, 27).

He explained that when God made man, He didn't make him Jew or Arab or American. He made him a human being. And he indicated that what we need is for man to become, not a member of a certain race or culture, but what God originally made him: MAN.

Colossians 3:11 says: *In this new man of God's design there is no distinction between Greek and Hebrew, Jew or Gentile, foreigner or savage, slave or free man. Christ is all that matters, for Christ lives in them all* (PHILLIPS).

I believe through the *man* Jesus Christ you can become fully human again. You can become a new man, a whole man. By putting on Jesus Christ, you can be what you were born to be—you can do what you were born to do!

February 9

I Love You

God made man to communicate—to talk. Yet one of the greatest problems in relationships is communication. I remember dealing with a young couple whose marriage was in trouble. I sensed that although they were married, there never had been any real to-getherness.

I asked the husband, "Have you ever said to your wife, 'I love you'?" He said, "Well, by my *actions* I have—providing her a home and taking care of her . . . ."

"But," I said, "have you ever *said* it?"

"No, Brother Roberts, not in so many words."

"In the Garden, God and man walked and talked together. This is what God intends for you as a husband and wife." Then I asked, "Is it possible for you to recapture the feelings you had for her when you were newlyweds and just say, 'Honey, I love you'?"

Slowly he took his wife's hand, looked into her eyes, and said, "Honey, I love you."

Tears rolled down her cheeks and she said, "I'm so glad you finally *said* it."

This is the togetherness God made us to have in all of our relationships. And it is nurtured with positive, loving expressions. God Himself extends His love to us with WORDS: *You are precious . . . and honored and I love you* (Isaiah 43:4 RSV).

February 10

More Productive to Give

When I was a young pastor, I used to wonder what Jesus meant when He said, "It is more blessed to give than to receive" (Acts 20:35). Our needs were so many that any small gift thrilled us. To me, it seemed to be more blessed to *receive* than to give.

Then one day I learned what Jesus meant. While facing a need myself, I was deeply impressed to give a certain amount of money to God's work. It was a real sacrifice. But after I gave it, I felt a warm glow all over. It was pure joy.

At two o'clock in the morning, a man from my church knocked at my door. He said, "Brother Roberts, when I reached home and started to bed, the Lord began dealing with my heart. For two years I have given very little. As I observed your giving, it suddenly came home to me about my own need to give. I have an irresistible feeling that I should give this to you." He handed me a sum seven times more than I had given! It was the exact amount I needed for my urgent need.

When I started thanking him, he replied, "Don't thank me. I'm a wheat farmer, and I know by experience that the yield I get from my land is in direct proportion to the seed I plant. This is just seed

I've been needing to plant for a long time."

In his heart, this man had been withdrawn from the church for two years. His seed-giving was also withdrawn. Like the seed-money Jesus told about in the parable on giving, it was "buried" (Matthew 25:14–28). He had let his farm run down. After he started giving again and assuming his proper place in the church, everyone saw a profound change in his life. He resumed tending his farm. He found a new joy in being with his family and became one of the most enthusiastic men in the church—a man of strength to all of us. He is still a partner with me today, and still practices seed-faith.

As I reflected on how God multiplied my gift seven times over, I began to realize what Jesus meant when He said, "It is more blessed to give than to receive." I understood that He was saying, "It is more *productive* to give than to receive." For what we receive is not multiplied. Only what we give can God multiply back—whether it's a piece of money, a word of encouragement, patience, a smile, or a prayer we pray for someone. That's what Christianity is—giving and receiving.

February 11

The Ministry of Angels

There shall no evil befall thee . . . For he shall give his angels charge over thee.

Psalm 91:10, 11

Angels are far more active in our lives than we realize. Once, early in my ministry while away from home on a crusade, I woke suddenly in the middle of the night, knowing my family was in trouble. I dropped to my knees and prayed, "Lord, I'm fourteen hundred miles away from my family, so I can't help them. Please send an angel to protect them." Soon I became peaceful, and I knew God had answered my prayer.

When I got home, my wife, Evelyn, told me she'd been awakened one night by someone trying to break into the house. She was terrified, but she prayed, and after a few minutes the intruder left. I asked when it happened. It was the same night the Lord had awakened me and I'd prayed for Him to send an angel to protect my family. I believe He did.

Being human, you sometimes face problems you just can't work out. But at those times you can expect the angels of God to minister to you. You may sense their presence as a surge of strength, a clearness of mind that helps you solve a problem, or as a joy that spreads through your being. You may see it as miraculous protection. But however you experience it, the ministry of angels is another way God shows you that He cares for you!

February 12

Make It Right

He that covereth his sins shall not prosper: but whoso confesseth and forsaketh them shall have mercy.

Proverbs 28:13

We honor Abraham Lincoln today not only as a great president but also as a great human being. Yet we know that, like all of us, he was fallible.

The story goes that one night a Colonel Scott, whose wife had died suddenly, came to Lincoln asking permission to go home for the funeral.

The president snapped, "We are at war. Sorrow is the lot of all. You must bear your share."

Early the next morning, however, Lincoln was at Scott's doorstep, apologizing. "I treated you brutally last night," he said, gripping Scott's hand firmly, "and I beg your pardon. I've come this morning to make it right."

Deeply touched, the colonel said, "This is very kind of you, Mr. President."

"No, it's not," Lincoln answered. "I'd never have forgiven myself if I had not righted this wrong."

The thing that makes you stand out from the crowd is not that you never make a mistake, but that when you do, you are willing to admit it and do everything in your power to make it right.

Read Matthew 5:23, 24.

February 13

Give Your Seed Corn

I was deeply impressed by a statement Gerald Ford made at his Presidential Inauguration. He said, "America is eating too much of its seed corn." He indicated that many of the problems in our nation's economy are a result of our consuming too much ourselves and not giving as we should.

This reminded me of when I was a little boy and our family lived on a farm. We children had to help my father in the fields. And one of the hardest parts was the harvesting of the corn—pulling it from the stalk, shucking it, and putting it in the barn.

In those days we gathered the corn in wagons pulled down the rows by mules or horses. When my brother Vaden and I would bring a wagonload to the barn, Papa would have us climb up in the wagon to pitch the corn into the barn.

One day we were throwing it in right and left (and at each other sometimes) when Papa suddenly stopped us. He said, "Wait a minute, boys. Be careful with that corn. Take the biggest ears and pitch them into a special pile over here. Put the rest in the barn."

We were just little boys and didn't know the difference, so we asked, "Why, Papa?"

He said, "Because those big choice ears are my seed corn. That's what I'm going to plant next year. We'll eat the other corn and sell part of it. But we are not going to eat our seed corn. We want to plant the best so we'll have a good crop."

Papa knew what every good farmer knows—that what he planted was what would be multiplied back to us. He understood the Scripture that says, "Whatsoever a man soweth, that shall he also reap" (Galatians 6:7).

What is our Lord saying in this Scripture for us today? He is saying, "Give Me your 'seed corn'—the best part of your life. Give Me your best, then ask Me for My best. For what you give is what is going to be multiplied back to you."

February 14

Always Sweethearts

There was a time when it seemed that Evelyn and I were growing apart. I was completely absorbed in my rapidly growing ministry, and she was busy with our four small children. It was not that we loved each other any less. We were just learning to live without needing each other.

One evening after Evelyn had tucked the children in bed I said, "Evelyn, I want to talk . . . ." She looked at me a little puzzled and said, "What about?"

"Well," I said, "I think we are growing apart."

"What are you saying?" she exclaimed. "I love you as much as ever, and I know you love me. I think we have a perfectly normal life, except that you have to travel and I have to be at home with the children."

I said, "That's just it, Evelyn. I don't want us to have just a *normal* life. That isn't enough for us. I want us always to *need* each other—to always be sweethearts."

She thought a moment, then said, "I think I see what you mean, Oral. I guess we are just so busy doing the good things and the right things that we're taking each other for granted."

That night as we prayed together we dedicated ourselves to each other anew and asked the Lord to help us always to be one together and one in Him and in our ministry. As we prayed, it was like the Lord wrapped us together in His great love. It was as though there had never been a gap. After thirty-nine years of marriage, we are still sweethearts and expect to be always.

The Bible indicates that through marriage we get a glimpse of what our relationship with God is to be like (Ephesians 5:22–33). So not only in marriage, but also in our love relationship with the Lord, it is important to always be sweethearts—to always love and need each other.

This is why God has said in His Word: *I remember how eager you were to please me as a young bride long ago and how you loved me . . . But I have this [one charge to make] against you, that you have left (abandoned) the love that you had at first . . . Think about those times of your first love . . . and turn back to me again.* (Jeremiah 2:2 LB; Revelation 2:4 AMPLIFIED; Revelation 2:5 LB).

February 15

Things My Parents Taught Me

Two of the most powerful influences on my life have been my own father and mother, Ellis M. Roberts and Claudius Priscilla Roberts.

Both of them have died—Mamma in 1974 when she was eighty-nine years old and Papa in 1968 when he was eighty-seven. But I still feel their influence upon my life. You see, you don't learn just one time from your parents. You remember. And as you dwell on the things they taught you, they become a deeper part of your life.

In the next twelve devotionals I'm going to honor my parents by sharing their lives and some of the things I've learned from them. The Bible says, "Honour thy father and thy mother: that thy days may be long upon the [earth]" (Exodus 20:12). I want to live long upon the earth, but I want to honor my father and mother for a reason other than that: Because they taught me so many things that may be possible influences in turning your life around, as they have mine.

February 16

Someday You'll Understand

I rejoice at thy word, as one that findeth great spoil.
Psalm 119:162

One of the first memories I have of my father that influenced my life is seeing him sitting in an old cane-bottom chair leaned up against the side of our house. He was reading the Bible. I came around the corner and saw him. I stopped. I heard him chuckle and saw him nod his head. Then I saw tears well up in his eyes. I said, "Papa, why do you cry when you read the Bible?"

He wiped his eyes and said, "When I read the Bible, sometimes the Lord just touches me, and I can't keep the tears back." He said, "Oral, someday when you know Christ for yourself and you start reading the Bible seriously, you'll understand."

Many years later that happened to me. It happens to me still. I'll be reading the Bible and the tears will roll down, and I remember Papa saying, "Oral, someday you'll read the Bible for yourself and God will touch your heart."

February 17

A Little Stuttering Boy

As a boy I was a stutterer, and people often made fun of my attempts to talk. One time, after a particularly humiliating experience, I slipped away by myself, wondering if I'd ever amount to anything. Then I overheard Papa and my Uncle Willis talking. Uncle Willis said, "One day one of your sons will preach just like you, Ellis.'' (Papa was a preacher.) He went on, ''Vaden will be the one who'll preach.'' Vaden was two years older than I was.

Papa said, ''Well, Vaden will make his mark in the world, but he won't preach. This little stuttering boy here is the one God has called to preach.''

Uncle Willis said, ''Oral preach! Why, he stutters so bad he can't even talk. How can he preach?''

Papa said, ''God will take care of that.''

Here was a boy whose self-image was lying in the dirt, and Papa picked it up and gave it back to me. He helped me square my shoulders and believe. Oh, I didn't pay much attention to Papa's words about God calling me to preach. What I liked was the tone of his voice. Papa believed that little stuttering boy was going to amount to something! He taught me that no matter how small or insignificant you feel you are, to God you are somebody!

God promises: . . . *you will succeed because of my Spirit, though you are . . . weak* (Zechariah 4:6 LB).

February 18

You Can't Turn God's Love Off

When I was fifteen years old, I felt there was no future or hope for me as the son of a poor preacher. So one day I simply announced to Mamma and Papa that I was going to leave home. Mamma cried and Papa threatened. But when they saw they couldn't stop me, Mamma put her arms around me, and with tears coursing down her cheeks she said, ''Oral, wherever you go I'll be praying. You'll never get away from my prayers.''

What she was saying was, *''You'll never turn my love off. And you'll never turn God's love off.''* And that meant a lot to me.

The Bible says, ''Even if a mother would forsake her nursing child, I will never forsake you'' (Isaiah 49:15 PARAPHRASED). See also Psalm 139:7–10.

My parents taught me the wonderful truth that no matter how far you run, you can never turn God's love off!

February 19

"Why Was I Born?"

Millions of people wake up every morning and don't want to get up. They're lying down—physically and spiritually—because they don't have a purpose in life. They don't know why they were born.

I remember my dad telling me that when he was a young man he used to lean up against the fence on the farm where our family lived, look out over the horizon, and wonder what was out there and why he'd ever been born. He said, "Oral, I didn't amount to anything until God began to deal with me and show me that He had a meaning and purpose for my life." Papa passed on to me how important it is for us human beings to have a reason for being.

Saul of Tarsus was a man who had lost his reason for being. He lay on the ground, blinded by a light from heaven, hurting inside because he'd been fighting against God. But God said to him:

> *Rise, and stand upon thy feet: for I have appeared unto thee* for this purpose, *to make thee a minister and a witness.*
> Acts 26:16

God was saying to him, "Get up, stand up, and stay up, for I have a purpose for your life."

Are you feeling down, wondering why you were ever born? God is saying to you: *Get up, stand up, and stay up, for I have a purpose for your life!*

February 20

Prayer *and* Medical Science

Less than a year after I left home, I was brought back, dying of tuberculosis. Papa did two things that are very important. He called our family doctor, who brought in two other doctors, and they began to work with me. Then Papa said, "I'm going to write everybody I know who knows how to pray. And I'm going to ask those who can to come and pray for you."

Here were three compassionate medical doctors helping Oral Roberts. And from time to time people drove up in their cars and came in, and Papa would have them pray. He surrounded me with these two delivery systems of God's healing power. He didn't call them that. He just knew that God had given us doctors and the power of prayer for our healing. And my life was spared.

Today I'm involved in healing through prayer and medical science, because they are both God's delivery systems. They are the ways and instruments God uses, for He alone can heal. All healing is divine healing—my father taught me that. He gave me a wonderful image of the medical profession, and he gave me a wonderful image of the power of prayer to heal. And I hope I reflect that in my life today.

The Bible says, "They that [are sick] . . . need . . . a physician" (Matthew 9:12). It also says, *"The prayer of faith shall save the sick"* (James 5:15).

February 21

God Is a Good God!

[Jesus] went about doing GOOD, *and healing all that were oppressed of the devil.*

Acts 10:38

As I lay for months bedfast with tuberculosis, neighbors and friends came to see me. One day some people came who said God had tracked me down. God had put this disease on me.

They were really turning me off because I wasn't a Christian. Here they were telling me God had put tuberculosis on me. And it gave me a terrible view of God—that He runs around slapping people down with tuberculosis or cancer and sending them to hell.

Pretty soon my mother got stirred up, and she said to the leader of this group, "The devil afflicted my son. God didn't do this to my boy. God loves my son. God is good. And if you can't say something good, I think you ought to leave."

When they left, Mamma came in and sat down beside my bed. She said, "Oral, God's not like these people say He is. Sure, maybe the afflictions have made you stop and think, but they didn't come from the Lord. The Lord wants to heal you and give you life."

God is a good God! I've said that around the world. And I can trace it right back to my mother. She was the first one to tell me how good God is.

February 22

Just Talk to God

Pray continually.
1 Thessalonians 5:17 NIV

When I was a child, Jesus Christ was an integral part of our family life. I actually thought Jesus lived in our house, that He was a member of our family. All problems, great and small, were taken to Him. Mamma and Papa had a habit of waking up early—around five o'clock in the morning—and we children would hear them talking, usually about God or in intimate conversation with Him.

I couldn't understand this for a long time. But when I had tuberculosis and was given only a short time to live, my mother said, "Son, you must pray."

I said, "Mamma, I don't know how to pray. I don't know what words to say."

I remember her reply so well. "Oral, you don't have to know how to pray. You just open up your heart and tell God how you feel."

I said, "Mamma, is that prayer?"

She said, "That's prayer."

I've never been able to improve on Mamma's simple formula for prayer.

February 23

I Saw Jesus in Him

My father was instrumental in leading me to Christ. One night, as I lay dying of tuberculosis, he came in and said, "Oral, I'm going to kneel and pray, and I'm not going to stop until you give your heart to God."

Then he, Mamma, and the nurse knelt and prayed. After a while Mamma and the nurse finished. But Papa remained kneeling at the foot of my bed. He was a big man, and he had a powerful voice. And he was pouring out his soul to God because his son was dying and he was lost.

I looked down at him. I saw the tears streaming down his cheeks. I heard him talking to God about me—about Oral. And suddenly it hit me: I saw the likeness of Jesus in his face. At that same moment a warmth came up through my feet and my legs. It was the presence of God. I could feel it. And I heard myself saying, "God, I'm sorry. Forgive me. Save me. Come into my heart."

Soon we were all hugging one another and crying and laughing and praising God. A new creature had come into existence, and he had my name!

When someone becomes a Christian he becomes a brand new person inside. He is not the same any more. A new life has begun!

2 Corinthians 5:17 LB

February 24

God Will Do It Again

It shall come to pass in the last days, saith God, I will pour out of my Spirit upon all flesh.

Acts 2:17

When I was a young minister, I asked my father, "Papa, do you think the time will ever come when the great miracles of Christ will be repeated?"

He said, "Yes, sometime before the Lord returns we'll see this."

Now, he could have said, "No, I don't think so." I'd met many people who didn't think God was going to pour out His Spirit on mankind again. But my father sensed it was coming. He didn't know then how much his reaction would influence me.

Years later, after I'd begun a worldwide ministry and many people's lives were being touched and healed, my father said to me, "Oral, do you remember when you asked me why there were no healings and why the gifts of the Spirit were not in operation, and I told you that some day God was going to pour out His Spirit in a great way again?"

I said, "Yes."

He said, "I've lived to see that day."

I remember that as if it were yesterday. My father could look beyond me as a son and see the Lord—see the Lord working, which is most important of all.

February 25

Don't Strike Back

When I became a Christian, I thought everybody would be tickled to death that I had been saved and healed. I thought when I told people God was good and God would heal, they would think it was great. Instead, I got opposition. I was struck on every side. I'd pick up a newspaper and they'd say such bad things about me that I wanted to strike back—you know—tell them off.

One day my mother said, "Son, I want to tell you about criticism. Don't ever strike back." Of course that was the first thing I wanted to do. But she said, "Oral, don't ever strike back."

Then she said, "Here's how to handle criticism. Ask yourself if it's true. Are you guilty? If you are, change. And if you're not, leave it in God's hands." The final thing she said was, "If you're right, if you're doing God's work, you don't have to defend it. God will vindicate you."

Now, every time I pick up a newspaper that says something good about this ministry, I think about my mother, who told me God would vindicate me if I wouldn't strike back. The Bible says:

> *No weapon that is formed against you shall prosper, and every tongue that shall rise against you in judgment you shall show to be in the wrong.*
>
> Isaiah 54:17 AMPLIFIED

February 26

Stay Little

One day my mother came to my house. She was troubled about something. She put her arms around me and said, "Lean down." I'm over six feet tall. My mother was a quarter Cherokee Indian and only five feet tall. She pulled me way down to her, kissed me and wet my face with her tears as she said, "Oral, keep little in your own eyes, and God will bless the world through you."

You see, my mother could see through me. She could see that maybe I wanted to be somebody big. Maybe she could see pride coming up. And she knew that "pride goeth before destruction, and an haughty spirit before a fall" (Proverbs 16:18). She could see that if I would keep little in my own eyes and try to be humble, God would use me to bless others.

My mother went to heaven some time ago. She was eighty-nine years old. Before she left to be with God, she said it to me again: *Son, stay little in your own eyes.* Has a man ever received better advice?

February 27

Obey God

I think the thing my mother said to me that meant the most was something she said a thousand times. She always said, *"Oral, obey God.* The price for disobedience is so great." She said, "Never look back. Go forward with what the Lord puts in your heart."

Throughout my life I've been asked by God to do many things, none of them small. So it's been tough to obey God. But each time Mamma said, "Obey God." When I started this ministry in 1947 and the going got rough she said, "Obey God." When I announced we were going to build Oral Roberts University, I had no money, and few people, if any, believed I could do it. Mamma said, "Obey God." When I announced that we were going to build the medical and dental and law schools here at Oral Roberts University, I could feel her saying, "Obey God." And even today, as we are building the City of Faith, a great medical complex that merges God's healing streams of prayer and medicine, I can still hear her say, "Oral, obey God!"

I want to tell you, it means something to obey God. It's easy to say, but it's tough to do. But one thing about obedience, it's a million times better than disobedience. Because when you're disobedient to God you can't rest. When you obey God it may be tough from the outside, but inside there's a peace, a peace from God "that passeth all understanding" (Philippians 4:7).

February 28

Conquer Your Fear

Ye shall not need to fight in this battle: set yourselves, stand ye still, and see the salvation of the Lord with you.
2 Chronicles 20:17

As a boy I was always afraid of dogs. I had a newspaper route in Atoka, Oklahoma, and when I saw a dog coming, I would run away. At one house there was a dog I was particularly afraid of. That dog had run me off every day for a month, and one day I made up my mind that it wasn't going to happen again. I was going to conquer my fear.

That evening as I approached this particular house, I said to myself, "I'm not going to run. I'm not going to be afraid." When I got within fifty steps of the house, here came the dog, running pell-mell toward me, barking ferociously. I stopped and stood still. The dog dashed toward me and slid up to my shins. I stared at him and he stared back. Dumbfounded, he took one sniff, turned, and ran!

That was a great experience in my life. Many times since then I have reminded myself that other fears are like that dog. When the devil comes near you, he knows if you're afraid. And if you are he will dominate you with that fear. What can you do? You can walk up to your fear in the name of Jesus, take a stand, and say, "Devil, do what you will, for I am not afraid of you. God is on my side." And fear will leave you every time!

February 29

An Extra Day

A man received a greeting card which read, "God give you one year of happiness, 12 months of prosperity, 52 weeks of success, 365 days of good health, 8,760 hours of joy and gladness, and 525,600 minutes filled with His peace, love, joy, and blessings!"

"I was so impressed with this unusual greeting," he said, "that I got to thinking—time is God's unique daily blessing to each of us. And Leap Year has 366 days instead of 365. One extra day. A special gift from God."

Into each year God puts 52 *exciting weeks* to be filled with loving, precious memories. Every week He hands us 7 *new days* of opportunities to do good and to lift up people. Morning after morning, God's matchless grace is renewed with 24 *fresh, unspoiled hours* to serve Him. Hour after hour we are presented 60 *vital minutes* of inspiration, impetus, and creativity. Every day God gives us 86,400 *beautiful seconds* to love, forgive, bless, act, respond—to do in faith unto others as He has done unto us. Time is God's gift.

> *Look carefully then how you walk, not as unwise men but as wise, making the most of the time, because the days are evil.*
>
> Ephesians 5:15, 16 RSV

MARCH

March 1

God's Property

When praying for a person, I often say, *"Devil, take your hands off God's property!"* I emphasize this point because I feel the devil is causing some bad things to happen all over the world. He's attacking people with all kinds of sicknesses and torments, with hunger, with unemployment, with loneliness, with a feeling that nobody cares. And people need to hear a voice saying: "Devil, you're a defeated foe. Our Savior defeated you on the cross."

They need to hear someone say: *"Greater is he [God] that is in you, than he [the devil] that is in the world"* (1 John 4:4).

The Holy Spirit has been dealing with me to come right out and say this stronger than I've ever said it before. First, because it helps me and, second, it helps those I say it to. So I want to say it again, and I ask you to say it with me: *"I belong to God. Devil, in the name of Jesus, take your hands off God's property—ME!"*

Some people get frightened and don't have the nerve to say that. They feel they might be saying it in their own power. But every time you say those words in Jesus' name, you're giving the devil a command that's really straight from the Lord!

March 2

It Applies to Loved Ones

When you tell the devil to take his hands off you—God's property—you can also apply this to your business, your home, your loved ones, and friends—all those close to you.

Many times I've heard my wife, Evelyn, speaking in the name of Jesus, and saying, "Devil, let us alone." And she would go to the kitchen door and open it and tell him to get out of our house. You see, a lot of people don't understand that the devil is a personality—evil personified.

Another thing Evelyn did, especially while the children were growing up, was—when one of them was sick or something was wrong—she would pray for him, and I would hear her say, "Devil, you're not going to do this to my child." And this was scriptural. Acts 16:31 says, "Believe on the Lord Jesus Christ, and thou shalt be saved, *and thy house.*" God has promised us our household.

I constantly ask God to help my loved ones. And when I'm praying for them, I command the devil to take his hands off my children, off my grandchildren, off my friends, or off some partner I'm praying for—because I believe that's the kind of prayer the devil understands. When you belong to God and you know it, and you let the devil know you know it, it makes all the difference in the world!

March 3

No Wonder

No wonder the Psalmist marveled at God's workmanship and exclaimed: "I will praise thee; for I am fearfully and wonderfully made" (Psalm 139:14).

For did you know that . . .

- The human skeleton has more than 200 bones?
- All the blood in your body is pumped through your heart once every minute, and your heart beats about 100,800 times a day?
- Your body has more than 600 muscles and about an equal number of nerves?
- Your heart handles 5,000 gallons of blood a day—almost enough to fill a railroad tank car?
- The normal adult body contains approximately 24 trillion red cells, which carry oxygen to nourish tissues? Laid edge to edge they would stretch 116,000 miles—halfway to the moon!

God who created us has also intricately fashioned us with purpose, that we might conform to the image of His Son Jesus Christ. Oh, this is not easy! For there are many times in certain situations when we do not know what God's purpose for us is. It is then that we need faith—faith enough to be faithful. For in the end we will see His plan perfected in us.

March 4

The Rest of Jesus

He is able also to save them to the uttermost that come unto God by him, seeing he ever liveth to make intercession for them.

Hebrews 7:25

Several years ago, when our granddaughter Marcia was only three years old, my wife, Evelyn, was baby-sitting with her. Marcia wanted to be told a story. She loves Bible stories, so Evelyn told her about the birth of the baby Jesus, His life and ministry after He grew into manhood, and finally about His death on the cross and His resurrection.

"When I finished," Evelyn said, "Marcia pleaded, 'Tell me another story.' "

Evelyn asked, "Well, Honey, what would you like to hear about now?"

"Tell me the *rest* of Jesus," she said. I thought, *O Marcia, you have expressed what so many people are feeling today.* They are hungry to hear about "the rest of Jesus." The letters that come across my desk are saying, "Brother Roberts, tell me more about Jesus and what He is able to do. Can He help *me—now?*"

Jesus' birth, His life, His death, and His resurrection were only the beginning. The Bible says that Jesus is the same yesterday, today, and forever. That means the existence of Jesus is just as real today as it was when He walked the shores of Galilee, and His power just as relevant to your needs—*now!*

March 5

Knowing God As a Person

There was a time in my life when God seemed indefinite, vague, and far away. But as I studied the Bible, especially the four Gospels and the book of Acts, I came to know Jesus in the way the Bible presents Him—as a person. And I came to realize that I could know God through Jesus, for Jesus came to show us what God is like.

The Jesus I know is a man of power, compassion, and action. He was infinitely approachable. He walked and talked with all kinds of people, never limiting Himself to His own small group, as we often do. He wanted men to live freely and fully.

Jesus was strong in body, sound in mind, forceful in personality, and compelling in His teaching. He went from town to town, preaching in the temple and marketplace, on the seashore and in the mountains. He reinforced His message through healing the sick, controlling the forces of nature, changing the water into wine—meeting people's needs.

Jesus wasn't the weak, motherly man so often portrayed to us. He was a man's man, keenly alive and vibrant. And He said, ". . . he that hath seen me hath seen the Father" (John 14:9). When you meet God, you encounter more than a great spirit or idea or concept. You embrace the *man* Jesus. He is what God is like.

March 6

God Ain't Poor No More!

Many people think it's God's will for them to be poor—to suffer financially and socially. That's one reason I ran away from home when I was fifteen. My father was a preacher, and people's attitude was, "God, if You will keep the Reverend E. M. Roberts humble, we'll keep him poor."

People have linked poverty with being a Christian, because when Jesus became a man, He laid aside His heavenly riches and identified with us in every area of our human need. "Though he was rich, yet for [our] sakes he became poor, that [we] through his poverty might be rich" (2 Corinthians 8:9). But through Christ's death on the cross and His resurrection, He returned to His Father's right hand, where the Father *reendowed* Him with His eternal riches. The Scriptures speak of Christ's present glorified position in heaven, saying we have "all sufficiency" in Him (2 Corinthians 9:8).

God ain't poor no more!

We don't have to live a limited life, except for one thing—and that's death. "It is appointed unto men once to die" (Hebrews 9:27). Even then, God is going to raise us from the dead. We are hemming in the Lord when we say, "God can't do this," or "My problem is too big," because Christ is no longer limited by anything.

He is the unlimited Christ.

March 7

Biggest Box of Groceries

Faith is the substance of things hoped for, the evidence of things not seen.

Hebrews 11:1

Faith is a wonderful thing. It is mysterious, yet so practical. My father, the late E. M. Roberts, was a minister. He often grieved that he could not provide adequately for his family. He hoped for the day when people would understand the minister's needs.

I remember once, when Papa was away holding a revival, Mamma told my brother Vaden and me that she was sorry, but we didn't have anything to eat. We were on our way home from visiting a neighbor and Vaden said, "I don't think God is very good to us. Papa ought to come home."

I felt faith stirring in my childish heart. I said, "Vaden, you hush. God will take care of us. You'll see what the Lord will do."

When we got home, Mamma asked Vaden to open the door, but he couldn't because something was in the way. I helped him, and there was the biggest box of groceries we had ever seen. An hour later, with my mouth full of country ham and homemade biscuits, mashed potatoes, and gravy, I said, "See, Vaden, I told you God would take care of us."

Vaden grinned back at me and said, "Yeah, Oral, He sure did, didn't He?"

March 8

God's Reminder

Without me ye can do nothing.
John 15:5

During a question-and-answer period following my address to the student body of a college in the East, a young man asked, skeptically, "Mr. Roberts, you *say* you are healed—so how do you explain that little stammer you have sometimes?"

"I really can't," I said, "unless it is God's reminder that without Him I cannot talk at all."

Every time I speak it is a miracle, because I was born a stutterer.

Older boys often made fun of me and chased me home. Once when this happened, my mother took me on her lap and said, "Oral, someday you're going to talk. God will loose your tongue."

My mother's gift of love and faith bore fruit many years later. The night I was healed of tuberculosis in a public religious meeting, the man of God who laid his hands on me and prayed for me held the microphone in front of me and said, "Son, talk!" He knew that I had had a speech problem. When I started to speak, I discovered that God had set my tongue free. The words just flowed out of my mouth. So, I don't mind a little stammer now and then, because it reminds me that without God I can do nothing.

March 9

Put Your Heart In

I know, O my God, that thou dost test the heart . . . . With an honest heart I have given these gifts willingly, and have rejoiced now to see thy people . . . give willing to thee.
1 Chronicles 29:17 NEB

I remember something my mother once said that really affected me. I stopped by one day to give her some money, because she had a need. As soon as I'd handed it to her, I said, "Well, Mamma, I've got to go now."

She said, "Oral, I need the money, but do you know what I need most? For you to sit down and just talk to me and love me."

She was saying: *"Son, your money will feed and clothe my body and pay my rent, but it won't help my heart. I need your money, but I need more of you than that."*

There are times when giving money is not enough, for it is only a part of your existence. True giving involves the heart. It's giving your whole self—your time, your talent, your love, your compassion. For what is your money without your heart? And what is your time or your talent or anything else you give, unless you put your heart in it?

Somehow when your giving originates in your inner being, God's supernatural power flows through you, enabling you to meet the true needs of those whose hearts are hurting.

March 10

Use Your Talent

*He gave . . . talents . . . to every man according to his
. . . ability.*

Matthew 25:15

I believe I have stored up within me a certain kind and amount of talent. But what if I never use my talent? What if I never gave it as a seed? How would it ever be multiplied back to me?

The first sermon I ever preached was five minutes long, and I could have said it in two minutes. I held out for five. In that sermon I tried to talk about Jesus, but I got scared and stumbled through. But I had that call to preach inside me. And if I hadn't ever given that first sermon, I would never have preached.

The talent you *give*—or use—is what is multiplied back. If you give nothing, you get nothing back. Ask any farmer: "Do you plant seed?" *Yes.* "Why do you plant seed?" *To get a harvest.* "Do you ever get a harvest if you don't plant seed?" *No.*

What talent do *you* have? And don't say you don't have any. Within every individual, God has placed a certain kind and amount of ability. Whatever your special gift is, the way to develop it is to plant seeds. *Use that talent in some way.* Oh, you may fall flat on your face a few times, as I did, but in God's own time and way you will reap a rich harvest of joy and fulfillment.

March 11

A Real Fish Story

A funny thing happened to Evelyn and me while we were in Wyoming one summer and I was writing my book *How To Get Through Your Struggles.* We were near a trout lake, so she and I would slip off now and then and go fishing. The first few times we went, we didn't have much luck. Then one day we were visiting with some friends, and one of them said, "You know, Brother Roberts, when I go fishing, I catch fish."

"How do you catch them?" I asked.

"I take dominion over them. You know the Bible says, 'Have dominion over the fish of the sea' [Genesis 1:28], so I just tell those fish to get on my hook—and they do!"

The next time I went out in the boat, I said to the fish, "I take dominion over you. You get on my hook, and I'm going to pull you in."

Before I knew what was happening, a fish hit my line so hard it almost jerked my arm off. I reeled him in. I threw the line right back out, and again I said, "I take dominion over you, fish."

In less than an hour I had my limit of trout!

I went to the cottage and showed them to Evelyn. She got excited and decided she was going to go fishing. So the next day we were in the boat and I was catching fish right and left, but Evelyn wasn't catching anything. Finally, she said, "Oral, what are you doing that I'm not doing?"

"I'm taking dominion over these fish." I laughed when I said it, but I meant it.

She said, "Do you really believe in that?"

I said, "I sure do!" And I reminded her of what our friend had said.

About ten seconds later, I heard Evelyn scream, "I got one!" And, sure enough, she pulled a fish into the boat.

I said to her, "What did you do?"

She said, "I took dominion over it!"

Later that day, when I sat down to read my Bible and work on my book, I realized we had stumbled on to something very important. We can take dominion not only over the fish but over the struggles of our lives. When God created Adam and Eve, He gave them the power of dominion, telling them to take dominion over *all* things. That same power is ours today through the name of Jesus.

> *Behold! I have given you authority and power . . . over all the power that the enemy [possesses], and nothing shall in any way harm you.*
>
> Luke 10:19 AMPLIFIED

March 12

Go With God

> *. . . I am with you, and will protect you wherever you go . . . .*
>
> Genesis 28:15 LB

In many ways these are frightening times. Because of violence, people are afraid—afraid to go certain places, and particularly at certain times. But in our text, God is telling us He is concerned with our personal safety. He is with us. And He is our protection.

I remember once that I was concerned about getting on a certain plane I was to take overseas. I've ridden planes around the world many times, but on this occasion I felt a twinge of fear down in the pit of my stomach. So I began to pray: *"Lord, I want You to go with me on this journey and preserve me on this flight. Go with me."*

Deep within, it seemed I heard God say, "Go with you? Why don't you just go with Me?"

And I thought, *Of course, Lord. If You're going to be on board I know I'll be all right.* And I was.

Now whenever I start on a trip, I say, "Jesus, I'm going with You. If anything comes against me, it'll have to go through You first." That's a comforting thought!

March 13

There Is a Heaven

And he carried me away in the spirit to a great and high mountain, and shewed me that great city, the holy Jerusalem.

Revelation 21:10

I believe there's a heaven and a hell. Some people do not. But that's like believing you can step out in front of a speeding car and not be hurt. You'll be hurt just the same.

One way I know there's a hell is that there's one right here on earth. Everywhere you turn there's separation from God, which is what hell is. There's torment, which is what hell is. There's weeping, pain, frustration, and heartbreak, which is what hell is (*see* Matthew 8:12).

In the same way, I know there's a heaven. Sometimes it gets so close it kisses us. We feel the sunshine of its glory on our face, and we just know that we know that God is real.

We know heaven exists because there's a little heaven in our heart down here. Heaven is a place of *peace,* and we have God's peace in our heart now. Heaven is a place of *joy,* and we have the joy of the Holy Spirit in our heart now. Heaven is *life,* and we have the life of Christ in us now.

Heaven isn't some pie-in-the-sky theory. It's something you can experience—beginning today.

March 14

The Power of Moving Together

One of the intriguing mysteries of nature is a flock of wild geese flying in a V-shaped formation. When a group of aerodynamic engineers made a study of this phenomenon, they made an interesting discovery.

As the geese fly in the V-formation, the flapping of the wings of each bird gives an uplift to the one before and behind him, and he in turn receives an uplift from them. This lift creates approximately 70 percent more forward thrust, so that as a group, the geese can fly further than they can individually. If one goose slips out of formation and tries to fly on his own, he misses that uplift and falls behind. When he moves out on his own, he gives and receives nothing.

Do you see how God has built into nature itself the whole idea of people moving and working together? No wonder God said, "Love the Lord thy God with all thy heart, soul, mind, and strength. And thy neighbor as thyself" (Mark 12:30, 31 PARAPHRASED).

If we pull away from one another and try to make it on our own without regard for God, without regard for our fellowman, we lose something. The majority of our power is gone. And, oh! how many individuals have lost that. They are not part of the human race—not part of this forward thrust that God gives to people—

> who pray together . . .
> who sing together . . .
> who believe together . . .
> and who walk toward God together.

In these troubled days, God is trying to pull us together and show us that as we move with one another, we can go further and accomplish more than we can by traveling alone. He is telling us that if we will *walk side by side . . . love one another . . . give to one another . . . and feel for one another,* we will be stronger and have a much more powerful thrust in our lives, both as a group and as individuals.

March 15

It's Always Springtime

God who gives seed to the sower multiplies the seed sown.
                              2 Corinthians 9:10 PARAPHRASED

One of my favorite times of the year is springtime, because that's seed-planting time. It's a thrill to see farmers plowing up the ground and putting in the seed, knowing that in every seed they plant is the potential for a harvest—or what I call a miracle.

But *it's always springtime with God*. We don't have to wait for a special month or season of the year to plant seed. Every moment of every day is seed-planting time with Him. Many people don't understand that in their troubles they can seed for a miracle from God by giving of themselves.

You have planted seeds of faith . . .
      if you've ever loved anybody . . .
            if you've ever given money or time
                  and concern to someone in trouble.
And for *every* seed of faith you've sown, there's a due season for a miracle from God.

March 16

"Hilarious" Givers

One Sunday morning the church ushers grinned while passing the collection plates. Many of the people smiled back, but were puzzled. When the pastor began his sermon, the reason for the grins was obvious. He quoted this Scripture: "God loveth a [hilarious] giver" (2 Corinthians 9:7). Then he explained that the word translated "cheerful" is the Greek word *hilaros*—meaning "extremely joyful"—and this is the way the Lord wants us to feel when we give.

People often say to me, "Oral Roberts, I don't feel joyful when I give." And I know exactly what they mean. The thing that makes the difference for me is this: When I give, I know I'm opening up the door for God to give back to me. Each thing I give is a seed I'm planting with Him, and each seed has a harvest. I call it seed-faith.

In seed-faith you put in a seed, then you wait for God to multiply the seed back to you to meet your needs. You can come to the point where giving is a joy, where you no longer fret or worry or feel deprived when you give. You can be joyful—even hilarious—as you give, because each gift is a seed for a miracle from God. So don't give till it hurts—give till it feels good!

March 17

The Difference

Years ago a great orator toured America, giving readings from famous writers such as Shakespeare and Byron. One night he ended his performance with a dramatic reading of the Twenty-third Psalm. He gave it with such power and skill that when he finished the crowd burst into thunderous applause.

When the applause died down, an old gentleman rose slowly from his seat and walked to the front. People recognized him as a retired minister. He said to the orator, "How beautiful that was. Would you let me recite the Twenty-third Psalm, too?"

The orator graciously complied. And the old man, with a voice that wasn't quite so strong anymore, began: "The Lord is my shepherd . . . ."

When he finished, there was no applause, but people wept openly. The orator turned to the minister and said, "Sir, when I gave the Twenty-third Psalm there was great applause. But here you gave it and, though you didn't have the proper inflection or intonation, people are crying. What's the difference?"

The old pastor said, "Sir, I'm sure you gave it better than I did. But the difference is: You know the Psalm, I know the Shepherd."

I will give them an heart to know me, that I am the Lord.
Jeremiah 24:7

March 18

The Cat Seller

For if you give, you will get!
Luke 6:38 LB

A man who was interested in collecting antiques was browsing through a small antique shop when he noticed a cat eating out of a little bowl. His experience told him that it wasn't an ordinary bowl.

It was a rare antique. He thought, *This man doesn't know what he's got here.* He said to the storekeeper, "Mister, I sure like that cat. Will you sell him to me?"

"Well, I don't know about that," the man said. "I kind of like that cat myself."

"I'll pay you twenty-five dollars for him."

"All right, you can have him for twenty-five dollars."

The customer paid the man and picked up the cat. Then he reached for the bowl, saying, "The cat is used to this old dish. I'll just take it along."

"Oh, no, you won't," the storekeeper said. "That's the best cat seller I ever had!"

The world is full of "takers"—cat sellers and bowl buyers—who are trying to grab all they can for themselves. But the "givers" are the real receivers. God cannot multiply what you *take*. Only what you *give* can God multiply back to you.

March 19

Don't Give Up—Look Up!

Some time ago I was talking to a friend of mine who is a great giver. But something bad had happened in his life, and he broke down and cried. He said, "Oral, for years I've practiced seed-faith, just like you said. I've made a pattern of giving. I give my money. I give my time. I'm concerned about people."

As he wept, I cried too. And in a way I was embarrassed, because now it looked like what I had preached was false. All I could say was, "What I've told you is the truth. And what you've done is right. You have practiced the eternal law of our Lord. God is going to help you."

He said, "Well, He hasn't."

I said, "Have you thought of the Scripture: *Let us not be weary in well doing: for in due season we shall reap, if we faint not* [Galatians 6:9]? This means you'll reap if you don't get discouraged."

I said, "Let me give you an example. There is a due season when you harvest. If you plant wheat or corn, you don't go out to gather in the harvest until the *due season.* Another example: If you agree to work for a man for two weeks and then get paid—you work the two weeks first, *then* you get paid. That is your *due season.*"

"Well," he said, "when is my due season?"

I said, "I cannot tell you. Only God, our Source, knows." We were like two children sitting there crying. He hurt and I hurt. At last I said, "All I can tell you is two things: one, keep on sowing the seed; and, two, know in your heart there's going to be a due season. Expect a miracle."

"Oh," he said, "I've expected a miracle."

But I said, *"Keep on expecting a miracle.* Don't stop now. God is going to do what He says, but He's going to do it in His time and in His way. That's why we've got to learn His way."

Not long ago I saw my friend again, and he was absolutely radiant. Things had turned completely around for him. He had continued to plant his seeds of faith, and his due season had come.

God has a due season for you. It may start today, or it may start next week. But I can promise you from the Bible, it's coming! Expect it. Look for it. If you get too discouraged, you may not recognize your harvest when it comes. Discouraged people don't see miracles coming. So—*don't give up—look up!*

March 20

That Certain Grin

Now faith is . . . perceiving as real fact what is not revealed to the senses.

Hebrews 11:1 AMPLIFIED

On May 6, 1973, Oral Roberts University conferred an honorary doctorate on my longtime friend, the Reverend Rex Humbard, of Akron, Ohio. Rex related a story that day which explains something about faith. I want to share his story with you.

"Years ago," he said, "when Oral and I were playing golf, he had a difficult shot. There was no way to get the ball around the tree that stood between him and the green. Oral sized up the situation and said, 'Rex, I'm going to hit the ball hard enough so that it will have the height to go over the trees. But it's going to be spinning so that it will bring itself back and fall right on the green.' Then he hit the ball."

Rex continued, "I watched it spin, pull over a little, go over the trees, and drop on the green. Very politely Oral turned to me and gave me *that certain grin.*

"In the late forties, when my son had a collapsed lung, I came in a line for prayer and his healing. Oral laid his hands on him and prayed. Then he turned to my wife and me and gave us *that same grin*. My son was healed.

"Later I was on this campus—before there were even any buildings here. Oral told me of the vision God had given him and how one day there would be a great university here, and *he grinned again*.

"Because of the faith of this man of God and the degree that he has bestowed upon me—*with that certain grin*—I think I'll be a better man."

I know the grin Rex was talking about. It's my own expression of a "knowing" inside—a faith I have in God. I've often said that faith is not something you try to make yourself believe; it's something you cannot doubt. Faith is a knowing that comes into your heart. You come to a point where you know that you know that you know that you know! That's when you're in faith.

When you don't have that knowing, don't do anything. Just wait upon the Lord. But when you have it, that's the time *to make decisions, to negotiate, to advance.*

And if you will move forward then, the King of kings and Lord of lords will work miracles in your life!

March 21

The Rx for a Marriage in Trouble
by EVELYN ROBERTS

The other day I looked in the paper and saw where a Christian couple that Oral and I knew was getting a divorce. And this bothered me. I think our family and our marriage should be more important to us than anything else in the world. It grieves me when we who are Christians cannot sit down together and communicate with each other and keep our marriages intact.

Too many couples, when faced with the first problem following marriage, begin looking for someone else. The grass across the fence may look a little greener, as the old saying goes, but it's no different from the grass on this side.

Oral and I have not attained the perfect marriage. We are not angels; we are just human beings. We have to work at making our marriage work. If Oral has said or done something that hurts me, he comes back and says, "Honey, I'm sorry. I made a mistake. Let's sit down now and talk this over." And I do the same with him. That isn't always easy. So I have a lot of respect for Oral, because he will not let something fester in his heart or his mind.

James 5:16 says, "Confess your faults one to another, and pray one for another, that ye [or your marriage] may be healed." I believe this is the scriptural formula for a happy marriage and the prescription for one that is in trouble.

Not long before the death of my daughter, Rebecca, and her husband, Marshall, she and I were discussing the breakup of so many marriages among couples they knew. And I said, "Rebecca, may I ask you a question? How do you feel about your marriage?"

She said, "Mother, I want to tell you the truth. When Marshall walks in the door, I'm just as glad to see him as I was the day we were married."

I believe God wants every marriage to be that way. He never intended for the devil to come in and destroy our homes. When something is wrong, if two people can sit down and feel free to say what they need to say to each other and pray together and then love each other in spite of shortcomings, they can make a go of their marriage.

March 22

Love Breaks Down Walls
by RICHARD ROBERTS

A little boy was in a toy store, rummaging through the shelves of toys, when suddenly one fell to the floor and broke. The little boy was trying to fix it when the shopkeeper came up and said in a loud voice, "Young man, you put that toy back together!"

Because he was scared and confused, the boy's hands became so fidgety, he only made things worse. Just then a young girl walked up and put her arm around the boy. Whispering something in his ear, she helped him put the toy back together and back on the shelf. Then turning to the storekeeper she said, "It's okay, Mister! You see, he's my brother, and he understands me because I love it into him."

Because I love it into him. That's what God did. He loved us so much He gave His only Son to break down the walls between us and get through to us (*see* Ephesians 2:14).

Walls often get built up in our relationships. There's a lack of communication, a lack of understanding. But we can break down the walls between us by being tolerant and helpful toward each other, by just "loving it into one another."

March 23

White Fang

Jack London's books are among my favorites, especially the story *White Fang*. It's about a dog that was three-fourths wolf. White Fang's wild wolf nature asserted itself by snapping, growling, and attacking anything or anyone who crossed him. The animal was intelligent beyond belief, but he lived by the law of self-preservation and was controlled by a fury no man could master.

One day White Fang met his match of ferociousness in a huge bulldog, which would have killed him had he not been rescued by a stranger, Mr. Scott. Bystanders shouted, "Look out! He'll bite!" But Mr. Scott, who had a tender love for dogs, understood the animal immediately.

The man began calling White Fang's name and talking to him as he had never been talked to before, in a low voice, softly and soothingly. The animal snarled, then slowly lay back down, whimpering. There were depths in White Fang's nature which had never been touched. And when Mr. Scott began stroking and calling to the little dog inside the wolf-dog, his kind words and caressing hand touched the animal in the deepest levels of his wild being.

Slowly a miracle happened. In the light of Mr. Scott's love, the little dog inside the wolf rose up, asserted itself, and rearranged the total nature of the wild animal. He became a beautiful, loving dog. White Fang no longer had to fight and hurt those around him to fill the empty void within, because all the things he had fought to get became a gift to him from his love-master, Mr. Scott. And love became his discipline.

Ingrained in us by nature is the law of self-preservation. And that law is not always easy to balance with the problems we face. Sometimes we, too, feel like snarling and biting at others—the gas attendant, the man who's not paying us enough, the government, the family—and then we hate ourselves.

But there is also a spiritual nature in us that the Holy Spirit reaches out to touch and to caress. The voice of God in your heart calls to the spirit part of you that God made, to bring it into being.

When you respond, Christ's love overmasters you and transforms you in your total personality and being—and you enter a new world of love.

> *Christ's love controls us now . . . .*
> 2 Corinthians 5:14 LB

March 24

God Loves You—No Matter What!
by REBECCA ROBERTS NASH

There was a period in my life when I seemed wrapped up in hate. With the responsibilities of a home and little children to care for, and trying to be a good wife, I was frustrated. Eventually my frustration turned into hostile feelings toward others, because they didn't do what I thought they should. But mostly I felt hatred for myself, because I seemed unable to be the kind of person I wanted to be.

Then I heard my father, Oral Roberts, preach a sermon using Jack London's story *White Fang* as an illustration. It was like looking into a mirror! I saw myself as that wolf-dog, filled with hate and fear, being stroked with God's love until the love hidden deep inside me was brought out.

My husband, Marshall, also taught me a great lesson along this line. Knowing how I felt, he said, "Rebecca, I love you for what you are—no matter what. And I have faith in you."

He told me that again and again. And knowing he loved me, no matter what I did, gave me a great sense of security and confidence in myself. And that confidence gave me the courage to trust my judgment in making decisions. And finally it helped me get started on the road to liking myself.

I know now that God loves us just as we are—no matter what. We have the security of knowing that. And through God's powerful love, we can have the faith to believe we are able to do what we have to do and the courage to do it.

> *We know how much God loves us because we have felt his love and because we believe him when he tells us that he loves us dearly.*
> 1 John 4:16 LB

March 25

Lord, Sometimes I Get Desperate!
by SALLY JO SHELTON

Help, God! I'm desperate! Without You I'll never make it!

Like a child throwing himself into his father's arms for comfort and safety, I abandon myself totally to Your care.

Be kind and gentle with me, Lord, because so many times a day I find myself crying to You for help. Like a baby needs his mother, I need You in the tiniest details of my life.

Fill me to the brim with joy, O God, for I'm offering everything I am and have to You. If I'm keeping anything back, show me what it is and help me to give that to You too.

I am confident You will meet my needs, Lord, for You are Goodness personified. You're always ready to forgive and forget. Your mercy is so abundant it spills over on all who come to You.

So again I ask, Lord, help! Hear my urgent requests!

Whenever I get desperate, Lord, I always call on You for help because I know You will come to my rescue.

This prayer is based on Psalm 86:1–7.

March 26

I'm a Desperate Man!

A university student recently said to me, "President Roberts, most people look at you as a man of faith, somebody who can reach out and expect a miracle from God. Can anyone do this? If so, how?"

I said, "You're going to be surprised by my answer. I don't think you're going to reach out for miracles until you get in need enough—until you get desperate."

I'm a desperate man!

I live on miracles. I was desperate when God healed me of tuberculosis. My very life and breath are miracles. But I'm desperate every day. I can't carry on the tremendous responsibilities of the Oral Roberts University by myself. I can't carry on a million-dollar annual budget for television. I can't do those things. I *have* to have miracles. I *have* to have God. I'm clawing. I'm scratching. I'm reaching out. I just tell Him, "God, I've got to have You." I don't say it in polished terms, but somehow God hears. And I think like this, day and night.

There are people who say they don't believe in miracles. Do you know why? They don't feel the need for one. The key to receiving a miracle is the need—and *feeling* the need. When your back is to the wall and there is no one you can turn to, that's when you start thinking about the possibility of a miracle happening in your circumstances.

Jesus said, "He [*anyone!*] that believeth on me, the works [miracles] that I do shall he do also; and greater works than these shall he do; because I go unto my Father. And whatsoever ye shall ask in my name, that will I do, that the Father may be glorified in the Son" (John 14:12, 13).

Christ is speaking to us about our concerns—and He's saying, "Where your need is, is where I am."

I can never be grateful enough for the understanding I have gained of Jesus concerning the way He comes to a person at the point of his need, in the form of that need, and to meet that need "according to his riches in glory" (Philippians 4:19). Mahatma Gandhi said, "Not even God would dare to appear to a hungry man except in the form of bread."

Jesus came to me in the form of my need, which was healing. When I learned that God was concerned about me personally, I began listening. He got my attention. I know it may sound crazy, but it is through your need that you can begin to comprehend God and to open yourself up to Him as your Lord and Savior and as your Source of total supply for every area of your life.

Because of Jesus, a miracle can happen to anyone. Miracles start in *Him*. The God who gives me miracles and who raised me up from nothing is the God of the *now*. If He performs miracles for me, He can perform miracles for anybody!

March 27

God's Originals

Genesis 1:1 says, "In the beginning God created the heaven and the earth." Then you read a little later that God "created man" (v. 27).

Created.

Genesis is the only place in the Bible where the word *create* is used in this way. The meaning of it is that God made the heavens, the earth, and man out of *nothing.* Now that is a very important point. We read on in the next verses that God said, "Let the earth bring forth . . . let the waters bring forth." God made the rest of Creation out of *something* (vv. 11–20). It's as if you say that General Motors or Ford created your car. You don't mean they made it out of nothing. You mean they took previously existing materials and rearranged them into your automobile.

God made man's *body* out of dust—something that previously existed. But when God speaks of creating *man,* he speaks of the spirit of man, the living breath He breathed into man which made him a living soul and through which He implanted in him His own spiritual and moral likeness.

So when God created man, He made him an original. That means you as a human being are special—an original. *God's original!*

March 28

God's Masterpiece

You are *God's masterpiece* made in His spiritual image and likeness (Genesis 1:26; John 4:24). *"And the Lord God formed man of the dust of the ground, and breathed into his nostrils the breath of life; and man became a living soul"* (Genesis 2:7). From the moment of Creation, God showed that man's spirit—not his mind or his body—was to be the governing power of his life on earth.

Man became a living soul—a *spiritual being!*

Man's spirit was to have supremacy over the mind and body and bring them together into a unified, harmonized whole man, in which God would live. We see this in the Garden of Eden when God and man walked and talked together (Genesis 3:8). There was no sin, no sickness, no unhappiness. There was perfect fellowship between them. They were one, just as Jesus and His Father were one. It was God and man—the way God made us.

You see, your whole life is spiritually based. The problems or needs you have may look physical, but that's just the way they are manifested. Every problem begins in your spirit, and the solution begins in the spirit. So to get an answer for your problems, you've got to get back into the spirit—God's Spirit and your spirit—the way you were made.

March 29

God's Offer

The problems in the world are not created by God. They are created by people, who have choices. When God placed man in the Garden of Eden, He gave him the power of choice, elevating man above all Creation. The Lord said, "Of every tree of the garden thou mayest freely eat: But of the tree of the knowledge of good and evil, thou shalt not eat of it: for in the day that thou eatest thereof thou shalt surely die" (Genesis 2:16, 17).

But then the devil came and said, "Ye shall NOT surely die [3:4]—*God is not telling it to you straight, for you can eat of this tree and you will not die."*

Now the devil was not telling the whole truth, because he was referring to physical death, right on the spot. But that's not what God said. He said, "*You* shall die. That spirit I put inside you will die." Although God included ultimate physical death, He was talking about *spiritual* death. He was saying, "The moment you eat of this tree, the spiritual and moral image of God upon your spirit will disappear. And that's death!"

In the Garden, God offered man the choice of the kind of human being he wanted to be. Today you have the same choice. To choose to live by the spirit rather than by the mind is the greatest decision you will ever make on this earth.

March 30

God's Material

The tree of knowledge in the Garden of Eden was beautiful to look upon and good to the taste; *it appealed to the senses.* And when Adam and Eve ate of the forbidden fruit, the Bible says that immediately "they knew" (Genesis 3:6, 7).

In that moment, man's spirit was submerged, and he chose to live by his intellect. When the mind ascended, the spiritual part of man died.

In that moment, man chose to live on the sense level—what appeals to his sight, hearing, feeling, taste, and smell—on the materialistic, sensual level of life (*see* Romans 8:13).

From that moment, man decided he was going to manage his life and do what he wanted to do. No longer would he exist as God had made him.

From that moment, there was a disintegration of the personality of man—a separation of his spirit, mind, and body—and thus a lack of harmony and peace. This is why it is believed that 85 percent of our diseases are emotionally induced. The mind cannot cope with the frictions of life, and it passes off to the body its torments and incapabilities.

From that moment, man was no longer God's masterpiece. But, thank God, we are still *God's material!* And through Jesus Christ, God's Son, we can be completely restored.

March 31

God's New Creation

Following the fall of man, God immediately began a program to redeem man; that is, to restore the supremacy of the spirit over the mind. To do this, God sent His Son Jesus Christ to take away that which the devil had put on man and to put back on man what the devil had stolen away.

In the latter part of His ministry, Jesus began to talk about the Holy Spirit, who would help bring about this restoration. He said, "If any man thirst, let him come unto me, and drink. He that believeth on me . . . out of his belly shall flow rivers of living water" (John 7:37, 38).

Here Jesus is not talking about thirst for physical water. He is talking about a thirst of your inner man—a thirst for the spiritual life that died with Adam and Eve when they turned away from God. Like them, we have tried to run our own lives intellectually. We have built a civilization based on the mind and body, almost ignoring the spirit, while God made us spiritual creatures.

The spirit of man has died. And the only way you come out of that death is through repentance—through believing on Jesus. The Bible says, "Therefore if any man be in Christ, he is a new creature: old things are passed away; behold, all things are become new" (2 Corinthians 5:17). Jesus, through the Holy Spirit, quickens you and gives you a new life (*see* Romans 6:4; 8:11). Once again the spirit of man comes to the forefront. His mind and body, governed by and filled with the Holy Spirit, become a reintegrated personality, as God made him. And man is instantly a *new* creation—restored!

APRIL

April 1

The Greatest Miracle

Christ died for our sins . . . he was buried . . . and . . . he rose again the third day.

1 Corinthians 15:3, 4

In interviews with the press I have been asked, "Mr. Roberts, what is the basis for your belief in miracles?"

I base my faith in miracles upon the life of Jesus Christ Himself and upon the single greatest miracle of all time—the resurrection of His body and His life from the dead.

Think about Jesus Christ's life for a moment. He was the Son of God, yet He emptied Himself and became a human being—a man. He faced life exactly as you and I do today. He had the same needs and He felt the same hurts that we do. Yet He underwent the agony of death on the cross so that He could deliver us from the curse of sin and death. On the third day after His crucifixion, the eternal power of life, which is God, went into action—and God raised Jesus from the dead. Death couldn't hold Him.

This is the single greatest miracle of all time!

Do you realize what that means to us in the *now?*

You and I can expect a miracle today, based upon the greatest miracle—the resurrection of Jesus Christ.

April 2

Resurrection Is Continuous

. . . once the Spirit of Him who raised Jesus from the dead lives within you He will, by that same Spirit, bring to your whole being new strength and vitality.

Romans 8:11 PHILLIPS

Our whole expectation for miracles is based upon the resurrection of Jesus Christ. You see, the resurrection is continuous. It

77

didn't end when Jesus was raised from the dead. His resurrection is just the beginning of a continuous resurrection in your life. You not only have the hope of being resurrected from the dead in the end time, but you can also experience the miracle power of the resurrection every day of your life.

Jesus Himself reassures us, "Because I live, ye shall live also" (John 14:19). *Because this resurrection happened to Me, it will happen to you, too.* You see, the same Holy Spirit who raised Christ from the dead is present in this world today, making miracles available to meet the needs in your everyday life. Day by day, as you bring your problems to Christ and trust in Him as your Source, you can expect many miracles.

Yes, if you believe in a resurrection that is continuous—one that will ultimately bring about the restoration of your total life—you can believe in miracles for the *now*.

April 3

The Seed of Faith

Unless I die I will be alone—a single seed. But my death will produce many new wheat kernels—a plentiful harvest of new lives.

John 12:24 LB

The resurrection of Jesus Christ was *not* an accident. Jesus seeded for that miracle! The people thought that they had killed Him, but actually He put His life—both His living and His dying—in as a seed of faith that He was planting. That seed of faith was with Him when they laid His body in the tomb. God had built into that seed the miracle of life, and the third day the seed burst forth. It blossomed and brought forth Jesus from the dead.

The miracles you receive are not accidents. You don't get something for nothing. Miracles come because you have put in the *seed of faith.*

Every time you love, that's a seed of faith.

Every time you give, that's a seed of faith.

Every time you pray for someone, that's a seed of faith.

Every time you have a good thought toward someone, that's a seed of faith.

When you sow a seed of faith, you sow a seed of resurrection from the problem you are facing. It's a seed that holds in it a potential miracle for you.

April 4

The Most Important Thing

The most important thing in your life is a miracle—especially when you need one.

Jesus Christ expected a miracle. He said, "Destroy this [body], and in three days I will raise it up" (John 2:19). Do you see where His expectation was? He was expecting the greatest miracle of all time. Jesus Christ could submit to the cross and to death, knowing that the seed of faith which He had sown would be multiplied back into eternal life. Because Jesus could expect that miracle, even though all of the satanic forces of the world were hurled against Him, *we can expect a miracle.*

Of course, we expect a miracle on the basis that we are putting seeds of faith in and because we are doing exactly what our Lord Jesus Christ did.

And that brings us up to the thing that you are facing in your life now. I know how serious it is, because I know how serious things strike me. I don't think you and I are any different in this regard. Each of us has our problems. And whatever the problem is, it feels worse to us than it feels to anybody else. If you have a pain, it hurts worse than anybody else's does. But the important thing is: *Are you expecting a miracle? Are you expecting the power of the resurrection to live in you today?*

April 5

Roses Will Bloom Again

The wilderness and the solitary place shall be glad for them; and the desert shall rejoice, and blossom as the rose.
Isaiah 35:1

The desert, the Bible says, shall blossom as the rose. That reminds me of when I was in Israel and I asked my guide to take me through Sharon and show me the roses of Sharon. As we traveled, he told me a story about Sharon. It's a rather barren, desolate area of Israel. He said, "Mr. Roberts, this is where all of our great roses come from."

I said, "Yes, I know. It's in the Bible." In Song of Solomon 2:1, the writer was speaking of Christ, when he said, "I *am* the rose of Sharon."

What does this say to you and me? Isn't it saying that when we are down—when we think we've had all we can take—the works of God are not over? You may have suffered a loss. You may have a loved one that's in a desperate situation. You may have something wrong in your body. There may be a problem that's eating you up. But I say unto you, cheer up. God is alive. And He is not through with you . . . .

Roses will bloom again!

April 6

The Stingy Man

There is a story of a man who was so stingy and selfish that he wouldn't give anything to anyone or help anybody. He lived to himself and was miserable. Finally, his friends dwindled down to just one lone man who would have anything to do with him.

One day the two men were walking along a path, and a light rain was falling. They came to a narrow wooden bridge across a deep stream. The stingy man's friend lost his footing on the slippery bridge and fell into the water. He thrashed about, struggling to find something to grasp hold of, for he could not swim. He looked up to the stingy man, who just stood there. The drowning man's first thought was to yell, "Give me your hand!" *No,* he reasoned, *that won't do any good. He wouldn't give anyone the time of day.*

In desperation, the man stuck his hand out of the water and gasped, "Here, friend, *take my hand!*" The stingy man smiled, reached down, took the man's hand, and pulled him to safety.

In a way, this story is a picture of the human race. Down through time God was saying to man, "Give Me your heart. Give Me your life." But man was wrapped up in himself, his own desires, and his own way. He shut his heart to God's voice.

Seeing the hardness of man's heart, God stopped saying, "Give Me your life," and He said, *"Here, take Mine."* God wrapped up His love in His only Son, and through Jesus Christ gave Himself for us, that we might be saved.

> *Herein is love, not that we loved God, but that he loved us, and sent his Son to be the propitiation for our sins.*
>
> 1 John 4:10

April 7

The Lost Ring
by REBECCA ROBERTS NASH

One day I dropped my ring in the car, and try as I might, I couldn't find it. I searched under the carpets with a flashlight and still couldn't find it. Although the ring wasn't very valuable, it had sentimental value, and I wanted it back.

Several weeks passed, and my mind was occupied by other things. My husband, Marshall, had been working on a difficult real-estate deal. In fact, problems had caused it to drag on for months. We had talked about it at length and asked God to help work it out. Finally, an agreement was reached and a meeting was scheduled to sign papers and close the deal. When it was over, Marshall called to tell me how well it went and how everyone was happy with the way it had turned out.

That afternoon, driving to pick up the children from school, I was talking to the Lord and thanking Him for helping us, when I thought I heard something roll out from under my seat. I reached down and my hand fell on the ring I had lost.

I was so happy that I pulled the car over and stopped. Joy welled up in me. I was amazed and grateful, and I began to talk to God all over again: "Lord, You have blessed us so much. You are cared about these real-estate problems and helped us work them out. You have given us patience to wait when we thought we couldn't and now—finding this ring is *too much!*"

I think I know what the Psalmist felt when he wrote: "How precious is your constant love, O God!" (Psalm 36:7 LB). I'm continually learning that, in ways both great and small, God reveals His loving care and concern for you and me.

April 8

God's Risk of Faith

I shall not call you servants . . . for a servant does not share his master's confidence. No, I call you friends . . . .
John 15:15 PHILLIPS

Occasionally we all find it difficult to trust the Lord. But have you ever thought about how difficult it must be for God to trust us?

God took the greatest risk of faith of all time when He gave man the power of choice. Would man live the way God had made him—in togetherness, in unity and love? Or would he become a selfish creature, taking care of self and his own, but denying the being and existence of others? In giving man the power of choice, God was saying, "I believe in you. I will risk your having the power of choice." This was God's trust in humanity at work. Now that's the greatest faith ever known!

For, you see, now we can do with God's Creation what we will. We can pollute it or cleanse it. We can be reverent toward one another or irreverent. We can uphold God or we can smash His image in our spirit. That God has given us this power—and that we can use it every moment of our existence—means God not only loves us but He also believes in us. If God trusts man that much, then how much more we can trust in Him!

April 9

An Invincible Spirit

Hope is divinely built into each of us. When we talk about hope, we are talking of the invincible spirit of man that can defy all doubts, challenge all defeats, and rise to rare heights of courage and faith. And hope knows no age barriers. It's in little children; it's in youth; it's in the middle-aged, and in the very old.

I recall a ninety-two-year-old man who came into the prayer line at one of our crusades. I smiled and said, "Brother, aren't you too old to be healed?"

His eyes flashed, his shoulders came erect, and with a voice I remember to this day, he said, "Young man, one never gets too old for a good God to heal him." Then he told me that certain friends had ridiculed him for coming. "I fixed them by coming anyway," he said. "Today I will be healed."

When I laid hands upon his head and prayed, his response was electric with joy and belief. And as he walked away, his step was jaunty, his body was straight, and his heart was praising God!

Hope! To awaken hope within you, you need only to respond to God and put your trust in Him.

> *May the God of hope fill you with great joy and peace as you trust in him, so that you may overflow with hope by the power of the Holy Spirit.*
>
> Romans 15:13 NIV

April 10

What It's All About

Real life and real living are not related to how rich we are.
Luke 12:15 LB

A wealthy man and I flew across the country in his jet. We set down at a beautiful lake area, where he showed me a gorgeous home that he said cost him hundreds of thousands of dollars. Then with a smile he turned to me and said, "Oral, this is what life is all about."

I can't tell you how I had to sit on myself. I felt I should say something, but I didn't want to offend him. After all, I was his guest. But I really felt like saying, "If this is all there is to life, then I've sure missed it, because I hear from thousands of people who have everything their hearts could desire in the way of material things, but they're miserable." And the man I was looking at was miserable, too.

Jesus said: *Man shall not live by bread alone* (Matthew 4:4)—which means that basically man is a spiritual being. He has a body, but he is not physical. He has a mind, but he is not mental. We were made by God, and He left a place in the human heart for Himself that only He can fill—only He can satisfy. *Things* are only poor substitutes for God. It is when you start reaching up to God and out to others that you find the real meaning of life and what it's all about!

April 11

You Can Do Better

I have a wonderful friend who is different from all my other friends. He's always criticizing me. No matter how well I do or how much I accomplish, he always has one thing to say to me: "Oral, you can do better."

After Oral Roberts University was built, I remember how thrilled and proud I was. My friend walked up and said, "Oral, you can do better." The time we produced a television special that captured the imagination of millions of people across America, this fellow saw me and said, "Oral, you can do better." And once I preached a sermon that I thought was particularly outstanding. There he was: *Oral, you can do better.*

How can I feel that a critical guy like that is my friend? Proverbs 27:6 says, "Faithful are the wounds of a friend." I believe that God has put this man in my life because everybody needs to be criticized once in a while. We may not like it, but we all need it at times to keep our perspective.

I've not reached any degree of perfection in my Christian experience. And I feel that everyone can benefit from having this attitude of doing better—of reaching upward to God—and of:

> . . . *working toward that day when [we] will finally be all that Christ saved [us] for and wants [us] to be.*
>
> Philippians 3:12 LB

April 12

How to Take Criticism

Criticism is hard to take. But sometimes it helps you to become a better person.

In our crusade days we drew large crowds, but controversy swirled about me all the time. I had to face a lot of things that were said about me that weren't true. I still have critics today, but I think in some respects it is good, because it has made me really learn the Bible. It has made me study the life of Jesus. And it has forced me to lean upon the Holy Spirit. Above all, it has made me examine myself to see if I really believe what I preach.

Your critics help you find your weaknesses. You know, friends won't always do that for you. I don't have a lot of the weaknesses I had then, because my critics very carefully pointed them out and I plugged them up as best I could. Some, I couldn't plug up. Some, I'm still plugging up.

I've learned that when criticism and opposition come at you, you can take it and make it a force with which you examine your motives. Ask yourself if it is true. If it is, have the courage to change. If it isn't, put the criticism in the hands of God and leave it there. The Bible says: *It is a badge of honor to accept valid criticism* (Proverbs 25:12 LB).

April 13

Be Willing to Change

God's method changed.
Hebrews 7:15 LB

God is not married to or bound by methods but by His eternal principles. This was a direct and divine revelation to me at a time of almost complete desperation in my life and ministry. As 1967 came to a close, I stood among the falling remnants of the methods I had been using for twenty years in the healing ministry. Some of my methods, so beautifully used by God, had run their course.

What did I do? I obeyed God! I changed my methods but held on to the principles He had given me when I began this ministry in 1947. And I'm seeing miracle after miracle after miracle.

Most people fear change. They seem to feel that change means they will lose something. In my study of seed-faith in the Bible, I saw that those who used the seed-faith principles taught by Jesus did not fear changing their methods. If they had—the little boy who gave his lunch to Jesus, the fishermen who loaned their boat to Jesus, the widow who gave God her last few pennies—they would never have experienced their seed-faith being miraculously multiplied in their lives and, through them, multiplied to meet the needs of others. The fact was, they thrilled at learning new ways from Jesus. Being willing to change—to move with God—is essential to becoming a good follower of Christ.

Read John 6:9; Luke 5:3; Mark 12:42.

April 14

A Lesson in Faith

With men this is impossible; but with God all things are possible.

Matthew 19:26

It is said to be a scientific impossibility for a bumblebee to fly. Its body is too heavy, its wings too small. Yet the bumblebee flies anyway—and makes a little honey while it does it.

The bumblebee cannot reason. It cannot doubt. Man, so prone to lean on his intellect rather than looking to God, seldom rises above his human limitations. Yet it is possible to do so—through faith.

Faith used in the spiritual dimension can work miracles never before thought possible. I've seen faith in action change drunkards to loving husbands and fathers who provide for their families. I've witnessed miracles of healing through faith that have literally lifted the sick from their beds. I've known men who used their faith to prosper in their business, so that they might give more to God's work.

Faith is the link that attaches our human weaknesses to an all-powerful God who transcends all barriers. Faith transforms you—lifts you up—makes a new person out of you. *Faith turns life's impossibles into possibles.*

April 15

The Source of All Healing

But unto you that fear my name shall the Sun of righteousness arise with healing in his wings . . . .
                                             Malachi 4:2

Some people who believe in healing through prayer turn away from doctors. On the other hand, some who have great faith in doctors tune out prayer. With them it's an either/or proposition. But our Lord said: *They that are sick need a physician* (Mark 2:17). So I accept both prayer and medicine reverently.

Some time ago I became very ill with a kidney stone. If you've ever had this experience, you know how painful it is. My wife, Evelyn, called the Abundant Life Prayer Group to pray for me. She also called our family doctor. He came and gave me a shot. Then he said, "Oral, I've treated you medically; now I want to pray for you." He laid his hands on me and prayed a simple short prayer, but full of sincerity and faith.

In one hour I was okay. I don't know if it was because of prayer or because of medication, or both. It doesn't matter—I was well. To be honest, I don't make demands on God. If God wants to heal me through prayer, I accept it from Him. If He chooses to use a doctor as the instrument to bring healing to me, then I accept that. Or if it's a combination of both, I gratefully accept it. For the Source of all healing is *God.*

April 16

Childlike Faith
by RICHARD ROBERTS

Except ye . . . become as little children, ye shall not enter into the kingdom.

Matthew 18:3

I remember when I was about ten or twelve years old I had twenty-two warts on my left hand. My mother came in one day and said, "Richard, you're going to the doctor, and you're going to have those warts burned off."

That scared me half to death. When Dad came home, I told him about it. I remember he said, "Evelyn, you leave that boy alone. He and I and the Lord are going to take care of those warts." Dad and I went off into another room and had a very quiet simple prayer. I didn't know how God was going to do it, but I just believed that when Dad prayed, the warts would go away. Within two weeks every wart was gone!

The Bible speaks of the importance of having faith as a child, or childlike faith. I believe that means simply believing that God answers prayers.

April 17

The Practice Point

Ye shall be witnesses unto me.
Acts 1:8

The Sermon on the Mount is the essence of Jesus' teachings to His disciples. In the book of Acts we see the Apostles *at the practice point*. It says so: "The Acts of the Apostles." The time arrived for them to put into practice what Jesus had taught them and demonstrated before them. In Acts they themselves "came up to bat." They started "throwing the ball into the basket." They began to "hit the golf ball" in their own game. They commenced their own witness. This was their moment!

Einstein, the great Jewish scientist, said, "Christianity when actually practiced by Christians will cure all ills." All social ills—all physical ills—all spiritual ills—all financial ills! All followers of

Christ arrive at their *practice point,* where they must give Christianity to others as Christ lived it and gave it to them.

How do you begin? In joyful anticipation. In prayer that comes from your heart. In the study of Jesus and His life and works. In making Him your Source. In giving to Him first. In expecting miracles. That's the key. This is your moment to witness—your *acts!*

April 18

Your Lack Is Your Security

The eyes of the Lord are watching over those who fear him, who rely upon his steady love. He will keep them from death even in times of famine!

Psalm 33:18, 19 LB

I once dealt with a man who wanted to be employed by our ministry. He was well qualified, but in the final analysis he said, "Mr. Roberts, I don't think I can handle the job. It would require me to depend upon God as sort of an unknown source. On my job now, no matter what comes, I'm taken care of. I've got security. And at my age I've got to think about security for my family."

This is a dangerous position to be in—where you feel you have to stay at a place where there is no risk—where you think everything is going to be provided for you, come what may—where you don't have to have faith.

Did you know that your greatest source of security is in the things you lack—not in the things you have? For the things you have, if you're not careful, can become something on which you lean. I feel the worst thing a person could do for me is to offer to take care of all my needs, because it would take away my sense of trust in God. He has designed us to depend on *Him* as the Source of our security!

April 19

The Best Advice
by EVELYN ROBERTS

Parents often ask my advice about how to bring up their children. I haven't yet solved all my problems as a parent. But I think the best advice is this: Get a good grip on the Lord. Know Him for yourself. Then saturate your children with the Word of God (*see* Deuteronomy 6:6–11). If they have not been taught the Word at home and grounded in the faith, their minds become fertile soil for someone to come along and plant in them one of the Satan-inspired ideologies that have come out of this decade.

The world will make a desperate bid for our children. We can't stop this. But while they are in our care and under our control, we can build up an arsenal of Scripture and faith in their minds and hearts that no power can prevail against. The Word is living and real. It has the answer for every situation of life. You learn through the Word how to use your faith effectively and how to depend on God as your total Source.

No greater heritage can we give our children than to teach them how to pray and reach God when trouble strikes.

April 20

No Rocking Chair

Soul, thou has much goods laid up . . . . take thine ease, eat, drink, and be merry.

Luke 12:19

Man works hard with the dream in mind of someday retiring, leaning back and taking it easy.

When I made the official announcement that God had laid it on my heart that it was time to build the schools of medicine, dentistry, and law at Oral Roberts University, my darling wife, Evelyn, said, "You know, I thought I'd gotten to the age where I could sit in a rocking chair, do some needlepoint, enjoy my grandchildren, and relax and take life easy."

I know how she felt, because this project meant struggle. But I remembered the words of Paul in 2 Timothy 4:7: *I have fought a good fight. I have finished my course . . . .* Paul never quit fighting. He finished the race and he finished it in faith.

I believe God wants us to resist taking our ease. He wants us to shake ourselves, to put our shoulders back and our heads up. God wants us to believe that we can do the impossible. He wants us to have stars in our eyes and the wonder of a child in our heart. God's way is not the way of the rocking chair, but the way of continually reaching, believing, struggling, and achieving until we finish our course!

April 21

So Much Smoother!

There is something about offending someone and living in the strain of being unforgiven that is too heavy for a human being to bear.

I remember once when my oldest granddaughter, Brenda Nash, was about ten years old she came to spend the night with Evelyn and me. Our grandchildren love to come to our house, and we love to have them. But when Brenda came in, the usual joy of coming to see us was not there. Her little shoulders were slumped and she looked uptight.

Pretty soon the phone rang, and Brenda jumped up to answer it. We were listening, and we heard her say, "Mommy, I'm sorry, too." A little more talk, then, "Well, Mommy, I want you to forgive me, too." Apparently, Brenda and her mother had had a little dispute and the load of it was upon her frail shoulders. But when she hung up the phone, everything was different. She'd had a release in her spirit and soon we were having a marvelous time, as we always have with our grandchildren.

Maybe you too feel the need to plant a seed of forgiveness and say to someone: "I'm sorry. Forgive me." If you do, God will multiply it back to you. "Forgive," Jesus said, "and ye shall be forgiven" (Luke 6:37). When the healing power of forgiveness sweeps through your being, everything runs so much smoother!

April 22

A Delicate Balance

[Live] as free people . . . but [live at all times] as servants of God.

1 Peter 2:16 AMPLIFIED

It's one of the paradoxes of being a disciple of Jesus Christ that while on the one hand God is setting us free to become all that we are meant to be, on the other hand we are choosing to become servants, love-slaves of God, joyously giving Him complete control of our lives.

Freedom and servanthood. You'd think they'd cancel out each other. Yet not only do they coexist, they bring out the good in each other. For servanthood without freedom is bondage, and freedom without servanthood is license. But together they form a delicate but perfect balance.

The Apostle Paul put it like this: "Although I am free in every way from any one's control, I have made myself a bond servant to everyone" (1 Corinthians 9:19 AMPLIFIED). He also said, "You . . . were [indeed] called to freedom; only [do not let your] freedom be . . . an opportunity . . . [for selfishness], but through love . . . serve one another" (Galatians 5:13 AMPLIFIED). Through Jesus Christ we are free to choose to become servants of God and of each other. And it's in the freedom of servanthood that we find true joy and fulfillment.

April 23

Jesus Knows How You Feel

Jesus sits where you sit!

A woman once heard me make that statement on television and she wrote me and said: "Mr. Roberts, I believed in you until your sermon last week. Now I just can't accept you anymore because you said Jesus sits where I sit and He's gone through what I've been through. I'm a divorced woman. Well, Jesus was never divorced. So how can you say that? Jesus doesn't feel the alienation and loneliness that I feel. I no longer have a husband or a home. I don't know where I'm going to turn. How can you say that He's experienced what I've experienced?"

I wrote her back, "You are correct in one way. Jesus was not a divorced man. But Jesus felt alienation and loneliness. He *felt* it. The Bible points out in Hebrews 2:18 and 4:15 that Jesus is 'touched with the feeling of our infirmities,' for He was tempted and suffered the same things we do. Therefore, He is wonderfully able to help us. This makes it very clear that Jesus knows how we feel. He knows what loneliness is. It's hard to understand, but Jesus was man. I mean *human!*"

Think of any human feeling you've ever had—loneliness, the feeling that nobody cares, despair, frustration—and try to understand that Jesus experienced it for you. He walked through it, and He's come to walk you through it.

April 24

They Don't Mix

When bad things happen, we often ask, "Why did God let this happen to me?" But the question is: Why did the *devil* do this to me? Look. You can draw a line right down the middle of this page. Put the devil, with his badness, on one side and God, with His goodness, on the other side, and you in the middle—like this:

The   **YOU**   **Jesus Christ**
devil   **of Nazareth**

There is no goodness in the devil and no badness in God. The good things come from God and the bad things come from the devil. Jesus said, "The [devil] cometh . . . to steal, and to kill, and to destroy: I am come that [you] might have life . . . more abundantly" (John 10:10). The devil comes to steal from you: your faith, your love, your hopes, your talent, your time, your earning power, your right relationships, your health—everything good about you. This is why God says, "Resist the devil [so that] he will flee from you" (James 4:7).

Jesus said He came to give you life—*full and continuing life— abundant life!* Remember, the devil and Jesus don't mix! When bad things happen, put the blame where it belongs—on the devil!

April 25

New Roots

When I saw *Roots,* the great television series, I began to realize how important roots are to our lives. The series told how the black people were kidnapped and carried against their will from Africa to America under brutal conditions—torn away from their roots—and how one family traced its roots.

But, I thought, what happens once they find their roots? Is that all? Can going back into Africa and finding one's roots do anything more than establish your identity? Can it put money in your hand? Can it bring healing to your body? Can it save your soul? Can it straighten out your life? Or must all of us, whether we live in Africa or America or anywhere else on earth, look to new roots?

I believe that no matter what our color is or what our physical roots may be, we must have a better and deeper root system than just the nation we live in—and that root system is God Himself. In God, our roots are not left behind in a place, but they are within our innermost being, in the faith we have in God our Source. And that is always with us.

May your roots go down deep into the soil of God's marvelous love.

Ephesians 3:17 LB

April 26

Do You Have a Root System?

Blessed is the man that trusteth in the Lord . . . . For he shall be as a tree . . . that spreadeth out her roots by the river.

Jeremiah 17:7, 8

If you were to take a piece of wood—what we'd call a plank—and pound it into the ground, it would not reproduce itself. It might support something, but it would not grow or produce fruit. Why? Because it has no roots. It has no *root system*. But if you look at the tree from which that plank was cut, you would see that it had grown deep into the ground and its roots had connected with the soil and the water table. And because of the tree's root system, it had become a living thing, a producer of fruit, a multiplier of itself.

In Genesis 1:28, God said to man, "Be fruitful, and multiply, and replenish the earth." But how can we be fruitful unless we have roots? For without a root system we have no connection with the Source of all life, who is God.

When God is your root system, you are not just a piece of timber standing up in the ground, with no life-giving power of reproduction, of multiplication. As David said in Psalm 1:3, you are like "a tree planted by the rivers of water, that bringeth forth [its] fruit in [its] season."

April 27

Let the Winds Blow

Have you ever noticed that when seeds drop from a tree, they seldom stay at the base? The seeds could never take root and grow there, for under the tree there is too much shade. The seeds have to be blown away from the tree. Some drop at the base, but the winds take the others and blow them for hundreds of feet or yards, or even a quarter of a mile. There the seeds take root and develop a root system of their own. They become new trees. They produce fruit. And they in turn multiply by dropping their seeds, not at their base but to the winds. This is life.

It's a great temptation to drop your seeds at the base of your life, to cling to the things you create or produce, to build your life around yourself. You're the big guy. Nobody else counts. And so your life becomes empty and fruitless. You miss what life is all about. "For none of us liveth to himself, and no man dieth to himself" (Romans 14:7).

Our seed—the production of our lives—must be blown by the winds of the Spirit wherever He will, blowing it out where it can take root in somebody else's life so that it can reproduce and come back to us.

April 28

Our Root System Saved Us

As ye have . . . received Christ Jesus the Lord, so walk ye in him: Rooted and built up in him, and stablished in the faith.

Colossians 2:6, 7

My wife, Evelyn, and I have suffered in our lives, but until we lost our lovely daughter, Rebecca, and our dear son-in-law, Marshall, in an airplane crash, I don't think we knew what real suffering was.

God, our "root system," saved us, for the devil tried to mock me. He said, "Oral Roberts, you preach to others of hope. Now where is your hope? You have held many funerals to point people to Christ. Are you looking to Christ? You have told others whose loved ones have been snatched away by death that there is a God of comfort. Do you feel comforted?"

But I could fling the devil's mocking words back at him and say, "God knows something about this that I don't know." While my heart felt wrenched out of my body and the tears were streaming down my cheeks, I could say, "I have a root system. I have a Source. I have God."

And I know you can say: "I am like a tree planted by the water. I am rooted and grounded in Christ. He is my root system. He is my Source—and He will see me through every problem, every need, every sorrow!''

April 29

The Taproot

A tree has one special root called a taproot, which is larger than the other roots. It connects the tree to the soil, and from it the tree draws its nourishment, its life. Now if you were to destroy some of the smaller roots, they'd probably grow back and the tree would survive. But if you were to sever the taproot, then the tree would die.

In the same way, if you were to lose your job or if one of your loved ones should die, you'd hurt. But as long as you stayed connected with your Taproot—God—you'd recover. You'd make it.

When my wife and I suffered the loss of our precious daughter and son-in-law, Rebecca and Marshall Nash, part of our root system was destroyed. But through God we are overcoming that. Yet, if something were to sever our relationship with Jesus Christ—our Taproot—we'd never recover. Thank God nothing can separate us from our Taproot (*see* Romans 8:38, 39).

Jesus is the Taproot of our existence . . .
the Source of our total supply . . .
the everlasting Redeemer of our being . . .
the Nourisher of our life.

April 30

Rooted in God

God is your dwelling place.
Deuteronomy 33:27 RSV

God is your dwelling place! Moses reassured the people of Israel with those words while they were in the wilderness, wandering from one place to another, trying to locate.

Most of us can understand how these people felt, because we live in a mobile society. There is a rootlessness among people today. We move from job to job, from city to city, and predictions are that it will get worse. Our equilibrium is upset when we are uprooted and have to readjust to new surroundings. We tend to feel lost and unimportant. We are like the seeds thrown on rocky soil in Jesus' parable: "Because they had no root, they withered away" (Matthew 13:6).

But the Bible says: God is your dwelling place—or your *root system*. "In him we live, and move, and have our being" (Acts 17:28). Your body may move from one place to another, but you— the real you—lives in God. You are rooted in Him. People whose root systems are not in God don't really live, because they are cut off from the Source of life. But when Christ, God's Son, has come to live in your heart, you have new roots. You are wherever He is. And where you are, God is.

MAY

May 1

The Most Important Thing

On the Day of Pentecost, when the gift of the Holy Spirit was given, a great crowd gathered to watch the phenomenon. Peter stood and began to preach and explain to the crowd what was happening. As he spoke, the hearts of the people were deeply moved, and when he finished they asked, "What must we do to be saved?"

"Repent!" Peter said.

This was his first word to them—the first thing God said through a man after the Church came into being that day:

> *Repent, and be baptized every one of you in the name of Jesus Christ for the remission of sins, and ye shall receive the gift of the Holy Ghost.*
>
> Acts 2:38

So you can see that the most important thing in your life is not . . .

- Getting eight hours of sleep at night
- Eating breakfast in the morning
- Or even going to work.

These things are important. But God says the most important thing is for us to repent of our sins, to be baptized for the remission of sins, and to receive the gift of the Holy Spirit.

May 2

It Turns Your Life Around

When God says, "Repent," the thought can be so big that it is shattering. For God is saying that our pattern of behavior is dishonoring to Him—our thought pattern is wrong. And He calls upon us to repent; that is, to change our mind and heart from living in a state of wrong before Him. Not many of us want to change. We have built up a way of life, and it is set as hard as concrete.

Repentance is a complete change—*it turns your life around*. You are sorry because you have done wrong, and you ask God's forgiveness. But it is more than an intellectual change; it involves your heart—your innermost thoughts and being. You *stop* sinning. You confess your sins and forsake them (*see* Proverbs 28:13). Then salvation happens inside you.

Salvation is a Person—the man Jesus Christ. Through the Holy Spirit, He creates in you a new heart and a new spirit. You have a change of attitude, a change of habits, a change of thinking, a change of behavior—a change in your *entire* way of living. And it's all toward loving God and loving other people as you love yourself.

Repentance is a conversion experience—a beginning of following Christ and learning to become His disciple every day for the rest of your life.

May 3

It's a Daily Thing

Repentance is, first, an *act*—a step of believing on Jesus Christ as your personal Savior. And second, it is an *attitude* that you carry throughout the rest of your life.

Now we would like to think that we could repent one time and that would take care of our spiritual life for all time. And it does—for the whole past! But it doesn't take care of the future. For, you see, every day we live there is something we think or do or say that is not in harmony with the Lord. Jesus said, "He that believeth . . . shall be saved" (Mark 16:16). It's a *continual believing* on Jesus.

So, becoming a disciple of the Lord means living in an attitude of repentance. It means *daily* bringing your heart and your will to God and trusting in Him as your Lord. It means that you are against that which is wrong—whatever is unloving. Your heart continually declares: "I don't want the old way of life; I want the new way of salvation."

So the most important thing in your life is that you repent—and keep on repenting!

May 4

How You "Hear" God's Voice

Thine ears shall hear a word behind thee, saying, This is the way, walk ye in it.

Isaiah 30:21

After the death of our daughter, Rebecca, and her husband, Marshall, their three children—Brenda, thirteen; Marcia, eight; and little five-year-old Jon Oral—went to live with Marshall's brother, Bill Nash, and his dear wife, Edna Earle. There's love and faith in their home, and God is speaking to those children.

One day little Jon Oral said, "Uncle Bill, when you were my age, did God speak to you?"—And Bill said, *Yes.*

"Well, how did He speak to you? How did you know it was God?"—*Well, I don't know that I could put it in words, but, yes, God spoke to me.*

"Uncle Bill, do you think God would speak to me?"—Bill said, *Yes. Yes, He will, Jon Oral. You just listen, and God will speak to you.*

In a few days that little grandson of mine said, "Uncle Bill, God talked to me last night. God spoke to me."—Bill said, *He did?*

"Yes."—*Well, what did God say to you, Jon?*

"He said for me to share what I have with my sisters."—And Bill said, *Well, that was God all right, because only God will tell you to share what you've got.*

I believe God speaks to every person. His voice is all around you—in the Bible, in a sermon, in a prayer, in a song, in a book, in nature, in a word from someone. But primarily His voice is inside you. God's voice is a word He places in you—very special, most intimate and gracious. You do not have to hear it in the same way another person does, because God treats us as individuals. But if you listen with your will, with a determination to know God and obey Him, your heart will "hear" God speaking.

May 5

God Is for You!

God is for me!
Psalm 56:9

Ours is a world of competition. People feel forced to compete with each other in order to make it financially, socially, and otherwise. No wonder so many of us reach the point where we feel that the whole world is against us; that we're alone in our struggle to survive; that it's "just me against the world." But the Bible tells us that we are not alone, that God is with us, and that He is *for* us.

Sometimes we may feel that even God is against us because of our circumstances, but God is *for* us. When Jesus was on earth He was not against people; He loved people. God is against sin, but He's *for* the sinner. He's against fear, but He's *for* the fearful. He's against poverty, but He's *for* the poor. He's against sickness, but He's *for* the sick.

Jesus came to let you know that God is for you—that He cares what happens to you—that you are not out there in a lonely crowded world where nobody cares whether or not you eat, or have a steady income, or are healthy, or feel peace in your soul. Because God cares.

Say it: *God is for me! And if God is for me, who can be against me?* (Romans 8:31).

May 6

Leave Perfection to God
by REBECCA ROBERTS NASH

In a conference with my daughter's teacher, we were discussing how mothers and daughters can be so different. I said, "I haven't yet learned how to deal with that. I expect certain things from Brenda, and when I'm disappointed I tell her so."

The teacher said, "Oh, I hope you don't make the same mistakes I did. May I tell you what happened to me?"

She said, "I was the kind of person who expected perfection in myself and everyone else, and had very little tolerance for other ways or ideas, especially in my children. My daughter and I clashed all the time and had almost quit communicating at all. Then one Sunday my husband and I were in church, and an elderly gentleman was to play a violin solo. As he arose and began playing, I thought, *Oh, no, not him again! He plays so poorly and he has played that same song a dozen times. Why don't they let someone with real talent play?*

At that moment her husband leaned over and whispered, ''Just think of the hours of practice that have gone into that song!''

She continued, ''Suddenly a picture came into my mind of a little boy in knickers, standing before a music lectern practicing the violin, while outside his window all the other kids were playing ball. The picture of that little boy started other pictures in my mind, and it was as if a light bulb went on and I was able to see my daughter. There she was before me. Then I saw how *I* thought she should be. I do believe the Lord spoke to me and put a verse of Scripture in my mind—*The Lord will perfect that which concerneth me.* Later I found it to be from Psalm 138:8.

''The Lord showed me that He made my daughter and each of us to be an individual, not like anyone else. And He has a purpose for making us the way we are. Now why did it take me so long to see something as simple as that?'' she marveled.

From that day, she said, she has been able to change her attitude. And, although a difference in her relationship with her daughter didn't come suddenly, things are beginning to change and they are communicating again.

By the time the teacher's story came to an end we were both crying. ''My conferences don't usually end this way,'' she laughed. I hardly heard her, for I was busy praying, *Lord, help me to leave perfection to You.*

May 7

How to Release Your Faith

People often say to me, ''Oral Roberts, you're always saying: *Have faith in God. Expect a miracle!* What I want to know is how?''

I had this problem, too, until God showed me what I call the ''point of contact.'' The point of contact is something you do—and when you do it, you release your faith. I remember one woman who used my letter as a point of contact. She had been prayed for many times but hadn't been healed. Then one day she wrote me for prayer. She said, "I've come to the place I am no longer looking to you or any other person, just the Lord."

I prayed and wrote her back, and in a short time there came back a three-page letter, full of praises to God. She said that when she received my letter she prayed, "Lord, as I place this letter on my body I'm expecting *You* to give me a miracle." Then she said, "Something that felt like a warm liquid started flowing through me. And I knew God was healing me."

If you need healing, look to God as your Source (*see* Exodus 15:26). Then use a point of contact. Remember, a point of contact is something *you* do—a word, a prayer, a touch. And when you do it, you release your faith, and suddenly you know your miracle is on its way!

May 8

We All Get Lonely

One day I was with a friend in North Carolina, on a new golf course which had been chopped right out of a forest. The fairways were surrounded by trees. We came to one green where there were four trees isolated from the rest of the forest, and they were dead. Yet the other trees were glorious in color and beautiful to see.

"Why are these trees dead?" I asked.

My friend said, "Oral, when we cut the fairways out of the forest and left these trees alone, they got lonely and died." He smiled and said, "You remember the Scripture says: *It is not good that . . . man should be alone* [Genesis 2:18]. Well, it applies to trees, too. These got lonely and died."

How much like those trees we humans are! They say that the greatest hurt a person feels is loneliness, nonacceptance. Jesus experienced the pain of aloneness. He said, "Every man . . . shall leave me alone; and yet I am not alone, because the Father is with me" (John 16:32). Jesus showed us how to cope with the depression of loneliness: He put His mind on God, His Source of companionship. This consciousness, this awareness that God Himself is with you always—in good times and bad times—lifts your spirit and rids your heart of loneliness as nothing else can.

May 9

Worship the Source

I am the Lord that healeth thee.
Exodus 15:26

It is important to know the difference between the source and the instrument of healing.

People say, "The medicine the doctor gave me cured me." Not so. The medicine comes from God's natural resources, such as a plant or an animal; therefore, God is the *Source*. He just happened to heal through that instrument.

People say, "The natural forces of my body went to work, and now I'm feeling fine." True. But who created the body with built-in powerful healing forces? God, who is its Source.

People say, "This man or woman prayed for me and healed me." They prayed, but they didn't heal. God, who hears and answers the prayer of faith, did the healing. Prayer and faith are only instruments, or delivery systems; the Source is God. We must look beyond the instrument to the Source.

As a doctor once told me, "Oral, I've learned from the Bible, and from hearing you and reading your books, something that makes my practice a real joy. And it's this: I *value* the instrument of healing, but I *worship* the Source of it—*God!*"

I said, "Doctor, I've never heard it expressed exactly like that, but I believe it 100 percent!"

May 10

Like the Rest of Us

I remember one time, after we had finished making a television special on location, Evelyn went down to the laundromat to do our laundry. After it was dried she went to a grocery store so we could have something to snack on in our room. A woman saw her and followed in the background. As Evelyn was getting into the car, the woman rushed up and said, "Oh, Mrs. Roberts! You wash clothes and go to the grocery store just like the rest of us."

Later, when Evelyn shared this with me, she said, "If she only knew how human we really are."

I totally agreed.

That is one of the most wonderful things about Christ. He was human, too. He was God and knew no sin, yet He came to earth to share in our humanness. He became bone of our bone and flesh of our flesh (*see* Hebrews 2:14 LB). Jesus is the only One who can relate to everybody. And He's the only One whom everybody can relate to, because He sat where you sit and He felt what you feel. *Jesus knows what it feels like to be a human being.* As a man, Jesus is God, identifying with you at the point of your need. Jesus is God's affirmation of your humanness and of His power to give you a new and abundant life.

May 11

Miracles Are Coming

Miracles are coming toward you or passing by you every day.

God said this to me when I was thinking about people and their needs. It seemed I could see them hurting, feeling lonely, wondering why so many hard things were biting at them. And out of the depths of my soul, Jesus spoke, "Oral, tell people of My blessing and supply in these words: *Miracles are coming toward you or passing by you every day.*"

Then God let me see these miracles, as if they were flying toward me. If I was aware and sensitive to Him, I could receive every one of the miracles flying toward me. If I was not expectant in my heart, they would pass by me.

I thought of miracles I had been seeding for, one especially I had been needing for weeks. I suddenly realized God may have tried to give it to me before, but because I wasn't properly expecting, I hadn't been able to recognize this miracle and receive it. It had been passing me by. *I got my miracle that very day!*

Every one of us forgets to expect to receive. We feel forgotten, passed by. But you can have more miracles—you can! God's miracles are coming toward you to receive, or passing by you if you are not expecting. Only you can decide to be aware!

> *My soul, wait thou only upon God; for my expectation is from him.*
>
> Psalm 62:5

May 12

How to Deal With Loss
by EVELYN ROBERTS

Thirty-eight years ago a black-haired, blue-eyed baby girl was born to Oral and me—our firstborn. A few weeks following her birth, we took her to church and dedicated her to God. In essence, we were saying, "Lord, You have loaned us this precious baby. Today we give her to You and promise to teach her that Jesus loves her and wants to have a place in her life. We thank You for giving her to us, but we know she's really Yours."

The vows we made so long ago came back to my mind recently, as I was thinking how quickly time had passed since Rebecca came to live with us. And now she is gone from our sight, to be with God, who had given her to us.

One night as I was preparing for bed a sudden and terrible feeling of loss swept over me. I felt overwhelmed by it. And I began pouring my heart out to the Lord. "Jesus, why? Why did You take her when she was so young? I feel cheated for myself and for her three children. Jesus, can You understand how my heart aches?"

As clearly as I've ever heard anything in my life I heard His voice inside me, "Oh, yes, I know and My mother knows how you feel. Remember? I gave My life at age thirty-three. My mother stood and watched Me die on a cross. Yes, I understand."

"Lord, forgive me," I said. "How could I have forgotten for even a moment?"

Now, I know it's wrong for me to feel cheated. God never cheats us. He blesses us. And Rebecca was one of our many blessings. I believe that talking out my feelings to the Lord and hearing His words of comfort back to me have kept any bitterness out that might have built up inside me.

If you are grieving over some loss, you may feel cheated, as I felt momentarily. But if you can talk out your feelings with God and refuse to allow bitterness to live in your heart, the Lord will comfort you.

> *Blessed be . . . the God of all comfort; who comforteth us in all our tribulation, that we may be able to comfort them which are in any trouble, by the comfort wherewith we ourselves are comforted of God.*
>
> 2 Corinthians 1:3, 4

May 13

Send Your Problems Through Heaven First

*When ye pray, use not vain repetitions, as the heathen do:
for they think that they shall be heard for their much speaking. Be not ye therefore like unto them: for your Father
knoweth what things ye have need of, before ye ask him.*

Matthew 6:7, 8

Some time ago I spent a day in the Prayer Tower, reading letters from my partners who poured out their hearts in their prayer requests: "Brother Roberts, bad things are happening to me—My marriage is in trouble—I've lost my job—The conditions in the country are getting to me—Pray for me!"

When I saw the desperate needs of the people, I cried out in my heart: "Dear God, use me to communicate the Three Miracle Keys of Seed-Faith to people, so that they won't be underneath their problems, but will climb out on top of them."

I found myself praying hard. As I finished, phrases began going through my mind—phrases like: *Don't pray hard; pray easy. Prayer doesn't do it—God does! Tell the people to send their problems through heaven first.* I wasn't sure what these phrases meant at first, but I knew the Holy Spirit would reveal their meaning to each person who heard them, according to his need.

I left the Prayer Tower exhilarated. I knew then—and I know now—you don't have to pray hard if you are truly trusting God as your Source. He is going to take care of you if you send your problems through heaven first!

May 14

Something You *Do*

What do you do when you cannot expel bitter, angry thoughts from your mind? Some years ago an unflattering article was written about the Abundant Life Ministry. It really hurt me. And the man responsible was a friend of mine.

I tried to overcome the resentment within myself. But the more I thought about it all, the less I understood. One day I was on my knees in prayer and I heard words from deep inside me—I knew it was God speaking.

"Oral, write this man a letter and apologize."

What? I thought. *He should apologize to me.*

Nevertheless, I sat down and wrote the letter. It was hard. But when I had finished, I knew it was right. I recognized that I had had bitterness in my heart, which was worse than what the man had done to me.

Soon the man sent a reply that said, "Oral, I'm the one who should apologize."

God can heal our human relationships only when we have a spirit of forgiveness. Jesus taught that if ". . . a friend has something against you . . . go and apologize and be reconciled to him . . ." (Matthew 5:23, 24 LB). It doesn't matter who was originally at fault. Forgiveness is not only an attitude of heart but also something you *do*.

May 15

A Majority Vote

A great black preacher once said, "God always votes yes, the devil always votes no, and your vote decides the election."

In my own experience I know God has a will for what happens in our lives, the devil has a will, and so do we as individuals. But no matter how strong God's will or the devil's will is, our will decides it. Because God has given us the power of choice.

Even Jesus, in confronting the cross, faced the three wills. *First,* the devil's will was that Jesus disobey God's purpose for His life and by His own will put God aside. *Second,* God's will was that Jesus face the cross and let the Father plant His life as the "Seed of David," which He would raise up in the harvest of the resurrection—thus providing the power for our salvation and everlasting life. *Third,* Jesus' will was to decide whether to do the devil's will or God's will.

Jesus used His will to cast His vote with God's. He said, "Not my will, but thine, be done" (Luke 22:42). And that decided the way things went!

Your vote with God's makes a majority!

May 16

That Steady *Bump, Bump*

I've always loved horses, and when our four children were little I would ride with one or more of the kids behind me on the same horse. One day, when Richard was about three years old, he and I went riding together. I was making the horse trot, and Richard's head kept bobbing back and forth, hitting me in the back. I said, "Keep your head still, Richard."

"Aw wight."

But his little head kept right on bobbing.

"Richard Lee, I said to keep your head still."

The horse kept a steady trot, and Richard's head kept a steady *bump, bump.* When I told him again to keep his head still, he said, "But Daddy, it won't 'tay 'till." And who could argue with that?

The *bump, bump* of Richard's head reminds me of little irritating habits people have that bug us. But to expect people to change is often asking too much, just as I was expecting too much of Richard. Sometimes what we need for more harmonious relationships is to ". . . Be patient with each other, making allowance for each other's faults because of [our] love" (Ephesians 4:2 LB).

> *Dear Lord, help me to be more patient with the annoying traits and habits in some people which aggravate me. After all, they have to put up with mine.*

May 17

Bridging the Gap

> *. . . forgive, if ye have ought against any: that your Father also which is in heaven may forgive you*
>
> Mark 11:25

Forgiveness is more than saying, "I accept your apology." Forgiveness is a healing, a process of mending, and we can make it real in our daily relationships.

One way is to picture in your mind the one person who has hurt you the most. Now picture Jesus standing before an altar, beckoning to you. See Jesus coming to meet you. He puts His arms around you and hugs you warmly and lovingly, welcoming you into His presence. Then see Him beckoning to one who has hurt you. With an embrace equally warm and loving, He welcomes that person.

Jesus then places one arm around your shoulders, and the other arm around the shoulders of that one who has hurt you. And Jesus, bathing both of you in love, becomes the link which closes the gap between you.

That is the reconciliation Jesus can bring to each broken or strained relationship in our lives. Whether it's a deep hurt or only a minor annoyance, Jesus bridges the gap. His love can make forgiveness real in our lives and in our relationships—today.

May 18

God and the High Cost of Living

The other day my wife asked me to go to the grocery store with her. Before I go to bed at night I like to have a bowl of cornflakes. It's a habit I've had all of my life. So in the store I picked up my cornflakes and she got a loaf of bread, a half gallon of milk, and a few other items. At the checkout stand the cashier rang up the groceries and put them in a sack, which wasn't full. The lady handed me the receipt, and it was for $11.28. I checked each item, because I thought there must be a mistake, since it looked like we had only about $3 worth of groceries in the sack.

The cashier said, "Sir, is something wrong?"

"No," Evelyn spoke up. "He just doesn't know what the cost of living is. That's why I wanted him to come with me."

"Evelyn," I said, "is that all the groceries we get for eleven twenty-eight?"

"Oral, you just don't realize what's going on."

I began to think about that. Maybe I didn't know how high groceries are. But God does. And that makes me feel better. Because you and I can find a way to overcome the high cost of living when we learn how God does things. He specializes in shortages.

The answer is in the Bible. In Habakkuk 3:17–19 LB, the prophet talks about the shortages of his time:

> *Even though the fig trees are all destroyed, and there is neither blossom left nor fruit, and though the olive crops all fail, and the fields lie barren; even if the flocks die in the fields and the cattle barns are empty, yet I will rejoice in the Lord . . . .*

How could the prophet rejoice when everything was crashing down around his head? He is not saying, "I'm going to accept all this and rejoice." But, "I will rejoice *in the Lord*. I'll joy *in the God of my salvation*." Because in the next verse he says, "The Lord God is my Strength [my Source]."

That's how God operates in shortages. Though all things around you fail, you can rejoice in God and know you are going to get through it victoriously because *God*—your Source—will help you!

May 19

He Came to Cheer Us

Jesus spake unto them, saying, Be of good cheer.
Matthew 14:27

I remember as a small boy the first time I heard Will Rogers speak. We lived in Ada, Oklahoma. That year a drought came, and the farmers were being wiped out. We lived in town at the time, and food was scarce. I sold newspapers on the street. One day I ran down the street shouting this headline: WILL ROGERS IS COMING!

Will Rogers was able to cheer this nation. He was well-read, but his humor was direct and simple. The Convention Hall in Ada was filled with people from our county. They were from all walks of life. The blue collars and white collars all sat together. As a little boy, I sat there too. Will told a few funny stories, then opened his billfold and gave the first money to help those who were losing everything. Soon everyone there was giving. People left the hall that day no longer depressed. They were saying, "Will Rogers knows what we're going through. He came here to help us with our problems."

That's what our Lord did. He came to cheer us, to enter our human needs, to give Himself to us, and to get us to open our hearts to others. But Jesus didn't come just for one day. He came to be with us every day, in every need, and in every way.

May 20

Why Carry Them?

In 1948, when my ministry was just getting off the ground, a great theologian came to me and said, "Mr. Roberts, I want you to show me in the Bible where healing is in the Atonement."

The first verse I turned to was Matthew 8:17: "[Jesus] took our infirmities and bare our sicknesses" (*see also* Isaiah 53:4, 5).

"But that was two thousand years ago," he said.

"I agree," I said, "but that's when Jesus was here in the flesh. When else could He bear them?"

"I never thought of that as being on the cross," he reasoned.

"The thrust of Jesus' whole life was to go to the cross," I reminded him. "Think of any human need or feeling—any hurt, sickness, fear, loneliness, despair, or suffering—and realize that Jesus gathered these up and carried them with Him to the cross. He bore them there in His own body vicariously for us. *He bore them.* That's healing in the Atonement!"

You see, the old rugged cross is not just two pieces of wood. It is the stretched out, bleeding form of Jesus Christ, who took all of our needs and carried them in His own body.

So why should we carry them? Our Lord has already borne them for us!

May 21

My Greatest Discovery

The greatest thing God ever showed me—the greatest thing I know today—is that God is a good God!

I discovered this truth one morning as I was rushing to make an early class at a university I was attending while I pastored a church. I had just finished reading the New Testament through for the hundredth time, in a search for God's power and to discover Jesus as He really is. Without this background I might not have been prepared for my discovery.

I had resolved that each morning I would read something from the Bible. In my rush that day I simply opened the Bible at random to read, and it fell open to 3 John 2: *Beloved, I wish above all things that thou mayest prosper and be in health, even as thy soul prospereth.* These words literally astounded me. I could scarcely believe my eyes. This verse was simply beautiful. Yet, it had something more than beauty. It had power and it gripped my heart. For it was saying, "God is a good God!"

I saw too many people who accepted life's tragedies as God's will, and they didn't expect Him to change the inequalities of life. One was to be sick—another well. One poor—another rich. One happy—another miserable. And that was that. Religion was not divine deliverance but acceptance of life's inadequacies. But something inside me said this wasn't true.

The message in 3 John 2 is just as real to me now as it was then. It means that God is a good God and the devil is a bad devil. There is no badness in God and no goodness in the devil. The good things come from God and the bad things come from the devil.

It is a simple but powerful truth that you cannot believe God is blessing you, when at the same time you believe He is cursing you. It is difficult to believe His promise to supply all your needs if you believe He wants you to be poor. And how can you have faith that God will heal you when you believe He has afflicted your body?

The Word says that Jesus came to heal "all that were oppressed of the devil" (Acts 10:38). God wants us to have strong bodies, minds, and souls. He wants to prosper us—to lift up our spirits— and to give us strength for the responsibilities of life that He has entrusted to our care.

So look up and believe that God is a good God and that He wants to bless you. Think about it—accept it—open up to it—and you will see what God will do in your life and family.

May 22

We Have Time . . . If We Don't Hurry
by RICHARD ROBERTS

It had been a long surgery for the patient, and time was running out. But an artery still needed to be repaired. A young assisting doctor, who knew they only had a short time to finish, questioned the chief surgeon, "Do we have enough time to repair it?"

"Yes," the chief surgeon replied, "if we don't hurry."

Many times people ask me, "Richard, what are your plans for the future? What do you see for your life ten years from now?"

To me, the important thing is that I am doing what God wants me to do *today*. If my mind is on five years from now, I won't be able to do as well the work God has given me today. I feel what I am doing today is preparing me for what the Lord has in store for me tomorrow, and I must give my best today. We have time to do what the Lord has called us to do, if we don't hurry.

> *So don't be anxious about tomorrow. God will take care of your tomorrow too. Live one day at a time.*
> Matthew 6:34 LB

May 23

First Bale of Cotton

Of the firstfruits, ye shall offer them unto the Lord.
Leviticus 2:12

From the beginning, God taught the people that when they went out to gather in their grain, they were to give the very first they gathered to God.

In Pontotoc County, Oklahoma, where I grew up, the farmer who had the first bale of cotton got a premium price. So each farmer would watch his crop closely. He'd keep a close eye on the stalks that had the most bolls of cotton on them—those that were opening white and fleecy. Then he'd rush out and pick the first bale, put it in a wagon, and take it to the cotton gin. The farmer who got there first with the firstfruits would get about three times as much money for the first bale as anybody else would get the rest of the cotton season. That was the firstfruits.

In the book of Leviticus, instructions are given about the offerings the people of Israel were to give to God. Over and over it is pointed out that the offering was to be "without blemish." In other words: *Give God your best*. Why? Because what you give to God is what He multiplies back to you. This is God's way of doing things and your way of working with Him. That's why it is so powerful, even to causing your most needed miracles to happen.

May 24

Lord, Teach Us to Pray

One of the things about Jesus that stood out to His disciples was His prayer life. They were accustomed to much prayer in their Jewish religion, yet they saw in Jesus' life of prayer a fresh and more intimate approach to God. Doubtless some of them didn't even *like* to pray. There was nothing about prayer that turned them on. Once when Jesus had finished praying, one of His disciples was so deeply impressed that he said: "Lord, teach us to pray . . ." (Luke 11:1).

And Jesus responded by saying, "After this manner therefore pray ye . . ." (Matthew 6:9).

Jesus was not indicating that this was to be His followers' sole prayer—the only words we are ever to say in prayer. It is not to be a substitute for our personal expressions of prayer. Jesus meant that we are to pray *after the fashion* of this particular prayer, which we today call "The Lord's Prayer."

> *Our Father which art in heaven,*
> *Hallowed be thy name.*
> *Thy kingdom come.*
> *Thy will be done in earth,*
> *   as it is in heaven.*
> *Give us this day our daily bread.*
> *And forgive us our debts,*
> *   as we forgive our debtors.*
> *And lead us not into temptation,*
> *   but deliver us from evil:*
> *For thine is the kingdom,*
> *   and the power,*
> *   and the glory,*
> *   for ever. Amen.*
>   Matthew 6:9–13

May 25

God the Father

Our Father which art in heaven . . . .

The word *Father* referring to God was not used in the Old Testament. It was first used this way by our Lord Jesus Christ to signify the closeness that Jesus and God the Father had together. In fact, Jesus' favorite name for God was "Father."

I always called my father "Papa." I remember when I was hemorrhaging to death with tuberculosis and was brought home in the backseat of an automobile. My father looked in and I said, "Papa . . . ."

He said, "What's the matter, Son?"

"Papa, I've gone the last mile of the way."

Then Papa scooped me up in his arms, carried me into the house, and laid me on the bed. He said, "Son, you just lie there. We'll take care of you."

There was something about my father that was so deeply a part of my life. I've always been close to my mother but, oh, there was a relationship I had with my father that I cannot put into words. He stood for affection, for confidence, for protection, for love. He was especially near his children when they were ill or in trouble.

Papa! Jesus was saying, "Think of this kind of close relationship when you pray and say, 'Our Father—our Daddy—our Papa.' "

May 26

The Name of God

Hallowed be thy name . . . .

Jesus had a deep feeling about the name of God. He never used it irreverently. Jesus esteemed the name of the Father. "When you pray," He was saying, "reverence the name of God."

Many years ago a well-known newspaper photographer named Lee Krupnick had a habit of taking God's name in vain. It was so much a part of him, he did it almost without realizing it.

His wife became a Christian, and the name of Jesus was precious to her. She stood about all she could, then one day when Lee began to curse God she said to him, with the firmness that only a wife can have toward her husband, "Lee, don't ever curse the name of my Lord in my presence again!"

He whirled around and said, "What do you mean?"

She said, "Jesus changed my life. Although I love you, Lee, and I'm your wife, Jesus means more to me and has done more for me than anyone."

A strange quietness came over Lee.

Years later he told me this story and said, "Oral, that day something went into my heart—not merely my mind—but my heart. The Holy Spirit convicted me of my sins. And because the name of God—the name of Jesus—was hallowed to my wife, I came to know Christ."

May 27

In Heaven and Earth

Thy kingdom come. Thy will be done in earth, as it is in heaven . . . .

Jesus was very concerned about the nations or kingdoms that existed on the earth. But He was even more concerned about a higher kingdom—God's kingdom. For He taught us to pray, "Thy kingdom come."

Think for a moment of what would happen if the kingdom of God were to come to this earth. What if two nations who were at war with each other would sit down and say, "Why don't we ask what God's will is in this situation?" What if a family who is always quarreling and fighting with one another would stop and say, "What is God's will for us?" What if our community leaders would sit down and ask themselves the same question? If this happened, then we would all treat each other as human beings, and God's kingdom would come to earth.

Every time you pray, "Thy kingdom come," you are praying a revolutionary, radical prayer. You are praying that what is *in heaven* will come to be down here *in the earth*. And that starts with you and me—with our repentance and love. The will of God starts in heaven but it is lived out in us.

May 28

Supplying Our Needs

Give us this day our daily bread . . . .

I'm glad Jesus didn't leave *bread* out of "The Lord's Prayer." The hip folks today call money "bread." When Jesus said, "Give us this day our daily bread," He meant, "Give us this day our material needs." Jesus knew all about the physical necessities of life. He knew the worth of a widow's mite and what the loss of a coin meant to a housewife. He knew about clothes that needed mending and about not having a place to sleep at night.

Even after His resurrection, Jesus showed concern for His disciples' bodily needs when He came to them after they had been fishing all night. He knew they would be hungry, so He prepared breakfast for them and said, "Come and dine" (John 21:12).

Jesus is talking about bread—*about God's bread*. He's talking about a supply of your needs that really satisfies; about clothes that please you; about an automobile that works; about a house that becomes a home. He's talking about God meeting your needs. God wants you to have peace. He wants you to live out your days in health and happiness.

May 29

God's Forgiveness

And forgive us our debts as we forgive our debtors . . . .

In connection with this portion of "The Lord's Prayer" Jesus immediately added these words:

> *For if ye forgive men their trespasses, your heavenly Father will also forgive you: But if ye forgive not men their trespasses, neither will your Father forgive your trespasses.*
>
> Matthew 6:14, 15

Jesus indicated that the human race is guilty of trespasses—we are debtors.

We *do* things we ought not to do.
We *say* things we should not say.
We *think* things we should not think.

Each of us is a trespasser, and our forgiveness must come from God. There is one Forgiver—and that is God. Men may or may not forgive us, but God *will* forgive.

A man once said to John Wesley, "I'll never forgive."

Wesley replied, "Then pray that you will never sin."

In other words, the only way we are ever going to be forgiven by God of our trespasses is to forgive the one who trespasses against us.

May 30

Rough Waters

And lead us not into temptation, but deliver us from evil . . . .

Essentially, Jesus was telling us to pray, "God, don't forsake me when the going gets rough. Don't let me get into situations that are bigger than I am. Don't let me get in water over my head."

I heard of a fellow who was asked where he was going. He said, "I'm going to get drunk, and how I dread it!" That may sound funny, but it makes a point. You see, he wasn't enjoying drinking. But it had a hold on him. He wanted God's help, and when he said, "How I dread it," it was really a prayer.

That may not sound like a prayer, but a prayer can be just a sigh
. . . a groan . . . or a deluge of tears (*see* Romans 8:26; Hebrews
5:7).

In whatever way you express the sincere desire of your heart,
God will understand, and He will help you.

May 31

Eternal Power

*For thine is the kingdom, and the power, and the glory for ever.
Amen.*

When Jesus said these words, He was living in an outpost of the
Roman Empire. The Roman soldiers in their barbaric cruelty were
putting their burdens on the people and acting like Rome was going
to rule forever.

But Jesus looked beyond Rome—beyond every other kingdom
that would arise on the earth—and He said, *"Thine* is the kingdom.
There is something bigger and better and more stable than any
earthly kingdom," Jesus was saying. "And that kingdom is ruled
by the King of kings and the Lord of lords."

He was saying to you and me today: "You are surrounded by the
kingdom of God—an incomparable power that can set you free—a
glory that can fill your breast. So why settle for the transient things
of this world when you can have the permanent kingdom of God
within you? You can have the limitlessness of the Spirit of God
helping you to receive health again. You can have your soul
saved—your material needs met. *And this can start today!"*

JUNE

June 1

The Shepherd and His Sheep

The Lord is my shepherd; I shall not want.
                                      Psalm 23:1

My shepherd. The word *my* indicates a personal relationship. A shepherd and his sheep are very close. "The shepherd . . . calleth his own sheep by name, and leadeth them out . . . and the sheep follow him: for they know his voice" (John 10:2–4).

A *shepherd* is one who guides and leads the sheep. Jesus called us "sheep" because we don't know where to go ourselves. We need the Lord as our Shepherd to lead us where He wants us to go.

People have a lot of shepherds—or leaders. But *the Lord* is a different kind of shepherd. He is not only our Guide but also our Source for everything we need. People try to make a lot of different things their sources. But if we accept anything short of the Lord, it's really just a substitute. The Psalmist is saying, "The Lord is my Source."

A little girl once said, "The Lord is my Shepherd, and that's all I want." And it's true. If the Lord is your Shepherd, He *does* supply all your need. There is no lack! With the Psalmist you can say, "I shall not want."

June 2

Green Pastures and Still Waters

He maketh me to lie down in green pastures: he leadeth me beside the still waters.
                                      Psalm 23:2

Green pastures. The Psalmist could have just said "pastures," but it wouldn't have meant much. Because some pastures are old, brown, dried-up grass, rocky and full of briars. And there's no nourishment or rest in that. But can you think of anything more refreshing than *green* grass and *still* waters?

Still waters. After feeding the sheep and letting them rest for a while, the shepherd leads them to the watering place. Sheep will not drink from a rushing, noisy stream, so the shepherd first dams up the stream and makes it into a quiet pool—and then the sheep drink.

The Lord, our Shepherd, provides us quietness and refreshment. You see, He wants us to rest. There's a restlessness in our nation—a rootlessness—people on the go, moving here and there. They can't seem to be quiet. Of course, the Lord wants us to have action. But He also wants us to have times of quietness in Him— quietness in our heart, from which power is generated to have godly action going on in our lives.

June 3

Soul Restoration

He restoreth my soul: he leadeth me in the paths of righteousness for his name's sake.

Psalm 23:3

One bad thing about sheep is that they have a tendency to stray—to just follow their noses. They put their heads down and start grazing, and away they go. Sheep are said to have such poor sense of direction that they will graze right up to, and over, a cliff. So if a sheep strays, it's in danger; and the shepherd has to go out and find it and restore it to the flock.

Aren't we often like that? We simply wander off from our Shepherd. But though we may stray again and again and again, when we say, "Lord, forgive me," He brings us safely home again (*see* Ezekiel 34:16).

The soul—that inner part of us—can go astray like a sheep. It can be lost. But God, who made our soul, can fully restore it. He can and He does! The Bible says, "All we like sheep have gone astray; we have turned every one to his own way . . . but are now returned unto the Shepherd . . . of [our] souls" (Isaiah 53:6; 1 Peter 2:25).

June 4

Through the Valley

Yea, though I walk through the valley of the shadow of death, I will fear no evil; for thou art with me.

Psalm 23:4

I recall when my wife, Evelyn, and I first moved to Tulsa. Our son Ronnie was four years old. Just a few blocks from where we lived, a terrible murder had been committed only a couple of weeks before. One night I was gone and Evelyn and the children were alone in the house. Ronnie couldn't go to sleep. He called Evelyn in by the bed and said, "Mother, I'm afraid that man is going to get in this house and murder me."

Evelyn said, "Oh, no, honey. Jesus is watching over you. He won't let that happen! He has assigned your own personal angel to stand by your bed all night. You don't have to be afraid."

He said, "Well, okay. If that's the way it is, then I'll go to sleep." And he went right to sleep.

When it comes to the valley of the shadow of death, we're all little boys and girls. But the Lord tells us that when we go through that valley we need have no fear, because we're not alone. The Lord, our Shepherd, is with us. He takes the fear away!

June 5

That Rod and Staff

Thy rod and thy staff they comfort me.
Psalm 23:4

When a shepherd in Israel takes his sheep from one pasture to another, he uses his rod and staff to beat off the snakes and the wild animals—anything that endangers his sheep. This is exactly what the Lord, *your* Shepherd, does for you.

The shepherd's staff has a crook to it, so when a sheep starts getting out of line, the shepherd just reaches over and puts that crook around the sheep and pulls it back where it belongs. Did you ever feel the Lord pull you back in line?

I have. I *have* to have God's authority in my life because, like sheep, I get to going in every direction. I don't always like His authority, but I need it. I must have it. For I have found that where there is authority and discipline there is also security.

Discipline hurts sometimes. But when you know God is in charge of your life, you can relax with a sense of security. God's "rod and staff" are an encouragement and a comfort that let you know that God is always there with you to beat your enemies away and to keep you out of trouble.

June 6

An Inside Feeding

Thou preparest a table before me in the presence of mine enemies.

Psalm 23:5

When your enemies are trying to get the best of you, it's good to know the Lord is there, feeding you, strengthening your inner man.

I'm reminded of a man who was being falsely accused and was to be brought before a group of his superiors to defend himself. He realized he would probably lose his job, and he was frightened. But while he was on his way to the conference, the Lord gave him Psalm 23:5: "Thou preparest a table before me in the presence of mine enemies."

So the man recited this verse over and over. And as he sat down and faced the men who were going to question him, he continued saying it under his breath. To his amazement they all started talking about something else. Finally one of the men said, "There's nothing to substantiate this accusation. Let's forget the whole thing." And turning to the man he added, "Don't you think it's time to go back to your job?"

The man said he has always believed that because of that Scripture he didn't lose his job.

June 7

Joy Runs Over

Thou anointest my head with oil; my cup runneth over.
Psalm 23:5

Oil is a symbol of the Holy Spirit. As a young boy, David, the Psalmist, was anointed with oil by the Prophet Samuel. Later

David's life was filled with danger, temptation, hardships, and anxieties. Yet because of that special anointing, he was always able to rejoice in the Lord. He sang, "Shout with joy before the Lord, O earth! . . . come before him, singing with joy . . . . the Lord is God! He made us—we are his people, the sheep of his pasture" (Psalm 100:1–3 LB).

Israel is a hot country, and under the blaze of the noonday sun, the sheep become weak and lifeless. Also briars often scratch their faces. At the end of the day, the shepherd goes among the sheep with a vial of oil and pours it on their heads and into their wounds. The oil goes all over them, refreshing, soothing, and healing them.

When we're in such a tangle with our adversaries and problems that we don't know what to do, the Lord anoints us with His Holy Spirit, and the joy of the Spirit runs down the sides of our souls—out of the cup and into the saucer!

June 8

Goodness and Mercy

Surely goodness and mercy shall follow me all the days of my life: and I will dwell in the house of the Lord for ever.
Psalm 23:6

A good shepherd never leaves his sheep. At the end of the day, he calls them one by one into the fold. After they are all accounted for, he lies down at the door and personally keeps them safe.

God cares and provides for us as surely as a shepherd cares for his sheep because He is "the *good* shepherd" (*see* John 10:11–14).

Somewhere people have gotten the idea that everything bad that happens is an act of God. For example, if you're sick, God made you sick. But we know that God is good. James 1:17 says, "Every *good* gift . . . cometh . . . from the Father." And Psalm 23:6 says, "*Goodness* . . . shall follow me all the days of my life." Goodness and mercy surround us because the Good Shepherd is always near.

This verse reminds us that the Lord, our Shepherd, is going to be with us *always*. He's forgiven our sins of the past. He's with us today. And we don't have any fear for the future, because we're going to dwell in the house of the Lord *forever*.

June 9

There Is a Power . . .

And Jesus [said], *All power is given unto me in heaven and in earth.*

Matthew 28:18

There is a Power that isn't limited. There is a Power beyond this universe, far beyond the sun and stars, who also walks upon this earth in the person of the Lord Jesus Christ—coming here through the Holy Spirit, through His angels, and through His Holy Word. There is a Power that can sweep back obstacles, destroy overwhelming odds, and even things up for us; a Power that can enable us to live the kind of life we would love to live.

There is a Power that is not of man, that can reach the lowest alcoholic and take the very appetite, the burning thirst, from his being. There is a Power that can pick up a twisted cripple and make him walk again. There is a Power that can take sightless eyes and make them see once more.

There is a Power that can reach into the lowest hell and pick up the vilest sinner and make him pure enough to be the father of any child. There is a Power that is beyond our imagination, so great, so wise, so wonderful, yet so close—fingertip close to us—that we can reach out and take hold of it, pull it into our lives by faith, and find ourselves living in a brand-new world on this earth. This Power is God.

June 10

Honest Doubts

Faith begins with doubt. You have to have some honest doubts in order to have great faith; otherwise, you are presuming. And presumption means nothing. Faith means you have investigated. You have solid evidence. But to get that evidence, you first have doubts.

Remember Thomas, one of the Twelve Apostles, who doubted the Lord's resurrection? He said, "Except I shall see in his hands the print of the nails, and put my finger into the print of the nails, and thrust my hand into his side, I will not believe."

Thomas is our kind of guy. The others didn't voice their

doubts—but they ran off anyway. Thomas was an honest doubter, and he's the one to whom Jesus made a personal appearance, and said, "Thomas, reach hither thy finger, and behold my hands; and reach hither thy hand, and thrust it into my side: and be not faithless, but believing."

Thomas took one look and confessed, "My Lord and my God!" (*see* John 20:19–29). All Thomas' cynicism faded when he saw reality—Jesus!

So don't be discouraged if you sometimes have doubts. It is natural—a part of growth. Honest doubting is better than indifference. It indicates that you are seeking.

June 11

Being a Christian Is Not Being Perfect

The just shall live by faith.
Galatians 3:11

Are you attempting to live by your faith? I'm not talking about being perfect. None of us has reached perfection. Sure, we make mistakes. Sure, we stumble and fall, but we get up and go on.

Christianity is not living in perfection every day, for we stumble from time to time. But it means the thrust of our life is toward God. It means that we have faith in Christ as God's Son, who has come into our heart to make us a new creature, and we are reaching up toward God to live by our faith, rather than by compromise or doubt. It means we have new roots, a new root system, and our roots are in God Himself.

Maybe you have never known God. You've been groping through life. You've broken God's laws and you're suffering and paying a terrible penalty for it right now. You've never repented and asked Christ to change your heart, to make you a Christian, to come into your life and live in you.

If not, this is the moment when God is speaking to you to change the way you've been living, asking you to commit your life to Him.

I'm going to ask you to repeat this prayer and let God give you a new life beginning right now:

> *O Lord, I'm sorry for the way I've lived and disregarded You, and I repent. Take away this heavy load, this awful burden, from my heart and set me free. Give me Your peace.*

*Deliver me from every wrong desire and every bad habit
that binds my life. Come into my heart and change it. And
now I receive Christ as my Savior and Lord of my life. And
by Your grace, Lord, I will serve You all the days of my life.
Amen.*

Remember, Christ saves you and Christ keeps you saved. Begin today to build your life around Him.

June 12

Healing Is for the Total Man

I believe healing is for the whole man. It's for anything in your life. So many people associate healing with just the body, but our body is only a part of our existence. We are spirit, mind, and body. We're all a package. Whatever is wrong with any part of us makes us ill and, to me, healing is for the totality of man. It is for any part of his being:

    his spirit
    his mind
    his body
    his marriage
    his relationship with his children

God gave me a miracle with my youngest son, Richard, who went away from me as I went away from my father when I was a teenager. Richard now sings on our weekly "Oral Roberts and You" television programs and quarterly specials. Oh, but he was going the other way. Then a miracle happened.

It was a healing!

Richard wasn't ill physically, but he received a healing from God in his spirit. And now instead of saying, "Dad, get off my back"—which he once said to me—he says, "Dad, I'm by your side." And any father will tell you that that's the sweetest news he ever heard!

*[May] the very God of peace sanctify you wholly; and . . .
your whole spirit and soul and body be preserved blameless
unto the coming of our Lord Jesus Christ.*

                                                    1 Thessalonians 5:23

June 13

The Desperation Point

Have you ever watched a little child trying to tie his shoestrings when he hasn't quite mastered it yet? He diligently draws up the strings to make sure they are even, makes a loop with one string, twists the other around it, and pulls. But it doesn't work. So he tries again—and again. Finally, out of sheer desperation, he turns to his mother and lets her take his fingers in hers and help him tie the bow.

We all like to consider ourselves self-sufficient. We like to think, *I can handle life by myself. After all, others do it, and so can I.* But inevitably the day arrives when you come to the end of your personal strength and resources, and suddenly you realize you can't do it all yourself. You reach the desperation point and you pray the prayer God always hears: *God, help me. I can't make it without You!*

How it hurts when you've come to the end of yourself—when you've tried your hardest and you've failed. But there is something good about it. It pulls you toward God. It teaches you to rely on Him, to draw from His strength, and to pray: "I am poor and needy: make haste unto me, O God" (Psalm 70:5).

And He does!

June 14

We Forget
by REBECCA ROBERTS NASH

One day when my son, Jon Oral, was two years old, I was busy working in the house and trying to keep an eye on him at the same time. I missed him and called. He didn't answer. He wasn't in the back yard or the front yard, and I started to get panicky. I ran through a neighbor's yard and out into the street, calling his name, but getting no answer. Just as I started back through the gate I heard, "Mommy! Mommy!"

"Jon," I cried, "what are you doing here?"

He ran up to me and hugged my legs and said, "Mommy, I find you."

Apparently he had called me and, not being able to locate me in the house, had gone outside searching for me. All the time he was looking for me, I was in the next room!

Are you lonely or in trouble and it seems God is far, far away? He isn't. He's right there with you. Christ said, "Lo, I am with you alway, even unto the end" (Matthew 28:20). The main reason we become afraid is that we forget this marvelous truth.

June 15

Stagecoach Driver

In the days of the old stagecoach, companies had a hard time getting good drivers for the hairpin curves of the Rocky Mountains. They were losing too many stagecoaches, so they sent out a call to the East Coast, "Send us good drivers." Several men came and applied, saying how well they could drive—how near the edge they could drive the stagecoach without going over.

One young man said, "I withdraw my application. I can't drive like that. And if I could, I wouldn't." The owner said, "How would you drive, son?" He said, "Mister, I'd see how far away from the edge I could stay and keep that stagecoach from turning over." The owner said, "I've been looking for a man like you. You've got the job."

Godliness is not seeing how closely you can brush shoulders with the world and still hold onto Christ, but how far away from the spirit of the world you can live. That does not mean isolation—going off somewhere and becoming a hermit. Jesus' prayer for all those who believed on Him was, "I pray not that thou shouldest take them out of the world, but that thou shouldest keep them from the evil" (John 17:15). Jesus was talking about being in the world, but resisting and refusing to be a part of the world's spirit.

June 16

Push the World Back

"Life isn't worth living. I wish I were dead." Did you ever say that? That's what the Prophet Elijah said in a time of discouragement. He sat down under a juniper tree and said, "It is enough: now, O Lord, take away my life" (1 Kings 19:4). Elijah surrendered his will. He lay down inside.

Perhaps that's where you are. Maybe your problems have piled up and you don't see any way out. You may be walking around on two feet, but inside, the man isn't standing and walking. He is withdrawn from life, he's no longer interested in people, and he wishes the whole thing were over.

This feeling of wishing to die can be surrendered to a desire to live. One of the things God did was appeal to Elijah to rest. The Lord had Elijah sleep, and He awakened him two or three times and had him eat. Then the Lord sent him to a place where he heard the still, small voice of God.

How long has it been since you took time off from your affairs? The man who lives inside—how long has it been since he stopped and calmed down? When did he put up his hands and push the world back for a few hours and pillow his head on the promises of God and rest?

> [God says:] Wait on the Lord: be of good courage, and he shall strengthen thine heart: wait, I say, on the Lord.
>
> Psalm 27:14

June 17

Something Good Will Happen!

> . . . always be expecting much from . . . God.
> Hosea 12:6 LB

You can dwell on your problems until you get so low that the devil can climb on your shoulders and keep you down. But an attitude of expecting something *good* to happen to you changes your perspective and brings the problem-solving power of God into your life.

Sometimes we are like the old boy who had a flat on a country road at night and didn't have a bumper jack. He saw a light in a distant farmhouse and said, "That farmer will probably have a jack." So he trudged about a mile to the farmhouse.

All the way he was building up a morbid expectancy: *I understand farmers are suspicious of strangers at night. In fact, I've heard they sleep with a shotgun by their beds. That farmer had better not chase me off his property!*

By this time the man had reached the farmhouse. He knocked on the door. The farmer stuck his head out and asked, "What do you want?" The man blurted out, "You can keep your old jack!"

In the same way don't we, by our attitude of doubt and negative anticipation, rob ourselves of God's gifts? Regardless of how much miracle power God has, it is effective in our lives only when we cease being negative. Fully expect something good to happen—and it will!

June 18

Get Back Into Joyous Living
by RICHARD ROBERTS

The disciples were continually diffused with joy and the Holy Spirit.

Acts 13:52 AMPLIFIED

The distinguishing mark of the Christian is *joy!* Joy from deep inside that is not dependent on circumstances.

When we don't have joy, it may be that we are harboring bitterness. Jesus taught, "If you are offering your gift at the altar and there remember that your brother has something against you, leave your gift . . . . First go and be reconciled to your brother; then come and offer your gift" (Matthew 5:23, 24 NIV).

Personally, I find it hard to function when I have bitterness in my heart. So whenever I find myself feeling resentful toward another person, I try to make it a point to be reconciled with him so that I can get back into joyous living with God. I challenge you to do the same.

If someone holds something against you, go and ask forgiveness. And if you hold something against someone, in the same manner forgive him. This action will cleanse you inside and allow the Holy Spirit to fill you with joy.

June 19

Our Keeper

The Lord is thy keeper . . . The Lord shall preserve thee from all evil.

Psalm 121:5, 7

Two cars drove into a service station from opposite directions. One driver recognized the other and walked over to his car. "Say,

Jim," he said, "the Lord is really watching over me today. Just a few miles back a huge truck went out of control and started heading directly toward me. At the last second the truck swerved back into its own lane and barely missed me. It's wonderful how the Lord protects us!"

"It surely is," agreed Jim. "He protected me today too."

"What happened?"

"*Nothing*," answered Jim. "None of the trucks I met went out of control."

We are inclined to take for granted those times when *nothing* happens. But this, too, is God's divine protection. His tender mercies are over us every moment of every day, not just in times of danger or crisis. Sometimes we see the evidence of God's care; sometimes we are not aware that we have been protected. Our Keeper and Protector, though unseen, is very real.

June 20

God Always Has a Purpose
by EVELYN ROBERTS

Since Christ suffered in the flesh . . . arm yourselves with the same . . . purpose . . . . For whoever has suffered in the flesh . . . has stopped pleasing himself . . . and pleases God.

1 Peter 4:1 AMPLIFIED

I think that as Christians the greatest thing in the world we can try to do is to please God in everything we do. Now that's hard to do! Sometimes we try to do things to please ourselves, not even considering what God's will is for us. I've done that so many times in my life. I've gone ahead like a bull in a china closet, butting my way through. But when I stopped and let the Lord work things out the way He wanted to, they always worked out for the best.

For over a year I worked on my book titled *His Darling Wife, Evelyn.* (Of course, it's mainly about Oral, but since he always introduces me as his "darling wife, Evelyn," that's what I named my book.) At the end of the summer, the manuscript was just about ready for the printer. I was really hoping I would get it into the hands of the publisher by September and it would be out by Christmas. But when I called New York I found that I was too late, because the quota of books to be published by Christmas had already been filled. I was really disappointed. I wanted that book so badly for Christmas!

Then I got to thinking, "Well, Lord, I guess You really had another purpose in mind. It was my purpose to get it out, but it was not Your purpose. Evidently You have something greater for me in the spring than at Christmas."

That spring when the book was published, it was a huge success.

I firmly believe that everything that happens to us happens in God's purpose. There's nothing that happens to us by accident. Now maybe at the time we can't see it, but God always has a purpose. This is why in 1 Peter 4:12 AMPLIFIED the Apostle Paul goes on to say: "Beloved, do not be . . . bewildered at the fiery ordeal which is [testing] your quality, as though something strange . . . were befalling you."

We cry and moan and fuss when things don't work out as we have planned them. But God wants us to be quiet in our spirit and to pray; *Lord, I don't know what Your purpose in all of this is. But if it somehow glorifies You and fulfills Your will and purpose for my life, then this is what I want too.*

June 21

Not a Bad Question

One day Peter, as spokesman for the disciples, said to Christ, "Behold, we have forsaken all [we've given everything], and followed thee; what shall we [receive] therefore?" (Matthew 19:27).

Now that's not a bad question! A lot of people might think it's bad to ask, "What are we going to get? We've been giving. We've been giving up this and that in order to follow You, Jesus, to take Your ways rather than our ways. Now what are we going to get out of it?"

You might think that Jesus would have rebuked Peter. But He didn't. He said to him, "Verily I say unto you . . . every one that hath forsaken houses, or brethren, or sisters, or father, or mother, or wife, or children, or lands, for my name's sake, *shall receive an hundredfold, and shall inherit everlasting life*" (Matthew 19:28, 29).

Jesus responded, "Because you've followed Me and because you've not let any of these things stand between you and Me, even to the extent of giving, you're going to receive a hundred times what you've given—and everlasting life."

God is a debtor to no man. When you give, you can *expect* to receive!

June 22

Know **That You Know**

I know whom I have believed.
2 Timothy 1:12

Years ago a brilliant but eccentric professor of mathematics assigned a problem to his students. The next day he asked various ones to go to the board and write down the solution. But to each one he said, "I'm sorry, that's wrong. Please be seated."

Finally, a student who had studied all night went up and wrote down an answer that had already been refused. The professor said, "That's wrong. Didn't you hear me say before that it was wrong?"

The young man said, "Yes, sir, I did. But it's the correct answer."

"Are you sure?" the professor asked.

"Yes, sir, I'm absolutely sure."

Then the professor smiled. "You're right," he said. "It *is* the correct answer."

When the other students protested, the professor explained, "People are looking for solutions to their problems. They want the right answer, but they also want to know that the person who gives them the answer has confidence in it. This young man has demonstrated that he *knows* that he knows the solution!"

That is how faith in God works. You come to a point where you *know* that you know that in God you have the solution to your problems.

June 23

Keep Your Light Burning

Ye are the light of the world.
Matthew 5:14

A famous man once told the story of how he found himself to be a guiding light to an elderly lady living alone on a hillside opposite his home. He had purchased an old abandoned house on a mountain slope in an unsettled area to use on holidays to "get away from it all." One day he and his wife tramped down to the valley and to the small house on the other hillside. There they met the old lady. "Be ye the windows with the light across the valley?" she asked. When they said yes, she told them how much their light meant to her.

"Be ye going to stay and keep your light burning, or maybe not?" she asked anxiously. From that day the man and his wife decided to keep the light burning in their window, even when they were gone. They even removed the curtains so more light would shine out.

We are not always aware that others desperately need and want light—the light that we have in the window of our Christian experience. Whether people ever tell us that they are blessed through our lives or not, we may be assured that if we have Christ, we are the light on the hillside. We are the light in the window that someone is watching.

June 24

I Believe . . . You Can Touch God

I believe it pleases God for you to
   interrupt Him with a need.

You can reach out and touch God . . .
   in the silences of your life . . .
   in your deepest emotions.

You can touch Him . . .
   when you are in a crowd
   or if you are alone . . .
   if your bills are piling up
     and you can't pay them . . .
   if you are troubled . . .
   if you are young or old . . .
   if you are scared and frightened.
God is there!

"But God is so busy," someone says.
   Yes, He is busy . . .
   but His business is You!
          See Hebrews 4:15, 16

June 25

I Believe . . . God Is in the Now

God is in the NOW or He's never been.
God is here or He's nowhere.
God loves you or He doesn't love anybody.
God is concerned about your existence,
    or He's never been concerned about the
    existence of anyone.

See Hebrews 13:8

June 26

I Believe . . . God Is a Good God

Every day God's goodness confronts and surrounds us—
    in the beauty of the sunrise and the
      blue sky . . .
    in the harmony and profusion of all
      nature . . .
    in the song of the birds and the glory
      of the flowers . . .
    in the majesty of the stars and the
      stillness of the evenings . . .
    in a baby's smile, a mother's tender
      touch . . .
    in all the wonderful things our Lord
      surrounds us with each day of our
      lives.

I believe He speaks to us in His goodness
    and calls us to Him. And as surely as
    day follows night, our acceptance of His
    goodness will bring Him to our side.

See Psalm 86:5

June 27

I Believe . . . The Cross Is Giving

A good everyday explanation of the cross is *giving*.
Jesus said, "If any man will come after Me,
   let him deny himself,
   and take up his cross daily,
   and follow me."

The cross is something you do.
Every time you give . . .
   A little bit of you dies.
   You die to self.
   A little bit of that part of you
   that wants to run your own life . . .
   that wants to leave God out
   and not include others . . .
   dies.

On the other hand,
   every time you give of yourself . . .
   love, energy, talents, time, or money . . .
   a big part of you comes alive,
   and you share in the joy of the resurrection
   that follows on the heels of the cross.

                                                See Luke 9:23

June 28

I Believe . . . Everyone Has Faith

God has given every man the "measure of faith."
But not everyone directs his believing toward God.
One person may put his faith in himself and his
   own ability.

Another may direct his faith toward money and
   what it will get him.

Still another person may put his faith in a career
   outside of God's will.

All three are putting their faith in something other
   than God. So theirs is misdirected faith.

I believe the highest purpose of faith is for it
to be directed to God through Jesus Christ to
meet human need.

See Romans 12:3

June 29

I Believe . . . God Speaks to Each Person

God's voice is all around you.

His voice is in the Bible
in a sermon . . .
in your prayer life . . .
in a song . . .
in a book. . .
in nature . . .
in a word from someone.

But primarily His voice is inside you.

God's voice is a word that He places in you . . .
very special . . .
most intimate and gracious.
If you listen with your will . . .
with a determination . . .
to know God and obey Him . . .
your heart will "hear" God speaking.

See Revelation 3:20

June 30

I Believe . . . God Is Present in Time of Trouble

It's when you are in trouble that God's face shines the brightest. That's when His face emerges above the storm clouds.

It's when you're in trouble that God appears to you the strongest. That's when you see Him standing there in the shadows.

It's when you are in trouble that you feel the strong hand of God—taking possession of your mortal frame—lifting you—putting your feet on the solid rock, Christ Jesus.

See Psalm 46:1

JULY

July 1

Only So Far

One of the hardest things for people to understand is human suffering. Why do accidents happen? Why do we lose our jobs? Why does sickness strike our bodies?

A classic example of human suffering is Job. According to the Bible, Job suffered as a result of *what the devil did to him*. One day the devil came to God and falsely accused Job of being a phony. "Let something happen to his family or his possessions. Let him get sick and feel pain," he challenged God. "Then You'll see his faith is not for real." Although God allowed Satan to test Job's faith, He set a limit on how far the devil could go: *Spare his life!* Satan stripped Job of his wealth, wiped out his family, and struck his body with dreadful boils—yet "In all this Job sinned not, nor charged God foolishly" (Job 1:22).

Yes, the devil is involved in human affairs. Many times he strikes innocent, righteous people. The Bible says that he walks around "as a roaring lion . . . seeking whom he may devour" (1 Peter 5:8). But we are not at Satan's mercy. He can only do as much as God allows him to do. God is Master of the situation. And with our trust in Him, His great purpose will be worked out in our lives.

July 2

As You Believe

Much of Job's suffering was, by his own admission, *caused by what he did to himself*. While viewing the collapse of everything dear to him, Job admitted, "The thing which I greatly *feared* is come upon me, and that which I was *afraid* of is come unto me" (Job 3:25).

138

Job put into words what he actually had done to himself. *I feared—I was afraid!* It's good to admit this. Get it out of your system. Confess it to God. Just say, "God, I'm scared." Job believed terrible things were going to happen—and they did. This is what constitutes fear—believing the wrong things, instead of believing God!

Much of the suffering in the world can be traced to fear. But there is one thing the devil can never take from you. *And that's your faith!* In the crucible of suffering, Job got control of his believing. He cried:

> *Though [God] slay me, yet will I trust in him . . . . For I know that my redeemer liveth . . . . when he hath tried me, I shall come forth as gold . . . . I know that thou canst do every thing . . . .*
>
> Job 13:15; 19:25; 23:10; 42:2

Job swung his believing in the right direction, and God "turned his captivity."

July 3

God Reverses Circumstances

Job suffered also as a result of *what men and circumstances did to him.* First, his children were killed in an accident. Then his business collapsed. Next, he was struck down with sickness. And his wife rejected him. Even his friends blamed him for everything that had happened. The fact was, these things were beyond his control. He was struck, blow by blow, until he was utterly alone and helpless as far as man's power was concerned. This is what people call the winds of chance, or being a victim of circumstances.

But Job did not allow his circumstances to hide the face of God. Instead, he clung to his *Source.* He prayed for his friends who had hurt him, and he forgave them. Job opened up his heart and let the cleansing love of God wash his soul, until he could really give of his heart, of his love, of his forgiveness, and of his prayers.

The Bible says that when Job prayed for his friends, God reversed his adverse circumstances. God multiplied back all Job had lost—health, family, possessions—giving him *twice as much as he had before!* (*see* Job 42:10).

God is not limited by your circumstances. He can deliver you.

July 4

Freedom Is . . .

Freedom is not a physical state of being. It is deeper than that. For even if you are free, you can be bound inside.

Freedom is of the spirit and mind. It is release from within.

Freedom is to look upon another man's wealth and not covet—to look upon another man's wife and not lust—to look upon another man's home and not desire it.

Freedom is to look upon problems and not panic, to look upon needs and not be afraid.

Freedom is to look every man in the face and know that you are a person in your own right.

Freedom is knowing that God is real to you—that whether you live in a ghetto, or work on a job that is unpleasant, or suffer trouble in your family, you feel a relationship with the Power that is the answer to everything—the power of God.

Freedom is knowing Jesus Christ, because in Him you are free from the bondage of self.

July 5

Let God Do What He Can Do

. . . Everything in the heavens and earth is yours, O Lord, and this is your kingdom. We adore you as being in control of everything . . . your hand controls power and might . . . .

1 Chronicles 29:11, 12 LB

I remember a young man who went to Spartan Aviation in Tulsa, Oklahoma, to learn how to fly. He did very well in his first lessons, and the day before he was to solo, he went up for a final training flight. The instructor put him through the different things they do on that last day, and finally he turned the controls over to him completely.

The young man was enjoying it as he held his hands on the controls and was able to maneuver the plane. (I've never had the experience myself, but I've been told by pilots that there are few experiences in life that are comparable to controlling a plane up in the big sky.) He was doing fine, when all of a sudden he hit what was apparently an air pocket, and the plane began to jerk and jump and fall. He was almost scared out of his wits, when he heard a calm voice and felt a pair of strong hands on top of his. The voice said, "Let me take over. Just turn it over to me."

Gradually the plane began to straighten out. When the instructor was sure the plane was under control he said, "Now you take the controls."

The instructor didn't interrupt as long as the young man was able to do what needed to be done, but he did come to him when he could no longer do what was necessary.

God is like that. God is not going to interfere with our lives in the experiences we can handle ourselves. He expects us to do that. But He also expects us to turn our lives over to Him in those moments when we can't operate, so we can feel those Hands and hear that Voice saying, "Here, turn the controls of your life over to Me. Let Me handle this."

I think the most important thing this says is to stay aware that Christ is the real Manager of your life. He's the Controller. He controls everything. He's going to let you do what you can do, but He wants you to let Him do what He can do.

July 6

The Mountain Climber

A friend of mine, who is a mountain climber, said, "Oral, do you know what a mountain climber does when he sees he can't make it down a mountain before dark?"

I said, "No, I've never climbed a mountain."

"One thing he doesn't do," he said, "and that's *enter the darkness*. When he sees he can't get to the bottom before the sun goes down, he stops." He said, "If the climber has a tent, he gets in it. But if he doesn't, he finds a crevice in the rock and ties himself in. And he stays there through the night."

"Isn't that awfully uncomfortable?" I asked.

"Yes," he agreed, "but it's not important whether he's comfortable or not. The important thing is for him to survive, to be there in the morning."

And I thought to myself, *That's how it is in our Christian life.* It's not important that we be comfortable in our trials. It's not important whether people say bad things or nice things about us. The important thing is that we take refuge in Jesus when dark times set in; that we stand strong in our faith; that we survive!

> *The Lord is . . . a rugged mountain where I hide; he is my Savior, a rock where none can reach me, and a tower of safety . . . .*
>
> Psalm 18:2 LB

July 7

Faith Is Not Complicated
by EVELYN ROBERTS

Faith is not a complicated theological "something." Faith is simply believing God will do what He says He will do in His Word.

One evening when our son Richard was about five or six years old and Oral was away in a crusade, Richard called from his room and said, "Mother, come here. I'm sick."

"What's wrong?" I asked.

"Oh, I have such a headache I can't go to sleep."

"Well, let's pray and ask the Lord to heal you."

We prayed and then I said, "Richard, you believe Jesus now and go to sleep."

After a while he called for me again. "Mother, the prayer didn't help a bit," he said. "My head still hurts."

This time I sat down on the side of his bed and said, "Richard, let's talk a moment. If you were to ask me to get you a glass of water, do you think I'd do it?"

"Yes, of course you would."

"Well," I said, "just as I'm willing to get you a glass of water, Jesus is willing to heal you. He said in His Word, *If you ask any thing in my name, I will do it* (John 14:14). Do you believe that?"

Richard thought for a moment, then he said, "Well, yes, I do."

So we prayed again, and in five minutes he was sound asleep. The headache was gone. It was nothing but simple faith. Doubt had been erased by faith in God's Word, by believing God would do what He said He would!

July 8

You Can Grow Bigger

In all these things we are more than conquerors through him that loved us.

Romans 8:37

In 1953, as Mallory, the British mountain climber, and his colleagues were making a heroic attempt to conquer Mt. Everest, Mallory fell. Today he is buried in the eternal snows of the great mountain. His companions returned to tell their story.

One of the climbers, addressing a large audience in London, told of all their hardships, the unbelievable circumstances, the struggle with the wind and cold, and losing their leader. It was a very emotional meeting. Behind him on a screen was a huge picture of Mt. Everest, so that during his talk he could show the levels the climbers reached and where Mallory had lost his life.

When the speaker finished his talk he turned to the mountain on the screen and began to talk to it, as if it were alive. He said, "Everest, we tried to conquer you once and you beat us. We tried to conquer you a second time and you beat us. But, Everest, listen to me. We are going to conquer you because you can't grow any bigger. *But we can!*"

You can grow bigger—bigger than any mountainous problem—if you really want to. Jesus Christ can invade and fill you and enable you to do it.

July 9

Red Sea Experience

God will make a way when there is no way!

When God put that thought in my heart, I was struggling with a difficult problem. I mean it was tough. Every time I tried to get a solution, I was blocked. There was no place to turn. There was no way.

Listen to what happened. Evelyn and I were eating a bite one evening. I was really feeling low, when the Lord put Exodus 13 and 14 into my mind. The Children of Israel had come to the Red Sea. The Egyptians were behind them to destroy them, and the sea was before them to drown them. Then Moses said, "Fear ye not, stand still, and see the salvation of the Lord" (Exodus 14:13).

Evelyn said, "Oral, that's it! The Lord is showing you how He will make a way for you!" Suddenly I knew everything was going to be all right. I had been thrashing about and not looking to God, my great Source of supply. Immediately the way opened up for me! I was able to walk right through the problem on dry land.

Whatever your Red Sea experience—whatever your most urgent need—there's no reason to panic. God will walk with you through the Red Sea and destroy the crushing problem behind you. You won't even get your feet wet! *Believe* that He will do it!

July 10

You Can Have a Part

When the Civil War was over, Robert E. Lee, general of the Confederate Army, was one of the men who stood out in both the North and South as a truly great Christian gentleman. To honor him, the people of Richmond, Virginia, had his statue made.

On the day the statue was to be put in place in Richmond, instead of using a team of horses to pull the statue to the public square, the people said, "Let us, the people who love this man, pull the statue through the streets into place."

They dismissed the schools and closed the shops that day, and people by the hundreds came. They tied long ropes to the statue, and as many as possible put their hands to the ropes and pulled the statue into place. Then they cut the ropes up into small pieces and gave one to each person who helped pull. Years later, if you visited the home of one of the helpers, he'd take out his piece of rope and tell you how he had a part in honoring General Lee.

One of the greatest thrills in life is to have a part in something greater than you are. And it's especially wonderful to have a part in God's work. The Apostle Paul says, "We are fellow workmen—joint promoters, laborers together—with and for God" (1 Corinthians 3:9 AMPLIFIED).

July 11

An Almost Magic Moment

Have faith in God.
Mark 11:22

I remember when, as a seventeen-year-old boy, I lay in bed, dying of tuberculosis. I could not believe that I would ever be well again. Then one day my sister, Jewel, came in and said, "Oral, God is going to heal you!"

A few days later my oldest brother, Elmer, came in and said, "Oral, get up! I'm going to take you to a meeting where a man is praying for the sick."

Jewel and Elmer had faith, and suddenly I had faith in their faith. That was an important moment in my life, when I went from no faith at all to faith in the faith of my brother and sister.

The moment came when I found myself face to face with a man who stretched out his hand to pray a healing prayer for a boy named Oral Roberts. Then my faith in the faith of my brother and sister was not enough. I had to transfer my faith in their faith—to having faith in the prayers of this man. But even that was not enough. I had to transfer that—to having faith in Jesus Christ. And when I did, I was healed.

It's all right to start out by having faith in somebody else's faith. But there comes an almost magic moment when you transfer your faith—when you center it upon the object of your deliverance— Jesus Christ of Nazareth. And that's when your miracle begins.

July 12

The Farmer and the Baker

Give generously, for your gifts will return to you later.

Ecclesiastes 11:1 LB

A farmer and a baker were close friends. The baker bought his butter from the farmer, and the farmer bought his bread from the baker. One day the baker became upset when he weighed his butter and found that it did not weigh a full pound. He said to the farmer, "My good friend, you are cheating me. I'm getting less than a pound when I buy butter from you."

"Oh, no," the farmer said, "I'm your friend. I would never do you that way! It's a pound."

When they couldn't settle it, the baker haled the farmer into court. The judge asked the farmer, "Why aren't you selling your friend, the baker, a full pound of butter?"

"I am, Judge," he said.

"Well, how do you know it weighs a pound?"

The farmer said, "Judge, the baker sells his bread in pound loaves to me. And I measure my butter according to his pound loaves."

The judge dismissed the case.

Jesus said, "With the same measure that ye [give] withal it shall be measured to you again" (Luke 6:38). *Or the measure that you give determines the measure of what you receive!*

July 13

God Is on Our Side
by SALLY JO SHELTON

Since God is on our side, who dares to pit himself against us? God withheld nothing, not even His only Son, but surrendered Him up to be crucified for us. Why wouldn't He also gladly supply everything else we need?

Who dares accuse us who belong to God? He Himself has acquitted us.

Who dares to put us down? Christ who died—yes, and even more than that, who rose to life again—is even now in conference with the Heavenly Father, pleading our case.

What can ever break the powerful bond of love between Christ and us?

Can problems or disasters?

Can oppression or shortages?

Can poverty or danger or conflict?

Of course not!

In spite of all outward circumstances, we are winners—and more. We are champions who cannot be beaten. Not because of our own ability and strength, but because of the supernatural power and help that Jesus so lovingly and generously provides for us. For I believe with all my heart and soul that nothing—absolutely nothing!—

- not death, not life
- not angels, not demons
- not governments, not organizations
- nothing happening now
- nothing threatening to happen in the future
- no height of achievement, no depth of despair
- nothing in all God's mighty Creation—

can ever sever us from the unconquerable love of God which comes to us in the Person of our Lord Jesus Christ Himself!

This devotion is based on Romans 8:31–35, 37–39.

July 14

Kiss of Forgiveness

And he arose, and came to his father. But when he was yet a great way off, his father saw him, and had compassion, and ran, and fell on his neck, and kissed him.

Luke 15:20

Remember the story of the young girl who played before the great maestro? Oh, she practiced! She wanted to learn that piece of music until it would get into her fingers, so that when she went on stage she could play it in perfect rhythm and harmony.

But when she went on stage and realized the great music master himself was there, suddenly her fingers were no longer nimble, but clumsy. She hit a wrong note, and a terrible discord went through the place. Everyone shuddered. And the girl, paralyzed with embarrassment and fear, sat with her hands covering her face and sobbed, unable to continue or to leave the stage.

Then someone moved, and all eyes turned. The great maestro himself had gotten up and was walking down the aisle, up the steps, across the stage, and over to the piano. He slid onto the bench beside the young girl, put his arm around her, drew her close, and planted a kiss on her cheek. No one had heard that note of discord quite like the master, but he was the first to forgive!

July 15

No Idol Gods
by RICHARD ROBERTS

The other night my wife, Patti, and I tucked our two daughters into bed, then listened while they said their prayers. Juli prayed first, and she really tickled us when she finished her prayer by saying, ''And, God, bless all the people in the world—and in all the other states, too.''

Then it was Christi's turn, and she really touched our hearts, because she finished her prayer by saying, ''And, God, don't let there be any idol gods. Just You, God,'' she said. *''You* be the only God.''

That reminded me that the Apostle John ended his first epistle by saying, ''Little children, keep yourselves from idols'' (1 John 5:21).

It's easy to think we have no idol gods, because we don't worship wooden statues. But those aren't the only kinds of idols. An idol is any person or thing that comes between us and God.

Like Christi, Patti and I want only *God* to be God, just like the song that says, ''Jesus, be the Lord of all the kingdoms of my heart.''

July 16

Healing Tears
by REBECCA ROBERTS NASH

He healeth the broken in heart, and bindeth up their wounds.
Psalm 147:3

''God, I don't think I can take it,'' my friend wept as she stood over her dead son. One of ten children, he had always been troubled. The year before, he had taken an overdose of drugs to try to end the pain of living. Now a self-inflicted gunshot had ended his young life.

Why? Why? The pain and suffering of a mother at the death of a child is great, but what she goes through when the death is a willful act is indescribable. Shock and sorrow rushed through her being again and again. Her family stood strong with her, and her many friends began to call and express their sympathy, saying they were praying for her. With God's help, this mother has come through her tragedy, manifesting the powerful truth that God really does heal the broken heart.

It wasn't easy. In the days that followed she experienced the stages of grief—feelings of guilt, anger, remorse, depression, and finally acceptance. "But," she said, "a peace slowly began to come over me, and with each day my heart was more open to God's love."

In a short time she was able to return to her job and once again able to laugh with acquaintances about the ups and downs of rearing a large family.

"There are times when I weep," my friend admits, "but now they are 'healing tears.' God has become a powerful Person to me, a hand on my shoulder. The prayers of those who care have lifted me up above the storm. I know God will take care of the future and I can trust Him."

Ironically, this devotional was published in the January/February/ March 1977 issue of *Daily Blessing* magazine immediately before the deaths of Rebecca and Marshall Nash, our dear daughter and son-in-law, on February 11, 1977. The devotional was read at their memorial service. It was as though these were Rebecca's very words to us at that moment. How sweet is the comfort of God— *O. R.*

July 17

The Impact of Disappointment

Thou hast had pity on the gourd . . . and should not I spare Nineveh?

Jonah 4:10, 11

Emerson wrote, "When it is dark enough, men see the stars." Yet we know that there are times in everyone's life when disappointment has the adverse effect. Instead of "seeing stars," men become angry and lose their balance. This was Jonah's problem. He had gone to Nineveh under God's command and preached a message of judgment. Then he retired to a hill to watch God destroy the people. But they repented and God spared them.

Jonah rocked under the impact of his disappointment. God caused a gourd vine to grow up to shield Jonah from the burning sun and to relieve his grief. But that night a worm killed the vine. When Jonah saw the withered vine, he was brokenhearted and wished himself to die. God gently reminded Jonah that he was showing more pity for the gourd than for the thousands of human lives in Nineveh which were spared because they prayed and God had mercy.

God gave Jonah the answer for disappointment. Not self-pity, but getting his eyes off himself and on God's mercy and compassion—and on people whom God loves.

July 18

Press the Button

In one of the skyscrapers in New York City, a group of people was waiting for an elevator. Finally someone said, "What's wrong with this elevator?" And another said, "That's how things are these days. Nothing works anymore." At the edge of the crowd a little voice piped up: *"Has anybody pressed the button?"*

Someone reached over and pressed the button which released the elevator, and immediately the doors opened. Everyone got in, laughing and talking, and up they all went.

The elevator was there all the time. They just needed to press the button. God is in your life. He is right there with you now. Have you pressed the button? Have you released your faith to Him? Have you looked up to Him and prayed?

Maybe you think, *I don't know how to pray. I don't know the right words.* Well, I've found you don't have to have a bunch of big-sounding words, if you'll just open your heart and reach down in the deeper dimensions of your being and press the button—call upon God.

> [*God says:*] *Call upon me in the day of trouble: I will deliver thee, and thou shalt glorify me.*
>
> Psalm 50:15

July 19

Absolute Obedience

In the deserts of the Middle East, the training of Arabian horses is a grueling process. The trainer requires absolute obedience from the horses. After weeks of putting them through their paces, he gives them a final test. He forces the horses to do without water for a couple of days, then turns them loose within sight of water. Just as they get to the water's edge—ready to plunge in—he blows his whistle. The horses that come to a complete halt are considered trained and ready for service. They stand there quivering, wanting water, but absolutely obedient.

Now this is a lesson that Christ is trying to teach us—*absolute obedience.* The Bible encourages us ". . . to endure patiently every trial and persecution, for they are his saints who remain firm to the end in obedience to his commands and trust in Jesus" (Revelation 14:12 LB).

Christ doesn't offer you an easy way. It's a disciplined way—a journey into discipleship. It's a training that goes on day and night. The Bible also says, "He that endureth to the end shall be saved" (Matthew 10:22). Christianity is not namby-pamby and soft. It takes great faith to obey, to recognize that God is your Lord and Master. But such obedience gives the rich reward of joy, peace, and life itself!

July 20

The Luscious Elberta Peach

While I was growing up we lived close to an uncle who made his living from his big orchard. He raised all kinds of fruit, but his pride and joy was the big luscious Elberta peach. People came from miles to buy his peaches.

I moved away, and it was several years before I visited my uncle again. I was shocked when I saw his orchard—or what reminded me of it. Only a few of the prized peach trees remained; they were scrubby and produced only a few small peaches.

"What happened?" I asked my uncle. "Did you have a storm? Or was it insects?"

Sadly he replied, "Oral, I simply did not pay attention to the trees. The fruit was my business. The fruit fed my family. I depended upon the fruit as the source of my supply.

"Then one year the crop was not so good; the next year it was less. I woke up and realized that the source of my supply was the *tree*—not the fruit! I saw that if I took care of the tree, the fruit would grow." Then his eyes lighted up. "I'm putting in a new orchard. This time I'll take care of my source."

God is your Source of supply just as the tree is the source of the fruit. If you cultivate your relationship with God—look to Him and trust Him—the supply of your needs, the answer to your prayer, will come because God as Source is "Lord of the harvest" (Luke 10:2).

July 21

God's Answer to Fatigue

If you have that "tired, run-down feeling" the TV commercials talk about, join the club. It's the plague of our day. You may think, *A vacation is what I need.* But time off from your regular routine does not always solve the problem. It's a common joke that you need a second vacation to rest up from the one you just took. Hard work in itself is a tonic for the body. But if it is not work that drains our energy, then what is it?

The strains and pressures under which we work and live: worries, fears, resentments, heartaches. These cause "soul fatigue," which is brought on because we do not enter into the rest God has provided for us. Hebrews 4:9 says, "There remaineth therefore a rest to the people of God."

When Jesus said, "Come unto me, all ye that labour and are heavy laden, and I will give you rest," He wasn't referring just to body fatigue. Notice this little nugget tucked into that verse: "Take my yoke upon you, and learn of me . . . *and ye shall find rest unto your souls*" (Matthew 11:28, 29).

That Scripture reminds us of a missionary in Africa who was driving down the road in a truck when he came upon a group of Africans carrying heavy baskets of wares on their heads. He stopped and picked the people up. After traveling several miles, he glanced back. To his utter amazement, his passengers were still carrying their loads. Stopping the truck, he asked, "Why don't you put those heavy baskets down while you are riding?"

"Oh, no!" they replied. "You've done enough. The least we can do is carry our own burdens."

Don't we do the same thing? God says rest is our heritage, but we don't reach out and take it, probably because we don't know how. Hebrews 4:10 tells us how: "He that is entered into his rest, *he also hath ceased from his own works!*"

In 1 Peter 5:7 we read: *"Casting all your care upon him; for he careth for you."*

God's answer to fatigue is so simple that we miss it! To enter into His rest we make a trade—our cares for God's rest. We cease our self-striving—carrying the weight of our cares and trying to solve our problems ourselves—and *we give them to God,* the Source of our rest.

Read Isaiah 28:11, 12; 40:28–31

July 22

God Is God in All of Life

The bread of God is he which cometh down from heaven, and giveth life unto the world.

John 6:33

Jesus said, "I am the bread of life" (John 6:35). *Bread.* One of the most common necessities of our everyday existence. In Jesus Christ God came *to earth!* Jesus Christ was not only God, but also a friend, a brother—a human being with human feelings. He loved people. He became tired, hungry, and sleepy. He rolled up His sleeves and worked. He sweat. He got His feet dirty.

Jesus was not diminished in His deity by where He was or by what He was doing—whether walking on a dusty road or worshiping in a synagogue, working in a carpenter's shop or attending a wedding feast.

What does that say to us? That God is God in all of life. And He is God in all of life *the same!* That means that you don't have to be in a church to experience God's love or to sense His presence. *God is God everywhere you go, in whatever you do, every day of the week.*

July 23

One Equals the Other

I was teaching a class on the Holy Spirit at Oral Roberts University. To illustrate a point, I asked one of my associates to give me a dollar bill. I put his dollar in my pocket, then took a dollar from my billfold, and handed it to him.

"Is that a fair exchange?" I asked.

"Yes," he replied.

"The dollar I gave you is as genuine as the one you gave me?"

"Yes," he said, "I have just as much as I had before."

My associate gave up a dollar. In return, he got another dollar of equal value. In the same way, when Jesus left the earth physically, He promised to send the Holy Spirit, who is equal with Him in the Godhead, to take His place.

"I will not leave you comfortless," Jesus said. "I will pray the Father, and he shall give you another Comforter [the Holy Spirit], that he may abide with you for ever" (John 14:16, 18). "Comforter" means one called alongside to help—one who warns, who admonishes, who helps us over our rough spots. It means one who gives us what we need at the time we need it.

The ministry of the Holy Spirit is built around Jesus Christ. Remember what Jesus said? "The Comforter, which is the Holy Ghost . . . *shall teach you all things, and bring all things to your remembrance,* whatsoever I have said unto you . . . . he shall testify of me . . . . he will guide you into all truth . . . he will shew you things to come. He shall glorify me" (John 14:26; 15:26; 16:13, 14).

If Jesus were still on the earth physically, He would be subject to human limitations. He could be in only one place at a time. He could help just so many people at a time. But through the Holy Spirit He is with each one of us all the time.

Therefore, Jesus said, "It is expedient for you that I go away: for if I go not away, the Comforter will not come unto you" (John 16:7). When Christ baptizes you with His Holy Spirit, He is sending another—equal to Himself—to take the place of His physical being. It is precisely as if Jesus were walking by your side in the flesh.

July 24

You Are Worth More Than You Think

In this was manifested the love of God toward us, because God sent his only begotten Son into the world, that we might live through him.

1 John 4:9

Several years ago I was sitting in our home in Tulsa, meditating on God's love and how He gave His only Son to die for us. This boggled my mind. I couldn't grasp it. As I sat there, I had a vision. It seemed to be actually happening: I heard my oldest little son, Ronnie, scream, "Daddy! Daddy! Daddy!" I jumped up and ran out into the yard where he'd been playing, just in time to see two men throw him into their car and take off.

I jumped into my car and began to chase them, but I lost them in the traffic. Beside myself, I drove and drove, until late that evening I came upon their car on a country road. I looked, and there on the side of a hill they had nailed my little son Ronnie to a cross and were jabbing it into the ground. I jumped out of the car, climbed through the fence, pushed the men aside, pulled my little boy off the cross, and held him in my arms. With the word *Daddy* on his lips, he died.

Out of the depths of my being I cried, "O God, what does this mean? Why did I have this vision?"

Inside my heart God spoke, "Oral Roberts, how many sons do you have?"

I said, "I have two, Ronnie and Richard."

He said, "If you were to give one of your sons to die on the cross for the sins of the world, you'd have one son left, wouldn't you?"

"Yes, if I gave Ronnie, I'd have Richard left."

He said, "Well, I had only one Son, and I gave Him. And that's what a human life is worth."

I said, "God, there's no way that any human life can be worth the life of Your Son, Jesus Christ."

He said, "You have no right to judge. You have no right to say that any human life is of less worth than My Son, whom I gave."

For a long time I sat there, stunned. But from that moment I began to see people in a different light. I've had a different feeling about the worth of a human being.

I believe that God has made each of us unique and irreplaceable. I believe there's something built into each human being that's more precious than all the silver and gold and diamonds of this world. I believe that if there had been only one person in the whole world, God would have sent Jesus to die for him. God wants us to believe that we are worth the life of His only begotten Son, Jesus Christ!

Can you take it in? I can't. It's beyond my comprehension. But we can try. Today God is saying, "You are worth more than you think!"

July 25

A New Relationship

Read John 2:1–11.

The first miracle of Jesus Christ was the turning of water into wine. It was the miracle of turning something very common-place—water—into something very rare and expensive—wine. Why did Jesus choose this as His very first miracle? What is its meaning to you in the now?

This first miracle of Jesus means that you can have *a new relationship with God.* In the Old Testament, when Moses was leading the children of Israel out of Egypt to the Promised Land, God gave him the power to perform miracles. Do you remember what the first miracle was that he performed, when Pharaoh refused to allow the Israelites to leave? It was the miracle of turning water into blood—a symbol of death and destruction (*see* Exodus 7:14–25). Throughout the Old Testament you see the symbolism of death.

But when our Lord Jesus came, He performed His first miracle to show us the abrupt change in relationship that a person now has with God. For Christ's first miracle was not the turning of water into blood, but the turning of water into wine. *Wine!* A symbol of life, of joy and gladness. This is what a first miracle of Jesus means to you in the now—*a new relationship between you and God.*

July 26

Jesus Is in the Midst

Read John 4:46–54.

The healing of the nobleman's son was the second miracle of Christ. It was performed in Cana of Galilee, where His first miracle took place. However, this miracle did not involve a poor family like the one that ran out of wine at the wedding and didn't have enough money to buy more. They faced a terrible shortage in their lives. This miracle concerns a nobleman's family, a family of great wealth.

One of the great meanings of this miracle is that Jesus comes to both the poor and the highborn. He comes to us, no matter what our station in life is, because . . . *Jesus is in the midst of life.* He comes to us in our health and in our sickness. And He comes to us in our life and in our death.

Many people seem to think that God is aloof, vague, unreal, mystical—so far away that He has no relationship to our human existence, to our toils, our torments, and the experience of our everyday lives. But I tell you this is not so. God is in the *now*. Whoever you are, He is in the midst of your concerns. God is at the point of your need.

July 27

Something Greater

Read Mark 3:1–5.

The miracle healing of the man with the withered hand says that *when Jesus heals a handicap in any person, He always has something greater in mind.*

God sees things differently than man does. For example, here was a man who had a limp, useless hand. But Jesus did not focus His attention solely on the man's hand. He first spoke to the man himself and said, "Stand forth."

A surgeon, who is a friend of mine, was talking to me about this particular miracle. He said, "Oral, as a doctor I would have automatically turned my attention to the man's hand. This goes back to my medical training. But as I read this story, I noticed that Christ did not touch the man's crippled hand. He seemed to view it as an extension of the man's entire personality. With the healing of the whole man, his hand was restored."

Then my friend added a statement that I thought was tremendous. He said, "More and more I believe medicine is moving in this direction—toward whole-man healing."

Isn't that exciting? Jesus is a restorer of the human being—the healer of your whole person—*body, mind, and spirit.*

July 28

Four Good Neighbors

Read Mark 2:1–12.

In the miracle healing of the man sick of the palsy, Jesus is telling us that *there are times when we have to help one another.*

In this story four good neighbors were concerned about their friend. These were men who were active in their community, but who were not too busy to become involved. Their concern was expressed in this particular instance by bringing a neighbor who was paralyzed to where Christ was preaching. It was the beginning of one of the greatest miracles that our Lord ever performed.

I wonder if this miracle would have happened if it had not been for these four men. There is so much good done in the world through people who help others. I believe that my own miraculous healing of tuberculosis and stammering happened—at least in part—because my parents, my sister, and my brother were concerned and were willing to become involved.

Everybody in the world needs a miracle of some kind. And what this great miracle says to us is that we need to get involved in the needs of the people around us. We need to become concerned for that one who needs a miracle. *It may be that God wants to use you to bring a miracle to your neighbor.*

July 29

Life Is Coming Your Way

Read Mark 10:46–52.
Have you ever felt that life was passing you by? Blind Bartimaeus felt like that. One day when he was sitting on the roadside near Jericho, Jesus passed that way. I'm a man who believes that Jesus passes everybody's way—that sometime in life He makes Himself known to every person. What you do in that moment when He passes your way determines the course of your earthly destiny, as well as your eternal one.

When Bartimaeus heard that Jesus was passing by, he cried out at the top of his voice, "Jesus, thou Son of David, have mercy on me." In that cry, Bartimaeus revealed that in his innermost being he felt that life had passed him by, but that if he ever encountered Jesus Christ, *life would come his way again.* Bartimaeus received not only his physical sight that day, but also his spiritual sight—for the Bible tells us that he "followed Jesus in the way."

The message of this miracle to you is that Christ is offering you the miracle you need. You know what that miracle is. At this very moment you can reach out to your Source—Jesus Himself—and receive what your heart cries for, because . . . *Jesus is passing your way.*

July 30

The Completed Miracle

Read Luke 17:12–19.

A completed miracle is a miracle together with a thankful heart. It is accepting something from God's hand and giving Him thanks.

In the great miracle of the cleansing of the ten lepers, we see ten desperate men who cried out to Jesus for help. Ten obeyed His command to go show themselves to their priest. And ten were healed. Nine of them were so delighted that they went on their way. But one was so grateful he came back, knelt down before the Lord, and gave thanks.

Some people think they don't get what they deserve, but this man was saying, "Lord, I got *more* than I deserve." This is the *completed miracle*—when God blesses you and you respond with gratitude.

This may be exactly the way your miracle will come about . . . by planting seeds of praise and thanksgiving for what God has already done for you.

You can enter an attitude of thanks and praise this moment. Look up to God and by faith thank Him for the miracle He has *already* begun in your life.

July 31

Touch and Agree

Read Mark 5:25–34.

When the woman with the issue of blood heard about Jesus, her first reaction was in her spirit, not in her mind. The Bible says, "She said *within herself*, If I may but touch his garment, I shall be whole" (Matthew 9:21).

You see, she was defeated through her mind, which said, *No more can be done.* But she got down beneath her mind, into her spirit, and there she found a whole new world. In that new world of her spirit, she was saying, "I'm going to touch Jesus, and I'm going to be whole."

When the woman touched Jesus, it wasn't a mere "finger-touching" type of thing. From *within herself* she was touching the man, Jesus Christ. For instantly He turned around and said, "Who touched me? . . . for I perceive that virtue [healing power] is gone out of me'' (Luke 8:45, 46).

There's a Scripture that says, ''If two of you shall agree on earth as touching any thing . . . it shall be done'' (Matthew 18:19). That's ''touching and agreeing.'' The woman felt in her body the beginning of a miracle, and she was healed!

Touch and agree! Today—touch someone with your hand or with your spirit and agree as touching some need on your heart—and believe for a miracle!

AUGUST

August 1

The Best for God

Out of all your gifts ye shall offer . . . the best thereof, even the hallowed part thereof.

Numbers 18:29

When we started building Oral Roberts University—beautiful structures of ultramodern architecture with space-age facilities—a man visited me. He said, "Oral, it is not right to build buildings like this. God teaches that we are not to have this world's goods."

I said, "Show me that in the Bible."

Well, he couldn't show me a Scripture to support his thinking. He was a product of his teaching. I said, "Sir, you can believe what you want. But God told me to build this university. And the beauty, the symmetry, and the commodiousness of the buildings are all harmonious with God's personality."

Many people do not understand that God wants us to live "the truly good life" (2 Peter 1:3 PHILLIPS). Therefore, they do not apply their faith, their hard work, and their initiative to receiving what God wants them to have. The person who clings to old worn-old teachings, traditions, and clichés is going to continue to be denied. But the person who understands God—who gives God his best and expects God's best—is going to be rewarded with God's fullness.

August 2

If I'm a True Friend . . .
by SALLY JO SHELTON

IF I'M A TRUE FRIEND, I put up with a lot; I help in any way I can.

IF I'M A TRUE FRIEND, I don't get jealous when someone close to me makes another friend or gets something I don't have.

161

IF I'M A TRUE FRIEND, I don't show off or brag; I don't act "holier than thou."

IF I'M A TRUE FRIEND, I always have good manners; I don't insist on having my own way.

IF I'M A TRUE FRIEND, I don't get my feelings hurt easily; I don't count the times another lets me down.

IF I'M A TRUE FRIEND, I'm never secretly glad when someone is treated unfairly; I'm always delighted when he gets the credit he truly deserves.

IF I'M A TRUE FRIEND, I accept a person for what he is—faults and all; I put my trust in him; I expect the very best of him; I stick by him even in times of hardship and misunderstanding.

IF I'M A TRUE FRIEND, my love doesn't ever fizzle out.

This practical application of 1 Corinthians 13:4–8 is particularly appropriate for this date—Friendship Day.

August 3

Two Laws of Life

When the three young Hebrew princes—Shadrach, Meshach, and Abednego—were uprooted from their beloved Jerusalem and carted away captive to the strange land of Babylon, they came face to face with an inescapable fact of life: *When you serve God you are going to be tested.* Not once, not twice, but again and again. Every day is a struggle. Every day the devil tries to steal away your obedience to God. Just like he did when he came against these three young men of faith.

They were told by the king, "You shall bow to my image or you will burn in my furnace" (Daniel 3:15). But they refused, for God had commanded, "Thou shalt have no other gods before me" (Exodus 20:3).

There are two laws of life: the law of faith and the law of compromise. These two laws confront us every day. Every day we're called upon to believe or to doubt, to give in or to take our stand for God. Satan whispers, "Bow or burn." But God says, "If you bow, you will burn. If you do not bow, you cannot burn."

Whatever you compromise to get, you're going to lose. It has no power to satisfy. But whatever you get by faith, you never lose. It cannot be taken from you. And it satisfies!

August 4

Life's Fiery Furnaces

Life's fiery furnaces—how hot they burn! The three young Hebrews learned how hot life's trials can get when they refused to compromise their faith and worship King Nebuchadnezzar's golden image. Furious, the king ordered them bound and cast into a furnace heated seven times hotter than ordinary (*see* Daniel 3).

Are you in a fiery furnace? Maybe it's a marriage that is going sour. Is it depression? Is it sickness in your body? Or grief? Those of us who have lost loved ones know how hot that furnace can be heated.

When the king looked in the furnace, he cried, "Did not we cast three men bound into the midst of the fire? . . . Lo, I see *four* men loose, walking in the midst of the fire, and they have no hurt; and the form of the fourth is like the Son of God" (Daniel 3:24, 25).

Sometimes we feel that God is away off in some mystical world. But He was at the point of the need of these young men. Jesus Christ Himself was in the flames, waiting to catch them in His arms. Whatever your fiery furnace is, the Lord is not a million miles away. He's in the now—coming forth in the urgency of your need to subdue the flames and rob the fire of its violence, so you will suffer no harm!

August 5

The Fire Is Powerless

"Who is that God that shall deliver you out of my hands?" King Nebuchadnezzar asked Shadrach, Meshach, and Abednego. Without the flicker of an eyelash, they answered, "Our God *whom we serve* is able to deliver us from the burning fiery furnace, and he will deliver us out of thine hand" (Daniel 3:15–17).

Some people can say, "Our God," but these young men said, "Our God *whom we serve*." Some people can say, "Our God whom we serve," but they said, "Our God whom we serve *is able*." Some people can say, "Our God whom we serve is able," but they said, "Our God whom we serve is able *to deliver us from the burning fiery furnace*." Some people can say that, but these men said even more: "Our God whom we serve is able to deliver us from the burning fiery furnace, and *HE WILL deliver us!"*

Shadrach, Meshach, and Abednego were not saying "God is able" just to bolster their faith. They knew who they were; they knew who their God was; and they dared to trust Him. The fire of our fiery furnace experiences is powerless before this kind of faith. They came out of the furnace without even the smell of smoke upon them, causing the king to say in awe, "No other God . . . can deliver after this sort" (Daniel 3:29).

August 6

The Laundry Isn't Done

A terminally ill woman was asked how she felt when she learned she was going back to the hospital, perhaps this time to die. "I wasn't ready," she said. "I thought, *O God, I can't die yet, the laundry isn't done.* Isn't that ridiculous," she said half laughing through tears.

Contrary feelings and mixed priorities are not limited to heavy events. We also have them in the grind of everyday living. Remember the story in Luke 10:38–42 of Mary and Martha, who had Jesus and His disciples as guests in their home?

Mary sat at Jesus' feet and drank in His words. Martha loved Jesus too, but it was a mixed devotion. The cares of this life had a great hold upon her. She was cumbered about serving a big dinner, and she complained to Jesus, "My sister just sits here while I do all the work. Tell her to come and help me."

But Jesus answered, ". . . Martha, dear friend, you are so upset over all these details! *There is really only one thing worth being concerned about.* Mary has discovered it—and I won't take it away from her!" (Luke 10:41, 42 LB.)

Jesus' answer might seem unfair, until you realize He was pointing out something very important about our priorities. In Martha's concern over having a delicious meal for her guests (a meal that could have waited a while), she unwittingly overlooked the spiritual feast that was spread before her in Jesus' presence.

Jesus once told His disciples, "I have meat to eat that ye know not of" (John 4:32). The very things Martha's heart searched for were resident in the Person of Jesus Christ—*calmness* for her troubled spirit, *peace* for her worried mind, *a joyful attitude* for chores being performed out of duty—but she didn't recognize it. Mary did.

The truths of the Son of God found an opening in Mary's heart, so that everything else lost its importance. Her priorities were straight.

Jesus was talking about our priorities when He said, "Seek ye first the kingdom of God, and his righteousness; and all these things shall be added unto you" (Matthew 6:33). Sometimes it seems contrary to all reason, but when we get our priorities lined up, the rest of life falls into place.

August 7

No Excuses

Frederick the Great once visited a prison and asked each prisoner about his crime. One convict after another denied his guilt and offered an excuse: "It wasn't my fault." "I was framed." "The judge was prejudiced against me."

Finally, after the king had talked to practically every convict in the prison, there was one man who actually admitted his guilt. Immediately Frederick called the guards. "Quick! Release this man, before he corrupts all these 'honest' men!" he ordered.

Ever since Adam blamed Eve for giving him the forbidden fruit, people have been making excuses and blaming others for things they have done wrong. But, you see, God is not looking for perfect, sinless people—for He knows there are none (Romans 3:23).

God is looking for people like the convict who admitted his wrongdoing without any excuses. These are the ones whom God can cleanse and use for His glory.

Lord, with the Psalmist I pray:

> *Have mercy upon me, O God . . . . Wash me thoroughly from mine iniquity, and cleanse me from my sin. For I acknowledge my transgressions: and my sin is ever before me.*
> Psalm 51:1–3

August 8

The Reprimand

A father recently related that his teenage son had been involved in an easily avoidable accident. The teenager was hospitalized for minor surgery. Apprehensive about his dad's reactions to the accident, the son confided in his mother: "Dad is really going to chew me out for this one." His mother tried to console him.

Later that evening the father visited his son and greeted him with a kiss. This unexpected display of love was more than the son could handle. With the realization of his father's love for him, he burst into tears. The reprimand he anticipated never came.

That father's reaction to his son's accident is like the way God deals with us—in love. In the midst of our mistakes and blunders we sometimes forget how loving and forgiving our Heavenly Father is. The Scriptures tell us that God is "rich in mercy" (Ephesians 2:4). He begins each day with a fresh supply of mercy. It is "new every morning" (Lamentations 3:23). We can remind ourselves of His mercy the next time we become fearful of God's reaction to some mistake we make. He deals with us in love and with mercy!

August 9

How to Stop Fear

The thing which I greatly feared is come upon me, and that which I was afraid of is come unto me.

Job 3:25

We are not born with fear, for God says, "I've not given you the spirit of fear. I gave you love and the power of a sound mind" (2 Timothy 1:7 PARAPHRASED). We create fear through wrong believing. We have faith when we believe right, fear when we believe wrong.

Fear is your having faith in something you don't want to happen—believing it so deeply that the bad thing actually happens. Faith is your believing God will come to you with good things— putting it in your mind and spirit and believing it until it happens.

God does not automatically lead you out of fear. This involves something *you* do. Exercising your faith is the first step in stopping fear in its tracks. In other words, you turn your life around by starting to have faith in the good things, and faith in God. Jesus said, "I am come that [you] might have life, and that [you] might have it more abundantly" (John 10:10). So why not start having faith for abundant life, believing good things will happen to you?

I want to pray for you, because I believe that God can heal fear. I believe that when you even have a good thought toward God, that's prayer. But it is even better to put into words what you feel in your heart—to say it, lay it on the line. Be absolutely honest. Admit to God, "I've been having faith for something bad to happen in my life and my family. I want to have faith in You, Lord—faith that abundant life will come to me."

Will you join me and let's pray together?

Our Father, we come to You in the name of Your Son, Jesus Christ of Nazareth. We believe in His power and His love. We believe that You are going to send good things into our lives. We pray that God will give us the burning desire to believe that abundant life from Christ is going to fill our spirits, our minds, and our bodies, and that this good is going to lift us up and give us new lives. Through Christ we pray, we believe, and we expect a miracle. We expect that miracle in our lives to begin today. Amen and amen.

August 10

The Scorpion and the Turtle

God is love.
1 John 4:8

A fable tells of a scorpion who came up to a turtle about to cross a wide river. The scorpion said, "Mr. Turtle, would you let me ride upon your back across the river?" The turtle said, "Oh, Mr. Scorpion, I can't do that, because you'll sting me and I'll die." The scorpion reasoned, "Mr. Turtle, I wouldn't sting you. You are my friend." The turtle said, "Well, if you promise you won't sting me, I'll carry you across."

So they plunged into the river. Halfway across, the scorpion stung the turtle. As they were plummeting to the bottom, the turtle cried out to the scorpion, "You promised! Why did you sting me?" And the scorpion replied, "I had to. You see, it's my nature to sting!"

What an analogy of how the devil comes to us! *Carry me on your back,* he says. "Oh, I can't, Devil. You'll destroy me." *Oh, no, I'm your friend,* he says. We think it won't hurt, so we go ahead. Then we are stung, because it's the devil's nature to destroy.

God says, "Let Me go with you. I'll give you life." How do we know? Because it's God's nature to give us life. It's His nature to raise us up and make us better human beings. God has no sting. He only has love, because that's what He is—LOVE!

August 11

God's Feet
by REBECCA ROBERTS NASH

One day Jon Oral, our five-year-old, asked me, "Mommy, can you see God?"

I said, "No, but you can feel Him."

A few days later Jon and a friend were playing in the backyard when I noticed them sitting on the grass gazing up into the clouds. I asked what they were doing and Jon said, "We were looking for God, but we only saw His feet."

I smiled.

Each of us is instinctively aware of God. Deep in our consciousness is a feeling of wanting to see Him with our eyes. Moses once asked to see God. But the Lord answered, "Thou canst not see my face: for there shall no man see me, and live" (Exodus 33:20). Until we have an immortal body that can stand to see God's glory face to face, He lets us see Him with our spirit.

Jesus said, "Blessed are the pure in heart: for they shall see God" (Matthew 5:8). To see Him you must have your heart—your inner eyes—open to Him. Those who look for God, whose hearts yearn after Him, can see Him and feel His wonderful presence.

August 12

Happy Christians

Happy are thy men, happy are these thy servants, which stand continually before thee.

1 Kings 10:8

When the Queen of Sheba went to visit the famous King Solomon, one of the most outstanding things she discovered in his kingdom was the happiness of his servants.

Her discovery is a beautiful picture of the kingdom of God. Those who serve God are happy people. Because of the condition of the world today, it is sometimes hard to find a person who is truly happy. But when you do, he is a person who really knows Jesus, for true happiness is being in the family of God.

Jesus said, "These things have I spoken unto you, that my joy might remain in you, and that your joy might be full" (John 15:11). Christians who are unhappy have not yet grasped the secret hidden in Christ's words—the secret of letting His joy dwell in us. If Christ dwells within our hearts and we allow Him full control of our lives, then *His* joy becomes *our* joy—and it is full and complete.

Someone has described the Christian's joy this way: "Joy is the flag which is flown from the castle of the heart when the King is in residence there."

August 13

The Lord Is My Lighthouse
by SALLY JO SHELTON

The Lord is my lighthouse and my rescue ship:
    what storm can terrify me?
The Lord is the anchor of my life:
    what person or circumstance can make me
    panic?

When bad things happen that would
    snatch away my peace of mind,
    strip me of self-respect, or
    rob me of health,
    they all fail miserably.

Though an entire army of problems closes in on
    me, my inner being is calm.
Though the whole world declares war against
    me, I still have confidence.

There is one request that I have made of the Lord
    —it is the longing of my heart—
that I may live in His presence continually,
that I may see with my own eyes His indescribable
    glory and loveliness,
and that I may come to know Him better and
    better.

Then when bad things come, they won't
     bother me because the Lord Himself will
     be my haven.
He will hide me in the secret place of His
     own eternal presence where nothing can
     touch me.
He will lift me above my problems.

At last I will triumph over all the old fears
     and doubts that have defeated me
     so long.
In joyful thanksgiving
     I will burst into songs of praise to the
     Lord.
I will tell everyone I meet how good God is!

This meditation is based on Psalm 27:1–70.

August 14

The Old Music Master

There's a story that has meant a great deal in my life. It's about a little boy who had outstanding musical talent. He had taken lessons from different piano teachers until he really knew more than they did. His parents heard of a famous piano teacher who was retired, and they went to him. But being old, he no longer wanted to take pupils. They pleaded with him to just listen to the boy play. Finally he agreed. As he listened, the old man straightened up and a glow came in his eyes. He said, "Yes, I'll teach him."

The years passed, during which the old music master poured his spirit into the boy's spirit. He taught him far more about music than the rudiments. He taught him that great music is the readable script of life. It's life itself, expressed through different tones upon a musical instrument. And the boy understood. He was not making sounds with his fingers alone. His whole inner being was being poured out through his fingers as he played.

One day the music master said, "Son, it's time for your debut." The word had spread that this young man had great promise, and the evening of his performance the auditorium was filled. There was a hush when he sat down at the piano. As he played, he leaned over the keyboard and poured his very soul into the music.

Before he finished, strong men wept openly. Women threw their purses at his feet. But not once did he look at the crowd. He kept his eyes focused on the balcony, where the old white-haired music master was nodding his approval and whispering, "You're on the right track, son. Just keep it up. Just keep it up."

What this young man did is the key to it all as a Christian—keeping your eyes upon Christ. Don't look at the crowd and what they are doing. Don't look at the circumstances. Keep your eyes on Jesus, "the author and finisher of our faith" (Hebrews 12:2). He is sitting at the right hand of God the Father encouraging you on, saying, "You're on the right track. Keep it up." It is then that you can be victorious.

August 15

Christ Makes You Great

Rod Laver and Ken Rosewall are two Australian tennis players who were great in the 1960s but who emerged as champions in the 1970s. It is interesting that, as a boy, Rod Laver was slowfooted, yet his coach nicknamed him "Rocket." And Ken Rosewall, who was spindly and small, was nicknamed "Muscles."

So today it is *Rocket* Rod Laver and *Muscles* Ken Rosewall, two of the greatest tennis players of the past fifteen years. But it was the greatness of their coach that made these two young men great, for they lived up to the self-image he projected for them.

The image you have of yourself helps to determine what you become—what you do with your life. If you have a defeated self-image, you *are* defeated. But if you project a mental picture of yourself as you want to be; believe it—and strive for it with all your heart—the "sufficiency" and enabling power of Jesus Christ, who resides in you, goes to work to bring it to pass (*see* 2 Corinthians 3:5; Philippians 4:13; 1 Timothy 1:2). For it is the greatness of Jesus that makes you great.

August 16

Where Is God?

Have not I commanded thee? Be strong and of a good courage; be not afraid, neither be thou dismayed: for the Lord thy God is with thee whithersoever thou goest.

Joshua 1:9

A little girl, who dearly loved God, lived with her grandfather, who was an atheist. One day when she came home from school, she found a note he had taped to her dresser mirror. It read, "God is nowhere."

Since she was just beginning to learn how to read, she had to read the note a syllable at a time. And so instead of reading it, "God is nowhere," she read it, "God is now here."

No matter who we are, there are times when our faith is tested. Often doubt creeps in and sneeringly says, "Where is that God you say is always with you?" Sometimes a skeptical friend speaks up and asks, "If your God is so real, why did He let this happen to you?"

But faith is stronger than any doubts or questionings. It clings to God's promise, "I will never leave thee, nor forsake thee" (Hebrews 13:5). In the most impossible of circumstances, faith stands firm and unflinchingly declares:

God is now here!

August 17

I Believe . . .

Healing is a touch of the resurrection in this life. Jesus told Martha, "I am the resurrection, and the life" (John 11:25). The resurrection is not a thing. It is our Risen Lord, waiting to give us fullness of life, to restore everything which has diminished us in any way, including our bodies. The resurrection is complete healing, it's immortality, it's whole-man life made eternal.

I remember a story my father told me: One day he went to a building site, where they were constructing a new house. He found an old lodestone, or magnet, made like a horseshoe and he got to experimenting, to see what it would do. He put it down among some shavings of wood, but nothing happened. Then he moved the magnet close to a pile of nails. As he did, the nails quivered and moved, then literally stuck to the lodestone.

Papa said, "Oral, that's like God moving in our lives. When you are healed, it is like a piece of metal being lured toward a magnet. Every now and then the Holy Spirit gets so close that we are pulled toward it and we get a healing, a miracle."

I believe when you experience a healing, it is a preview of the resurrection, when you will be healed in your total being.

August 18

Murphy's Law

Every good gift and every perfect gift is from above, and cometh down from the Father.

James 1:17

If anything bad can happen, it will! This is what the business world calls Murphy's Law. And a great many people believe in it. Many individuals, whether they know it or not, are practicing Murphy's Law. It's reflected in their whole attitude.

One lady said she always felt worse when she felt the best, because she knew how bad she was going to feel when she started feeling bad again. A man was having a very difficult time, and someone tried to help him. He said, "You let me alone. The Bible says: *In the world ye shall have tribulation.* Therefore, I'm going to 'tribulate.' "

This negative outlook on life has an insidious way of working into our thoughts, until we develop an attitude whereby we not only expect bad things, but we attract them. It becomes a magnetic force for bad to overtake our lives.

But God does not accept Murphy's Law. He only accepts a new kind of law—His own law. *If anything good can happen, He is going to bring it to pass!* Let your mind dwell on that thought. It can change your whole outlook on life!

August 19

You Belong to God

. . . you belong to Christ . . . .
1 Corinthians 3:23 LB

Recently I preached on the power of stating in faith: "I belong to God. Therefore, Devil, take your hands off God's property—*me!*" At that time I didn't know that sitting there listening was a young girl who would later be attacked by a rapist. I only felt I *had* to say what God wanted me to say.

A few nights later a man grabbed this girl and put a knife to her throat, threatening to kill her if she didn't yield to him. Suddenly the girl remembered who she was and to whom she belonged, and she said, "You can't do this to me. I am God's property!" Each time he would try to force her, she would say, "You can't touch me. I belong to God!"

Suddenly three strangers appeared out of the night, and the rapist ran. Later the police captured him. While being questioned, the man said, "It was strange, but when the girl kept saying, 'You can't do this to me—*I'm God's property,*' something stopped me. I couldn't touch her."

Maybe you are not being assaulted as this girl was. But right now you may be reminded of how, in some other way, the devil is trying to assault your life—how he is trying to take advantage of you. Remember you don't belong to the devil. *Tell him you belong to God.*

August 20

The Vase

. . . learn to put aside your own desires so that you will become patient and godly, gladly letting God have his way with you.

2 Peter 1:6 LB

I often relate the story of a very poor family, which had only one expensive treasure in their house, a very rare vase. One day the father received a telephone call to come home quickly, because his little son had his hand caught in the vase.

This family had an abnormal love for the vase, because it was the only nice thing they owned. So they worked long to release the child's hand, but without success. Then they thought to call their doctor, who could use his delicate instruments to free the child. But he, too, was unsuccessful. Finally, the doctor said, "All I know to do is to break the vase. Bring me a hammer."

When he drew the hammer back to break the vase, the little boy said, "Wait a minute! Would it help if I turn loose of the penny?"

Starting to solve the problems that we face in our personal lives begins by turning loose of sin, by turning from self and letting Jesus take control. Surrender in war means defeat. But surrender to God is a clear-cut victory, for this surrender brings joy and peace.

August 21

The *Big* Jesus Can

Jesus increased in wisdom and stature, and in favour with God and man.

Luke 2:52

The mother of three-year-old Beth was not feeling well, so she decided to lie on the couch while she kept an eye on the child at play. "Let's ask *Baby* Jesus to make Mommy well," the mother suggested.

"He can't," was Beth's matter-of-fact reply.

The mother blinked in amazement as Beth hesitated, then said, "But the other Jesus can—the *big* Jesus!"

Many of us have a tendency to keep Jesus as a baby in the manger. Bethlehem, placed in its right perspective, was the means of God's revealed entrance into the world. But it is only part of the full story of God's plan of salvation.

For in His childhood, as tender and beautiful as it was, Jesus never preached a sermon publicly, never ordained an apostle, never healed a sick person, never stilled the raging waves of stormy Galilee. In fact, as a child, Jesus never performed any mighty work. Luke emphasized in his Gospel that Jesus grew in wisdom and in stature and in favor with God and man. *He grew!* And He expects *us* to grow. We develop into mature Christians as we follow the *man* Christ Jesus.

August 22

The Bent Fender
by EVELYN ROBERTS

*The wicked borroweth, and payeth not again: but the righ-
teous sheweth mercy, and giveth.*

Psalm 37:21

I can't think of anything worse than a dishonest Christian. Oral
and I have stressed to our children and to Oral Roberts University
students: "Even if it kills you, pay your debts. Be honest."

Sometimes you can't pay a bill, but you can certainly go and talk
with the person or business you owe and say, "Look, I don't have
the money to pay my bill right now, but I will pay it as soon as
possible." That way, the person you owe is not offended and your
integrity is not tarnished.

Let me tell you a little incident that happened before Oral began
the Abundant Life ministry. We were living in Enid, Oklahoma,
pastoring a small church. One morning he backed out of the drive-
way and hit the fender of our neighbor's car. The car was parked in
the street. Oral could have gone on and the man would never have
known who hit it. But he stopped the car, got out, and knocked on
the neighbor's door.

We had been living there only about a month and had not met this
family. So Oral said, "Sir, I'm Oral Roberts. I live next door. I'm
the pastor of this church over here, and I backed out and hit your
car. I just want to tell you that whatever the damages are, I'll take
care of it."

The neighbor said, "Mr. Roberts, I'm Mr. Gustavus. I'm glad to
meet you." He said, "You know that I'm a car dealer?"

My husband said, "No, I didn't know that."

He said, "Why didn't you just go on and not tell me about the
damage? I never would have known who did it."

Oral said, "That's true, but I would have known. And I want to
take care of it."

Mr. Gustavus said, "Well, don't worry about it. I'll have the
guys down at the shop repair it."

That man turned out to be the man who helped us get our first
brand-new car. This was shortly after we had discovered 3 John
2—*Beloved, I wish above all things that thou mayest prosper and
be in health, even as thy soul prospereth*—which changed our lives.

It turned everything around for us and helped us to know that God wants to supply *all* our needs. But suppose Oral had not told this man that he hit his car?

August 23

Not Automatic

Many people think that if they give their heart to God, go to church, and hear the Word, everything will automatically work out. And in a sense it will, but in another sense it won't. A lot of Christians are miserable—uptight and joyless. Why? Because they have to deal with problems and needs here on earth; *and they don't know how*. They are not in heaven yet.

The Scripture says, "Ye shall know the truth, and the truth shall make you free" (John 8:32). But if you don't learn how to apply God's truth, it will not set you free. We have to learn how to appropriate the promises of God twenty-four hours a day if we are to be happy, victorious Christians.

God has a way of doing things. I call it *the miracle of seed-faith*. Seed-faith is a simple plan which God showed me. It comes from the Bible—scriptural and, oh, so powerful! I'm absolutely convinced that if you will apply the three miracle keys of seed-faith, you will get a lot more of your problems solved and your needs met. Seed-faith will change your life and keep it changed all the days of your life. Memorize the keys. Saturate your thinking with them:

- *God is the Source of your total supply.*   Philippians 4:19
- *Seed for your miracle.*   Luke 6:38
- *Expect a miracle!*   Mark 11:24

August 24

Learn How God Does Things

I believe that God created man (Genesis 1:26). Our response to life is through our spirit, then our mind and body, because God made us that way. If God created man, then we've got to know something about our Creator. We've got to know how He operates and then try to operate like He does. If we don't know how God works, we can't know how to do what He wants us to do. But when we learn how God deals with us, we simply fall in line with Him.

That is why I believe the plan of seed-faith cannot fail, because it begins and ends with God. He is your Source of *total* supply. Everything you do is an expression of your love in which you move out of self into the way of God—into seed-faith giving and receiving, sowing and reaping. You give *unto* God, then expect back *from* God, your Source.

I know that God is my Source. I am not to look to anybody else. Yet I find myself doing that. When I do, nine times out of ten I am let down. Aren't you the same way? That's because people and things are not our source. They are only instruments. There is only one way to turn when we have problems, and that's to God. If we can cultivate our relationship with God and learn how to put Him at the center of our life, He's going to take care of us!

Read Luke 6:38; Philippians 4:19; Acts 17:28, 29; Mark 11:24.

August 25

Seedtime and Harvesttime

In Genesis 8:22 God says: "While the earth remaineth, seedtime and harvest . . . shall not cease."

Seedtime and harvesttime—giving and receiving! This is God's eternal law. And it will not change, as long as the earth remains!

Have you ever had a harvest without first having seedtime? The Bible teaches that you never receive until you have given. You may think you have, but you really haven't. For everything you've received, somewhere, sometime you put a seed in. Somewhere you gave something.

Somewhere you patted somebody on the back, or you smiled, or you said an encouraging word, or you whispered a prayer for somebody, or you gave some money, or you made a little trip out of your way, or you gave someone forgiveness . . . .

All of these ways of giving are seeds of faith that you plant. Galatians 6:7 says, "Whatsoever a man soweth, that shall he also reap." What do you reap? A *harvest!* This is why I say, when you give, *expect a miracle*—because each act of faith is a seed planted, and it will be multiplied back to you many times!

August 26

"So-Loved" Giving

Seed-faith is loving and giving until it becomes your life-style, the way you react to life. You think it, feel it, talk it, do it. This is the pattern of existence that God Himself established, and it became a matter of the way He deals with man. Did you know God seed-faithed for you? He gave His Son Jesus, the seed of David, to go to the cross to be the divine seed sown for our salvation (*see* John 7:42).

"For God *so* loveth the world, that he *gave* . . ." (John 3:16). Love is expressed in an act of giving. You can give without loving, but you cannot love without giving. This poem, which Oscar Hammerstein gave to Mary Martin, expresses what I'm saying:

> A bell is no bell till you ring it
> A song is no song till you sing it
> And love in your heart wasn't put there to stay
> Love isn't love till you *give* it away.

I'm talking about something that's often hard to do. It's easy to love someone who loves you, but it's hard to love someone who hates you, because the human tendency is not to love. Only when you get God's love can you do it. That's why I think seed-faith is discipleship. I believe when you get into "so loving," nobody can keep you from giving. You want to give.

August 27

Your Depth

The depth of your giving is the success of your Christian living. There is no such thing as something for nothing. John 3:16 says, "God so loved . . . that he gave his *only* begotten Son." *His best!*

The depth of giving is NOT . . . holding down a job and working when the boss is around, then fooling around when he's not. It's not telling the truth when it's convenient and telling a lie when the truth is inconvenient. It's not trying to make a grade honestly, when the teacher is looking and then cheating when his back is turned. It's not putting your hand out, expecting something for nothing.

The depth of giving is . . . giving at the very depth of your being.

A depth that reaches to the deepest part of your soul, so that your love erupts and your compassion flows and your better self emerges. Every ounce of honesty—every part of your integrity—emerges, so that it might be multiplied into more integrity and more honesty.

God didn't ask something for nothing. He gave to the lowest and highest depth of His ability. When you see the depth of God's giving, you learn what your depth is—*your best!*

August 28

Focus Your Love

Why did God give His only Son? ". . . that whosoever believeth in him should not perish, but have everlasting life" (John 3:16). I believe God had a need. His need was to defeat the devil and recover the human family, which had been stolen out of His hands. God had that need and He gave for a desired result.

What was the desired result? God desired that no human would perish, but everyone would have life—abundant, eternal life. God was focusing His love.

For instance, I can take a magnifying glass and focus it on a piece of paper under the sunlight. If I hold it in one spot long enough, I can burn a hole in that paper. Now that's the only way I can understand what God did. He focused His love upon a certain thing He desired. And because of it you and I have been given eternal life.

Brother Roberts, are you saying I can focus my love in an act of giving upon a desired result in my own life? That's what I'm saying. This is one of the most revolutionary ideas I can think of. I believe that if you will learn how to so love that whatever you do is a seed of faith—an act of your deepest commitment to God—you can focus that love, just as you focus the sun through to a piece of paper. You can focus it for a desired result—a need—and God will meet that need the way it should be met.

August 29

Give in Expectation

Learn how to expect a miracle and don't be ashamed of it. That sounds simple, doesn't it? But the devil will fight you on this point because expectancy works miracles, and he doesn't want you to have any.

God gave and expected a miracle. How do we know that? In Matthew 1:21, we read: "And she shall bring forth a son, and thou shalt call his name *Jesus:* for he shall save his people from their sins."

By the very name that God gave His Son we know He gave in expectation of miracles. God was not just giving to the wind or scattering seed. He was giving with a direction of purpose. He was *expecting* men and women to be saved.

I've been taught all my life to give and expect nothing back. But God teaches us to give as a seed we plant, expecting to receive a harvest (*see* Luke 6:38). Galatians 6:9 says, "Let us not be weary in well doing: for in due season we shall reap, if we faint not." You have seed planted. It's in God's storehouse. It's got your name on it. You may be discouraged because the seed hasn't produced. God's time is not yet. Just as cotton and corn have a due season, the due season will come on your seeds of faith. Keep expecting. *God wants you to have miracles!*

August 30

Attach Your Heart

Have you ever given when you were forced to? You know, because somebody twisted your arm and told you, "You ought to—you owe it"? And they made you feel like a sheep-killing dog if you didn't? I have. I've given many a time when I know God didn't bless me for it because I didn't give out of my heart. And 1 Corinthians 13 teaches us that anything we give without love doesn't count. Say you sit up all night with a sick person. Fine. But if it isn't done in love, it's nothing. Our giving has to be motivated by the same love that motivated God when He gave His only Son for us.

God teaches us exactly how to give—and why:

> *He which soweth sparingly shall reap also sparingly; and he*
> *which soweth bountifully shall reap also bountifully. Every*
> *man according as he* PURPOSETH *in his heart, so let him*
> *give; not* GRUDGINGLY *or of* NECESSITY: *for God loveth a*
> CHEERFUL *giver.*

2 Corinthians 9:6, 7

God says to give as a seed you sow, not as a debt you owe. Attach your heart to it. Give *cheerfully!* The happiest person in the world is the seed-planter—the giver who gives the seed-faith way—because he knows that not only is the person's need going to be met to whom he gives, but God is going to multiply his gift back to meet his need, also!

August 31

Run With God

Seed-faith is a way of life—a rhythm of faith that helps you relate your *self* and your *need* to Jesus. This is an attitude you constantly practice, never breaking your stride.

The rhythm of seed-faith is like an athlete running a race. If you take three runners, all of them equal in ability, the one who wins is going to be the one who develops a rhythm, a harmony, so that as he runs, his body, mind, and spirit become a flowing whole. Every stride is backed by the force of his spirit, the determination of his heart, and the synchronized movements of his entire being.

The great dread of a runner is that he might stumble. For if he stumbles, it is difficult to regain his rhythm, and he may lose the race. Some people develop the rhythm of seed-faith—others stumble. They try it once or twice, to see if it will work, and then forget it. Seed-faith is not a way of life with them. And they wonder why their needs are not met.

What you and I seek is a rhythm of our faith, so that our spirit, mind, and body flow together toward God as a harmonious whole. *We "run" with God constantly* . . . looking to Him as our Source . . . seeking ways to give first . . . expecting Him to meet our needs—and He does! (*see* Hebrews 12:1, 2).

SEPTEMBER

September 1

Happiness Is . . . Being Like Jesus

[Jesus] went up into a mountain: And . . . his disciples came unto him: And he . . . taught them, saying, Blessed . . . .

Matthew 5:1-3

Blessed means to be happy, fortunate. It refers not only to outward prosperity, but also to inner well-being. We tend to think that doing is what makes us happy. But Jesus taught that our happiness stems from what we *are*, as well. And this is what Christianity is—*being like Jesus.*

In the Sermon on the Mount, Jesus gives us some guidelines on how to be like Him. We know them as the Beatitudes:

"Blessed are the poor in spirit: for theirs is the kingdom of heaven. Blessed are they that mourn: for they shall be comforted. Blessed are the meek: for they shall inherit the earth. Blessed are they which do hunger and thirst after righteousness: for they shall be filled. Blessed are the merciful: for they shall obtain mercy. Blessed are the pure in heart: for they shall see God. Blessed are the peacemakers: for they shall be called the children of God. Blessed are they which are persecuted for righteousness' sake: for theirs is the kingdom of heaven" (Matthew 5:3-10).

Happiness is being like Jesus!

September 2

Happiness Is . . . Being Poor in Spirit

My wife, Evelyn, says, "As I was growing up, this Beatitude bothered me, because I didn't understand what it meant. I thought, *Oh, no, Lord, I'm poor enough. Why should I have to be poor in spirit, too? Surely You're not going to say 'blessed' to me if I'm poor in spirit.* But since then, I've found out what being poor in spirit really means. It means to have total dependence upon the Lord. And I've also learned that it's not a sign of weakness. Rather, to feel the need of God is a sign of strength and spiritual maturity.''

Jesus said, ''[Happy] are the poor in spirit: *for theirs is the kingdom of heaven.''* What is the kingdom of heaven? The Bible says, ''The kingdom of God is not meat and drink; but righteousness, and peace, and *joy* in the Holy [Spirit]'' (Romans 14:17). And aren't joy and happiness what everyone is looking for?

Happiness is not being poor in that you don't have enough food to eat or clothes to wear—but in that you are conscious of your utter spiritual bankruptcy apart from God. Happiness is realizing that without God, you can do nothing, but with Him, you can do everything!

September 3

Happiness Is . . . Being a Mourner

The Lord has great compassion for us when we're grieving over someone we've lost or some misfortune that's happened. But in this Beatitude, ''mourning'' has a deeper meaning than that. Here it means to grieve with that godly sorrow that leads to repentance—a broken and contrite heart (*see* 2 Corinthians 7:10; Psalm 51:17).

But the meaning goes even further than that. It's a mourning not only for our own sins and shortcomings, but also for that of the whole world. It's allowing God to break our hearts with the things that break His heart, thereby motivating us to do His will.

There's a wonderful promise that goes with this: *They* shall *be comforted.* First, as we mourn over our own sin, we will be forgiven. Psalm 32:1 says, ''[Happy] is he whose transgression is forgiven, whose sin is covered.'' Then, as we mourn over the sin of the world, we will have the joy of helping others come to repentance as well. God says so in Psalm 126:5, 6: ''They that sow in tears shall reap in joy. He that goeth forth and weepeth, bearing precious seed, shall doubtless come again with rejoicing, bringing his sheaves with him.''

September 4

Happiness Is . . . Being Meek

Most people think of meekness as being like Caspar Milquetoast, the comic-strip character: a timid, weak, apologetic person, one who is habitually afraid to assert himself, readily intimidated by aggression or authority. But meekness is not weakness. Meekness is strength. It's submitting and relinquishing your will, your total self, into the hands of God.

Meekness is obedience to God. Moses was known as the meekest man in the Bible (*see* Numbers 12:3). Why? Not because he was the greatest. And certainly not because he didn't make mistakes, because he made a lot of them. When the Lord called him, he said, "O Lord, don't call me." But he was *submissive*. He *obeyed* God. And through Moses, God performed great miracles. No weakling could have led two million people out of Egypt, or had the faith and boldness to believe that when he stretched his hand over the Red Sea, God would open it up and let the people go through on dry land.

When we're meek, truly submissive to the Lord, not only shall we ultimately inherit the earth, but it puts us in an all-things-possible realm. Anything is possible when we are obedient to God!

September 5

Happiness Is . . . Being Hungry and Thirsty

One good sign of spiritual health is a continual hungering and thirsting after God. An insatiable hunger. You won't settle for cheese and crackers. You are so famished you could eat a ten-course dinner and still ask for more. You thirst and keep on thirsting. It's an unquenchable thirst. You aren't satisfied with a glass of water. You could drink the whole ocean. This is the kind of hungering and thirsting after righteousness Jesus talked about. You aren't satisfied just to be "saved." You want more and more of God.

However, righteousness is not something you can achieve or earn through your own efforts. It's a gift that you receive through faith (*see* Romans 3:22, 5:17). The gift of right standing with God.

Jesus promises that if you stay in this attitude of: "Lord, I want more of You, more and more and more," then you'll get more. *You shall be filled!* He vows. The word *filled* comes from the word *fodder*, which is what the farmers used to feed their cattle, to fatten them up. And this is what Jesus promises—fodder for your soul. Nourishment that will satisfy the deepest longings of your heart.

September 6

Happiness Is . . . Being Merciful

Time after time in the Bible we read about people coming to Jesus saying, "Lord, have mercy on me." The blind men, the lepers, the parents with demon-possessed children—why did these people come to Jesus? Because He had a reputation for being merciful. He never turned anyone away. In each case, He performed an act of mercy. He restored the sight of the blind. He cleansed the lepers. He delivered the demon-possessed.

A true follower of Christ is also to have a reputation of being merciful—of performing acts of mercy.

What is mercy? Another word for it is *compassion*. It is pity, that clothes itself in gracious deeds. When compassion sees a person in need, it not only feels for the person and identifies with him, but it also does something about it. Mercy is always active. It is kindness in action. It gladly forgives all who injure or offend it and returns love and understanding.

Proverbs 14:21 says, "He that hath mercy . . . happy is he." Why are the merciful happy? Because "they [in turn] shall obtain mercy" (Matthew 5:7). They give mercy, so they in turn receive forgiveness and help when they need it.

September 7

Happiness Is . . . Being Pure in Heart

When the label on a honey jar says: 100% PURE HONEY, it means that the honey has no additives, no contaminants. Similarly, when the Bible refers to a pure heart, it's talking about one that has no sin, that's free of pretense and selfishness.

However, unlike honey, the heart is not naturally pure. Jeremiah

17:9 says, "The heart is deceitful above all things, and desperately wicked."

David the Psalmist knew the secret of heart purity. Not that he never sinned. The Bible tells us that he did. But whenever he did sin, he repented. He confessed what he had done and prayed: "Create in me a clean heart, O God . . . Cast me not away from thy presence" (Psalm 51:10, 11).

The reward of the pure in heart is to see God. And to see God implies being in His presence. This is why David wrote:

> *Who shall go up into the mountain of the Lord? Or who shall stand in His holy place? He who has . . . a pure heart, who has not lifted himself up to falsehood.*
>
> Psalm 24:3–5 AMPLIFIED

September 8

Happiness Is . . . Being a Peacemaker

> *[God] hath given to us the ministry of reconciliation [of making peace between God and man, and man and man].*
>
> 2 Corinthians 5:18

So often we think of a peacemaker in a passive sense—a diplomat; a compromiser; a person who refuses to take sides. But peacemaking, as the Bible refers to it, means much more than that. It's active. It's not only peace*keeping* but peace*making*. It costs something.

The Apostle Paul was a peacemaker, in the active sense of the word. He reconciled Onesimus, the runaway slave, to his master Philemon. How? By telling Philemon, "If [Onesimus] hath wronged thee, or oweth thee ought, put that on mine account . . . I will repay it" (Philemon 18, 19). Paul wanted to reconcile these two men so much that he was willing to get involved. He was willing to pay a price himself. And this is the mark of a true peacemaker.

> *Blessed—enjoying enviable happiness, spiritually prosperous—are the makers and maintainers of peace, for they shall be called the sons of God!*
>
> Matthew 5:9 AMPLIFIED

September 9

Happiness Is . . . Being Persecuted

What? Happiness is being persecuted? Sounds crazy, doesn't it? Yet 1 Peter 3:14 says, "If ye suffer for righteousness' sake, happy are ye." And the Apostle Paul said, "I take pleasure in . . . persecutions . . . for Christ's sake" (2 Corinthians 12:10).

Now this doesn't mean we should seek persecution. It's inevitable. "All that will live godly in Christ Jesus *shall* suffer persecution" (2 Timothy 3:12). But we will be blessed only if we are persecuted for *righteousness'* sake, for *Christ's* sake; not for stupidity's sake, not for making trouble for ourselves.

Now, persecution is rough. Even when our suffering is for Christ, it's hard to "rejoice, and be exceeding glad" (Matthew 5:12). It's hard to be happy "when men hate you, when they exclude you and insult you and reject [you]" (Luke 6:22 NIV). But as you "love your enemies, bless them that curse you, do good to them that hate you, and pray for them which despitefully use you, and persecute you" (Matthew 5:44), the bitterness fades away. And in its place comes the joy of the Lord. It's an inner happiness you can't explain, but it's there nonetheless.

September 10

Trust

Have you ever wondered how birds keep from falling off their perches when they go to sleep?

Scientists say that the reason birds don't fall off is that they have a muscle in each leg which automatically tightens when they land on a tree branch. This muscle makes their toes curl securely around the perch and relaxes only when the birds consciously let go.

What a wonderful picture of how you can find the peace of mind you need to fall asleep at night! You have a muscle like the one the birds have—it's called *trust*. When you latch your trust onto God and His promises, you're secure. There's nothing to fear, nothing to dread. You can relax, knowing you are safe in your Heavenly Father's care.

Are not two sparrows sold for a penny? Yet not one of them will fall to the ground apart from the will of your Father . . . So don't be afraid; you are worth more than many sparrows.

Matthew 10:29, 31 NIV

September 11

"I'm Sorry!"

The Lord . . . saveth such as be of a contrite spirit.
Psalm 34:18

My brother, Vaden, is only two years older than I, and we were brought up almost like twins. Papa believed in taking his old razor strap and "laying it on us" when we boys got unruly. Vaden was a little stubborn and he didn't like to cry when Papa whipped him. Papa would first sit both of us down and talk to us. If that didn't help, he would use the razor strap. He wanted us to be sorry for our wrong. But Vaden would just look at him. If Papa whipped him, he would be sullen as an opossum and not say a word. Papa would keep whipping until he broke Vaden's stubborn spirit and made him say, "I'm sorry."

I caught on quickly. When Papa came toward me with the razor strap, I yelled like a Comanche Indian, "Papa, I'm sorry! I'm sorry!" As a result, I didn't get half as many whippings or whippings half as hard as Vaden.

When wrong has been done, the only solution is to admit guilt and ask forgiveness from God, who is faithful and just to forgive us and to cleanse us from *all* unrighteousness. From that moment, we are free and whole.

September 12

Set Your Own Pace

Two young women decided to get into shape by entering the aerobics physical-fitness program. They conditioned themselves by walking a mile each day, and after a few weeks they progressed to jogging. At first the two kept side by side as they jogged. However, one day one of the women pushed out ahead and started running, while her companion struggled along behind. About that time another runner passed the woman who was behind.

"Hard going, isn't it?" he called to her.

"It sure is!" the woman said breathlessly, pointing ahead. "I'm trying to keep up with my friend."

"Well, don't worry about that," came the encouraging reply. "Set your own pace!"

The secret to success in whatever you do isn't in keeping up with your neighbor. The secret is within you—in your own determination to do God's will. "Work out *your own* salvation," Philippians 2:12 says. You see, it doesn't really make any difference whether you're ahead of the next guy or behind him, as long as you're going forward and doing your best. If you're on the right track and you're trying, that's what concerns God. And that's all you need to be concerned about!

September 13

Heaven Strapped in Your Heart

They are not of the world, even as I am not of the world.
John 17:16

When the astronauts go to the moon, they carry the atmosphere of the earth in a little container strapped on their backs. Even while they are deeply involved in their work on the moon's surface, their breath and life are continually flowing into them from the earth's atmosphere. To be without it even for a few seconds would mean their sudden death.

Similarly, we live on earth but our origin is in heaven. We are made by God, in the image of God; therefore, our citizenship is in heaven. If we were to rely on the atmosphere of this present world for our existence, it would mean our spiritual death. Our very being depends on God.

It takes some doing for a person to be in the world but not of the world, as Jesus prayed we would be. But it is possible. The most victorious triumphant power on earth is a human being who makes God his Source—who doesn't withdraw from society or hide from the problems of life. Instead, he gets involved! He goes out where the action is and gives Jesus to the people. He is not afraid of man or any other power, because he carries the atmosphere of heaven strapped in his heart.

September 14

Let Your Heart Talk

A little girl sat on the edge of the sidewalk, picking the petals off a tiny flower. Her little boyfriend walked up. "Whatchadoin'?" he asked.

The girl just kept on picking off the petals:

He loves me. He loves me not.
He loves me. He loves me not.
He loves me!

"You love me!" she exclaimed as she picked off the last petal.

"Oh, I could have told you that," the boy said.

"Well, why didn't you?" the girl asked reproachfully. "Why didn't you?"

Speech is one of God's special gifts to us. It is one of the main ways we have of letting each other know how we think and feel. Yet many of us who can glibly wisecrack and joke are often afraid to tell others that we love them or appreciate them.

Jesus said, "Out of the abundance of the heart the mouth speaketh" (Matthew 12:34). *So let your heart talk!* If you love your husband, your wife, your child, your parents, your friends, tell them. If you think your employees do a good job, tell them. If you really appreciate them, it will help them just to hear you say it, and you'll be glad you did.

September 15

Become a Sow-*er*

He who gives the seed to the sower and turns [it] into bread
. . . will give you the seed of generosity to sow and, for
harvest, the satisfying bread of good deeds done.
                                        2 Corinthians 9:10 PHILLIPS

Seed-faith isn't just a matter of sowing seed once in a while, but of continuously sowing—of becoming a sow-*er*. To illustrate, you may go out into your yard or garden once in a while and dig a hole and plant a seed, but that does not make you a farmer. Or you may give once in a while, but unless you give continuously, you do not become a giv-*er*.

You see, it is the pattern of your life that determines the outcome of your existence. Everybody does good things, or sows good seeds, once in a while. But that is not nearly as significant as forming a pattern, so that the thrust of your life is to do good.

Now, suppose that you have not formed a pattern of constantly sowing good seed, but you want to start. Here is what I recommend: Not only start, but do it constantly. Make it an attitude of your life. Become a plant-*er,* a sow-*er,* a giv-*er.* And think of it as a joyous thing. Not as a debt you owe, but as a seed you sow.

September 16

Become a Follow-*er*

> . . . *be earnest, wholehearted followers of Christ who is the hidden Source of [our] faith.*
>
> 1 Timothy 3:9 LB

Jesus wants us to have an attitude of faith—of seed-faith.

Now what am I saying? I'm saying it's important first to start climbing the stairway of the Christian faith, but it's even more important to keep climbing—to stay on the stairway. Get a foot on the stairway, but don't take it off. Start climbing the stairs one at a time and *keep on climbing.*

For example, I could climb just one step and think I had done well and get off. That is, I could come to Christ and then back out and quit. Or I could come to Christ and then keep on every day, trying to have a good attitude, trying to serve Him, and trying to sow good seed.

What it all boils down to is making a commitment or a dedication of your life to the Lord *daily* and, secondly, a commitment to His way of doing things. This means you become a follow-*er* of Christ.

September 17

The Cumulative Effect

> *Honour the Lord with thy substance, and* . . . *So shall thy barns [storehouses] be filled with plenty.*
>
> Proverbs 3:9, 10

The nice thing about becoming a sow-*er*—a follow-*er*—is that the harvest becomes cumulative. That is, God builds a personal

September 19

"I Don't Remember"

An old, old story is told about Saint Gertrude the Great. One day she was crying her heart out when Jesus appeared to her. "What are you crying about?" He asked very gently.

"Oh, my sins, my sins!" she cried. "I'm so sorry for my sins!"

"What sins?" the Lord asked.

As she began to enumerate her transgressions one by one, the Lord said, "But I don't remember them." Then He made it clear to her that when she really regretted her sins and she confessed them, she was forgiven!

"If we confess our sins," 1 John 1:9 says, "he [God] is faithful and just to forgive us our sins, and to cleanse us from *all* unrighteousness." To have our sins so thoroughly and totally forgiven by God seems too good to be true. But it is a reality. And with our acceptance of God's forgiveness comes a release of tensions—a rolling away of burdens—the conquering of hostilities—a deliverance from fear—a whole newness of life!

September 20

Pearls of Wisdom

Pearls of wisdom often come from children. A couple and their nine-year-old daughter were riding along in the car. The husband was enthusiastically sharing with his wife the news of a big sale he was making and another one that looked pretty well wrapped up. "That will bring our income up to so much money by the end of the year," he said, "then we can do this and buy that . . . ."

The daughter, who was listening quietly, spoke up: "If you're making all that money, why aren't you guys happier?"

Already this little girl was beginning to understand the fallacy of thinking that happiness is something we get—something we can buy—to satisfy the yearnings we feel inside. To be happy, the human spirit must be fulfilled. This is what our Lord Jesus meant when He said, "Man shall not live by bread alone, but by every word that proceedeth out of the mouth of God" (Matthew 4:4).

Jesus went on to explain how we find true happiness. He said, "I am the bread of life: he that cometh to me shall never hunger; and

storehouse for every giver, in which He stores up the mira
we will need in each of our due seasons. *That is the cu*
effect!

I believe God has a personal storehouse, in which He sto
Oral Roberts' miracles—and He has a personal storehouse
God holds our miracles for His due season—for those
when we *need* a miracle.

If I had to depend on God to supply all the needs of Ora
University and this ministry all at once, I couldn't do it. I
have that kind of faith. It's too big a mountain. But I
working and sowing the seed for years. And the harvest i
tive. The miracles are happening. God keeps opening my
storehouse, in which He has stored up the miracles that
each of my due seasons. The cumulative effect is constar
effect. This is God's pattern for you, if you have been
planting seed.

September 18

A Burning in Your Heart

When the Lord speaks to your heart, He touches your
It is not only an experience of reason, but also somethi
feel. For example, not long ago a man said, "Mr. Rob
listening to your radio broadcast when you and your
about some difficulties you had had with your childre
discussed how they found God, a lump came into my th
then and there," he said, "I started back to God."

A similar experience happened to two of Jesus' disci
after His resurrection. A "stranger" joined them as
walking along the road to Emmaus. After they recogni
Jesus, He vanished. But note what they said to one an
not our heart burn within us, while he talked with us
and while he opened to us the scriptures?" (Luke 24:

A burning in your heart or a lump in your throat
speaking to you. These feelings may come while you
the Bible or praying—while you are hearing someone t
has done for them—while beholding some beauty of r
tening to a beautiful song. They are evidences to yo
God is real and that He is closer to you than your br

he that believeth on me shall never thirst" (John 6:35). Happiness is Christ living in your heart—centering your life around Him. He is the fountainhead from which all happiness flows.

September 21

Dandelions!

[God] hath made every thing beautiful in his time.
Ecclesiastes 3:11

A group of friends touring Switzerland agreed that one of the highlights of their visit would be to view a sunrise coming up behind the Swiss Alps. So early one morning they met to share this experience.

Slowly the sun inched its way up from behind the snow-covered peaks, causing the ground to glisten in the sunlight, like acres of diamonds. The group grew silent. Suddenly the sound of stomping feet broke the reverence of the moment.

"Dandelions!" muttered one of the men angrily as he stomped the ground. "Dandelions in my back yard! Dandelions in my front yard! Now dandelions in Switzerland!"

The beauty of God literally surrounded him, but he missed it. God has put beauty in each and every day—in people, things, incidents, places, feelings. Are you missing God's beauty because of the petty distractions of life?

Sure, life has its pesky dandelions—but it has its acres of diamonds, too!

September 22

A Form of Love

Whom the Lord loveth he correcteth; even as a father the son in whom he delighteth.
Proverbs 3:12

A mother stood in the doorway, watching her little four-year-old daughter playing with a favorite doll. The little girl turned the doll over her knee and spanked it, saying, "Even though I have to spank you, I want you to know that I still love you." The mother was hearing a live playback of the way she disciplined the child.

Discipline is a form of love. The idea of discipline is sometimes misunderstood. Many people associate it with punishment. But when God disciplines His children, it is for their training—not punishment. God is a God of love. No discipline is pleasant at the time. "But . . . afterward it yieldeth the peaceable fruit of righteousness unto them which are exercised thereby" (Hebrews 12:11).

God's correction of love removes the obstacles of undisciplined living which stand between you and a close relationship with Him. You are precious in His sight. Through correction, He reveals His watchful concern for you and draws you closer to Him. Be not weary of discipline, for it is the very groundwork of a happy, well-balanced, mature Christian. This is God's love.

September 23

"Too Young To Die"

If any man will come after me, let him deny himself.
Matthew 16:24

One night after prayers eight-year-old Teresa propped herself up in bed and said, "Mother, tell me again what you told me the other day about Jesus. I forgot."

Her mother leaned over and kissed her on the cheek. "Well," she said, "it's like this: One day when you are ready, Jesus will speak to your heart and ask you to give your life to Him."

Teresa was quiet a moment, then blurted out in protest, "But, Mother, I'm too young to die!"

We may laugh at such a literal interpretation of "giving your life to God." But becoming a truly committed Christian really does involve death. Not physical death. But death to our own selfish desires and ways. It involves a daily sacrifice of our will so we can do God's will. Romans 12:1 says, "I beseech you . . . by the mercies of God, that ye present your bodies a *living sacrifice,* holy, acceptable unto God, which is your reasonable service."

You may protest, "But I don't want to die to myself. That would be the end to everything I've ever wanted." Dying to yourself is not *the* end. It is *an* end, but it is also a beginning—the beginning of a whole new life. Not an easy life, but the most challenging, fulfilling life ever.

September 24

Think Big

Two women were on their way home from a concert where they had heard a famous violinist play.

"Wasn't it a wonderful concert?" one said.

"I didn't enjoy it at all," the other woman replied. "The stuffy air in there just ruined the whole evening for me."

Some people miss the music of life because they dwell on what's wrong with everything. They major in the minors! the petty things!

It has been said that God is uncomfortable with small thinkers. But it takes a personal realization of the greatness and majesty of God to release us from the prison of small minds and attitudes.

When Christ really gets your attention and you let His greatness permeate your heart and mind, you are not limited by a small mental attitude. You gain a whole new outlook on life. You think bigger, because the mind that was in Christ Jesus is in you.

> *Let this mind be in you, which was also in Christ Jesus.*
> Philippians 2:5

September 25

Life Is So Daily

A minister tells of driving by a bus stop one day and seeing a woman standing there wiping away tears. Concerned, he stopped, introduced himself, and asked if something was wrong and if he could do anything to help.

"Oh, no," she replied, "I was just standing here waiting for the bus and thinking of my problems. I'm so tired. But I've got to go home, cook dinner for my family, and then do the dishes and the laundry. In the morning I'll get up early, cook breakfast, get ready for work, then rush and catch the bus to my job again. It's the same every day. And I was just wondering how long I can take it."

She was like the man who, feeling the hardships of life, said, "The trouble with life is, it's so daily."

Jesus walked every foot of life as a man, facing the same type of human needs and frustrations that we do. It was in this arena of struggle that He said, "Come unto me, all ye that labour and are heavy laden, and I will give you rest" (Matthew 11:28). The good news of Christ's Gospel is that we don't have to struggle under the load of life's dailiness, trying to handle it all by ourselves. Jesus wants to carry the load for us.

> *Give your burdens to the Lord.*
> *He will carry them . . . .*
> Psalm 55:22 LB

September 26

The Good Shepherd

A friend of mine was in Israel recently on a tour. He was riding on a bus with his tour group when they came upon a flock of sheep. This is not too unusual in the Holy Land, but one of the ladies on the bus noticed something peculiar about this particular flock of sheep. They were not being *led;* they were being *driven.*

The lady became quite concerned and said, "Look at that shepherd. He is not leading the sheep. He is driving them and poking them, and whipping them! What's the matter with that guy? I thought a shepherd was supposed to lead his sheep."

The tour guide answered, "You're right. A shepherd does lead his sheep. But that man is not the shepherd. *He is the butcher.*"

What a graphic picture of Jesus' own comparison between Himself and the devil! He said, "The thief [or the butcher] cometh not, but for to steal, and to kill, and to destroy: I am come that [you] might have life, and . . . have it more abundantly. I am the good shepherd." (*See* John 10:1–18.)

One of the most important things you can know is this: It's the devil who slaps you around and makes you suffer—not God.

God is a good God!

September 27

"We Would See Jesus"

The story is told of a pastor who had an unusually successful ministry. But as the years passed, his concern for the people waned, and Jesus was not as real in his sermons. One Sunday he found a note on his pulpit which read: "Dear Pastor, 'We would see Jesus' (John 12:21). Your congregation."

After the service, the pastor returned to his study alone. There he prayed, "Lord, is it possible that my people are no longer seeing Christ in me?" In searching his heart, he had to admit that they were not. With new consecration he determined to recapture what he had lost and to preach Jesus with a passion and love he had never known before.

With his renewed zeal and love for God, the church began growing and people were coming to Christ again. One Sunday he found another note on his pulpit. It read: "Dear Pastor, 'Then were the disciples glad, when they saw the Lord' (John 20:20)."

The Holy Spirit operating in us provides an inner power that becomes an outward force to bring the reality of Christ to others. It is good to examine our lives every so often, to see if the glow of the Spirit is as bright as it once was.

September 28

No Magic in His Robe

While Christ was being crucified, soldiers gambled for His robe—a beautiful seamless garment. Ordinarily the clothes of the victim of the cross were divided four ways to pay the men who did the crucifying. But to divide Jesus' robe would destroy its value. So they decided to gamble for it (*see* John 19:24).

During Christ's ministry, many "besought him that they might only touch the hem of his garment: and as many as touched were made perfectly whole" (Matthew 14:36). The man who won Jesus' robe doubtless wore it on many occasions. But to him it was probably only the winnings of another gambling venture. If he did not come to believe in the *wearer*, he received none of Christ's benefits.

The robe of Jesus held no magic charm. Those who were healed by touching Jesus' clothes were healed because when they touched His robe, they touched Him—*Jesus*—with their faith. Their act of touching His robe was a point of contact for the releasing of their faith. And when they felt Christ's power, they directed its action toward their need. This is the goal and result of true faith.

September 29

The Visible Touches the Invisible

Not long ago a woman sent me a thrilling testimony. She said, "Brother Roberts, I wrote you recently and asked you to pray for my husband, who was in the hospital, receiving psychiatric treatment. I decided that your letter back to me would be my point of contact—that at the exact moment I received your reply, I'd release my faith for his healing. I did this and there was immediate improvement. In just three weeks my husband was discharged, and he has been improving steadily."

There were no healing properties in my letter to this woman, *for only God can heal*. She simply used my letter as her point of contact for releasing her faith in Jesus, and her husband was healed! This is scriptural. Read Mark 16:18; Acts 5:15; 19:12; and James 5:14, 15 for a few examples.

A point of contact is visible—something that helps you to touch the invisible God with your faith. It can be believing a Scripture verse, taking Communion, receiving prayer from a minister or friend, or setting the time and place for deliverance. Whatever your point of contact is, your believing becomes a single act of faith that reaches a point of no return and says: "I know whom I have trusted, and I am sure that he is able . . ." (2 Timothy 1:12 TEV). *In that moment, your miracle begins!*

September 30

Directed Power

The Bible tells about a woman with an incurable disease, who merely touched the border of Jesus' clothes and was healed. Though jostled by a huge crowd, Jesus asked, "Who touched me? Somebody hath touched me: for I perceive that virtue has gone out of me." (*See* Luke 8:43–48.)

The power of God, although invisible and immaterial, has a visible and material effect. Its results can be felt in the spirit, mind, and body. God's power is spiritual. Jesus likened it to the wind. It cannot be seen or explained but it can be felt (*see* John 3:8).

People sometimes say, "Mr. Roberts, when I watch your television program, I feel so close to God, and His power is so real."

Many describe the power of God as a quiet but definite sensation of exquisite joy and peace racing through their being.

Unquestionably, thousands of people have felt God's power and presence, but they have rejoiced and let it go at that. The most important thing about feeling the power of God is that you direct its action toward your greatest need. The woman who touched Jesus as a point of contact released His power for a definite purpose. She directed the healing virtue in Jesus from Him into her body. This is the secret of getting your need met.

OCTOBER

October 1

When You Become Restless

*As an eagle stirreth up her nest, fluttereth over her young,
spreadeth abroad her wings, taketh them, beareth them on
her wings: so the Lord alone did lead him.*

Deuteronomy 32:11, 12

When it's time for the mother eagle to teach her young to fly, she stirs up their nest. She removes the soft down and lets the eaglets down on the sharp briars, because if she doesn't, they forfeit their rights to be eagles.

Sometimes God stirs your nest. I remember, as if it were yesterday, when I was living in Enid, Oklahoma, in 1947—attending Phillips University, pastoring a nice church, raising a family. While I was in that little nest, God put a vision in my heart to build Him a school. And I picked out a piece of ground (about an acre!) where I was thinking about someday building the school. People asked me how long I intended to stay in Enid, and I said, "The rest of my life."

Then one day it seemed as if somebody pulled the rug out from under me. The people I'd been close to suddenly became unfriendly. The best friend I had—whom I'd worshiped with, prayed with, traveled with, played golf with, hunted quail with—suddenly everything was different between us. I wasn't at home. I felt like I would smother. It was God, pulling the soft cover away because He had something bigger for me to do. If I'd stayed in that small comfortable nest, my ministry never would have touched the world. God knew that, but I didn't.

You see, when God gets ready for you to move forward or to learn how to trust Him, He lets things happen to take away your ease. You become restless, discontented. The people you love and who love you seem to turn into your enemies, and the place you're in becomes cramped. You may not sleep well or be able to eat and

202

enjoy it. You become miserable—and so lonely.

This doesn't mean God has left you. It just means He is stirring your nest. He is wanting to lead you in a new direction and take you to higher things. He loves you and has something wonderful in mind for you!

October 2

How Big God Is!

O Lord God, thou hast begun to shew thy servant thy greatness, and thy mighty hand: for what God is there in heaven or in earth, that can do according to thy works?
Deuteronomy 3:24

Just as a mother eagle spreads her wings, revealing her powerful strength to her little ones, so God in the midst of His dealing with you lets you see how big He is and that He can take care of you.

That's what I saw in 1947, as I got out of the nest and was utterly alone. I began to look to God, because there wasn't anyone to look to but God. I began to search the Bible, to pray and devote myself to seeking God more than I ever had. It wasn't long until He showed me a vision of Himself. Oh, not something physical, but I began to realize how big God is, the far sweep of His eternal purpose, the majesty of His presence and power.

He gave me a recurring dream, in which He showed me that everybody is sick in some way. Everybody is crying inside about something that's hurting them. My heart felt like it would burst. I wanted to put my arms around all humanity and say, "Don't worry. God loves you. God can heal you." That was God taking me on His wings and showing me His bigness.

About that time a man whom I hardly knew walked up to me and said, "Mr. Roberts, you are not going to be in this town much longer."

"Why?" I asked.

"What you are preaching is too big for one small group," he said. "The world has got to hear this."

As I travel over the world, I often think about what that man said. *He was part of God's bigness.*

October 3

How to Rise Above Storms

In all their affliction . . . He lifted them up and carried them.

Isaiah 63:9 AMPLIFIED

A powerful built-in radar system enables the eagle to detect a coming storm long before the human eye or ear can. The mother eagle sits watching and waiting for the storm to hit. Then as the winds start blowing, she teaches her young how to set their wings so when the storm strikes, the winds that would destroy them lift them above the storm! God says He will lead us like that.

We can't always detect the storms that will come to us. But when bad things happen we can set our minds and our believing toward God and develop an attitude toward life that will help us rise above the storms. First, we can remember who our Source is: God! Second, we can keep on sowing seeds of faith—loving and giving even when losses are striking at us, giving out of our need, and giving for our desired results. And third, we can keep on expecting miracles, because we know that our God is an everlasting God and His eternal law of sowing and reaping will never change. (*See* Philippians 4:19; Luke 6:38; Mark 11:24; 2 Corinthians 9:10, 11.)

These three miracle keys of seed-faith living show you how to set your wings to rise above life's storms that strike—storms of illness, of opposition, of failure, of disappointment. They will not overcome you, but you will feel the power of God lifting you, until you're on top—above them!

October 4

Keep Getting Out of the Nest

I've found that getting out of the nest once is not the whole story. You have to keep on getting out. A dozen times I've thought we had reached the zenith in this ministry. Then I'd get uncomfortable in the nest and God would lay His wing down again.

One of the most uncomfortable periods of my life since 1947 was when God gave me the whole vision of the further dimension of Oral Roberts University—the schools of religion, medicine, business, and law—and the plan of cross-pollination of these four basic areas of man's life.

As God began to show me that I had to stop thinking He was through and that He had brought us to where He wanted us, the bigness of the vision frightened me, and I became ill in my body. I found myself begging God to uncall me and to take away my life. But God in His goodness let me face that—so I could get out of the nest again and up on His wing, where I belonged (*see* Psalm 91:4).

I'm sharing this personal experience with you because I know it parallels things that you've been through and will go through the rest of your life.

You are never going to develop unless you struggle. For God to use you, you've got to be willing to come out of the nest from time to time!

October 5

Miracles Follow Two Patterns

The Lord is good unto them that wait for him, to the soul that seeketh him. It is good that a man should both hope and quietly wait for the salvation of the Lord.
Lamentations 3:25, 26

Over the years as I have seen God work miracles, I have observed that they follow two patterns. Sometimes it almost stuns me, it's so quick. At other times, weeks or months will pass after I've prayed and seeded for a miracle before it happens. Then one day, there it is!

But, to be perfectly frank, most of my miracles do not happen quickly. I'm even tempted to look to human instruments rather than to God, my *Source*. Sometimes I'm tempted to actually believe God has forgotten me or doesn't care. Or I may find myself saying, "God, why is this happening to me? What have I done to deserve it?"

Then I try to remember that questions like these are the signs of a loser. A winner starts with different kinds of questions.

Who am I making my *Source* of total supply—man or God? Have I been seeding for a miracle as God says—cheerfully? Am I demanding that God send my miracle in my own way and time? Or am I trusting Him, as my Source, to send it in His own time and way?

Taking positive action like this, instead of eating my heart out and increasing my misery, has helped me to receive many miracles that people had told me were impossible. I'm learning to have a fierce, tenacious expectation for my miracle to happen, and at the same time to really trust God my *Source* to make it happen in His own way and time.

October 6

Hitting Slump

I remember a story about Casey Stengel, who was manager of the New York Yankees baseball team when they won ten American League pennants and seven World Series championships. One time Mickey Mantle, one of the Yankees' star players, was in a hitting slump. Each time he struck out, he walked down into the dugout and kicked the water cooler. After watching him do that time after time, Casey finally went over one day and said, "Mickey, it ain't that water cooler that's gettin' you out!"

That made Mickey think. Soon he came out of the slump and once again became a hitter of over .300.

During times of failure we all tend to blame it on outward circumstances or other people. "If I had a more understanding wife or husband . . . if I didn't have this handicap . . . ." In fact, this is what Adam and Eve did in the Garden of Eden when they disobeyed God. Adam blamed Eve, and Eve blamed Satan (*see* Genesis 3:11–14). But as long as we're busy making excuses, we never face up to the real reasons we aren't succeeding.

If you're in a "hitting slump," if you are failing at what you want to do most in life, your challenge is not to make excuses. By facing up to yourself and what you are doing wrong, you can determine to go out and, with God's help, do it right.

October 7

Fallen Among Thieves

The word *miracle* has fallen among thieves today. It is a lot like the man in the story of the Good Samaritan, whom Jesus described as falling among thieves (*see* Luke 10:30–37). That is, the secular world has taken the word *miracle* and attached it to such things as miracle drugs, miracle fabrics, miracle cleansers.

The word *miracle* has been robbed of its original meaning. In the King James Version of the Bible, the word that was translated "miracle" originally meant "wonder"—wonder of God: God moving in a human life and accomplishing something beyond human explanation!

Ours is a "self-help" generation. And this is good, because we've advanced and developed through self-help books. We've learned how to think in a positive way, and these things are instructive and helpful. But, in life, sooner or later we all come to a point where there is no more self-help. In fact, there is no help from any earthly or human source.

When there must be something done for us outside the realm of the natural—and we come to depend upon God for a wonder in our lives to meet our needs and solve our problems—then we will see the word *miracle* restored to its rightful place.

October 8

What Makes Us Better?

The goodness of God leadeth thee to repentance.
Romans 2:4

What makes us a better person? What makes us more loving and caring? Is it punishment? Is it one hard time after another? Is it crushing blows?

No.

It is love—God's love.

God does allow suffering, sometimes for reasons we don't understand. But it's God's love in the hard times that helps us to become better, more loving, more giving persons.

Was it the loneliness, the hopelessness, and despair that the disciples experienced at Christ's crucifixion that made them become strong "we'll-go-on-anyway" men? No, that just showed what insecure, frightened men they were. Rather, it was Christ's resurrection, His forgiveness and love that changed them into courageous go-getters.

God wants us to be better persons. He wants us to be the best we can be, so He sends us His love daily. Receive it with joy—regardless of the circumstances!

October 9

You Have a Choice

Would a God of love ever send anyone to hell?

Jesus preached the good news of the abundant life He came to offer. But He also taught that just as there is a heaven, there is a hell.

The lines are drawn for this, not only in God's Word, but also in the laws of nature. It's an accepted fact that nature will rise up and punish you if you break its laws. If you run a red light, you may get by the first time—even the second time. But if you keep on running red lights, sooner or later you'll hurt someone or get hurt.

The final judgment will not be because we've sinned but because we've remained sinners. There's a difference in telling a lie and in being a li-*ar*—in committing an act of adultery and being an adulter-*er*. The final judgment will be because we've formed a life pattern of being a sinn-*er*.

The Bible says, "Jesus came into the world to save sinners" (1 Timothy 1:15). God is a God of love. He doesn't send anyone to hell. Neither does He force anyone to go to heaven. You have a choice.

> *Seek ye the Lord while he may be found, call ye upon him while he is near . . . for he will abundantly pardon.*
>
> Isaiah 55:6, 7

October 10

Bulletin Fresh From Heaven

> *When they deliver you up, take no thought how or what ye shall speak: for it shall be given you in that same hour what ye shall speak. For it is not ye that speak, but the Spirit of your Father which speaketh in you.*
>
> Matthew 10:19, 20

The whole of the Christian's life is a thrust toward witnessing to people about Christ. Yet, have you ever wanted to witness, but you just couldn't find the words? Well, this is where the power of the Holy Spirit comes into the picture. You don't have to always depend on your intellect. Many times the Holy Spirit will drop the right words into your mind or heart at the right moment. And as you speak them, you give an inspired statement that is remarkable in its effect upon people.

For example, there are times when I am speaking on something I have prepared to give and all at once I feel the Holy Spirit move in me and inspire me. Then the words that come from my lips are not words I have learned. They are inspired statements; that is, God is handing me a bulletin fresh from heaven—something hot off the wire. When this happens usually someone will come to me later and say, "Mr. Roberts, as you spoke I felt the Spirit moving through me and communicating something from God to me."

Witnessing under the power of the Holy Spirit is what Christianity is all about.

October 11

"Gut-Level" Communication

Speaking . . . the truth in love.
Ephesians 4:15

"We just don't get along anymore."

"She really hurt my feelings."

"He makes me so mad!"

Relationship problems. We face them every day. How much more peaceful and effective our daily lives would be if we could only learn how to get along with people better!

Of course, there is no one easy step to having harmonious relationships. But the beginning of understanding between any two people is *communication*. Not on just a surface level—a "Hello, how-are-you?" type thing—but rather on what is commonly expressed as the gut-level. A level where you are open and honest with others about how you really think and feel.

You can use honesty or truth as a weapon to hurt the other person. But if you combine it with love, you will aim it not at hurting—but at opening up to the other person and letting him see you as you really are. When he sees that you are trusting him with yourself, he will be likely to open up to you in turn. And with both of you sharing your real selves, you will be far more able to resolve your conflicts.

October 12

God Loves You!
by EVELYN ROBERTS

At one of our laymen seminars at Oral Roberts University, I met a woman whose husband had died, and she said, "Mrs. Roberts, I'd like to see you for a few minutes."

I said, "Fine," and we sat down at a table to talk.

"Since I've lost my husband," she said, "everything inside me has dried up. I have no emotional feelings. I cannot feel sorrow. I cannot feel joy. I can't feel anything. I can't even cry."

"Do you believe God loves you?" I asked.

She said, "I don't know. I have never felt the presence of God in my life. Never."

I said, "Well, let's pray about it." I took her hands and began to pray, but I felt no response from her at all. Then I said, "Let's bow our heads again. I want to ask the Lord to show us what to do. I know He loves you. I know He is concerned about you. And He wants you to feel His presence." So we prayed again and I said, "Lord, just give me the key to this woman. I know that in everybody there is a key that opens up the inner man—that opens them up to You."

Suddenly I felt the woman needed love and concern. So I just reached out and put my arms around her. And I said, "Look, God loves you and I love you. I believe that if we ask the Lord to do something for you, He will do it, because Jesus said: *Ask, and it shall be given you; seek, and ye shall find* (Matthew 7:7). His Word tells you to *cast all your care upon him; for He careth for you* (1 Peter 5:7)."

We prayed again, and when I looked up, tears were streaming down her face. She said, "Wow! I felt something that time!" She came to me at the end of the seminar and said, "Mrs. Roberts, that prayer changed my life."

Well, I knew it wasn't the prayer. It was God who changed her life. God helped us to find the key that opened her up. She felt that somebody was concerned about her and she suddenly became aware that God loved her. One of the most important things for you to know is that *God cares for you. God loves you.* Then you can trust and believe in Him as the Source for your total life.

October 13

When You Don't Know How to Pray

Likewise the Spirit also helpeth our infirmities: for we know not what we should pray for as we ought: but the Spirit . . . maketh intercession for us with groanings which cannot be uttered . . . according to the will of God.

Romans 8:26, 27

Have you ever felt such a heavy burden on your heart that you were unable to formulate the words to fully express it to God? One outstanding dimension of the work of the Holy Spirit is that He makes intercession for us "according to the will of God."

The Holy Spirit who indwells you gathers up the longings and desires of your innermost being and expresses them to God through groanings and the prayer language of the Spirit. He searches out inhibitions, hidden resentments, repressions, and scars that are embedded in the human spirit. It may be a hurt or a grudge that you have carried ever since childhood. But whatever it is, you have assurance that . . .

- the Spirit knows your heart
- He knows how to pray through you
- He knows exactly what God's will is regarding your needs.

What quicker, surer way is there to touch God than to let the Spirit intercede for you?

October 14

"God Is My Best Friend"
by SALLY JO SHELTON

There is a friend that sticketh closer than a brother.

Proverbs 18:24

God is my best Friend.
    He cares about the things I care about.
    He loves me even when I'm unlovable.
    He is always there to listen and advise
        when I need to talk things over.

God is my heavenly Father.
  He holds me in the palm of His hand.
  He watches over me as the apple of His eye.
  He wants me to grow up to be like Him.
God is my Rock.
  He is my refuge when I'm afraid,
    my strength when I am weak,
    my surefooting when I stumble.
God is my Shepherd.
  He finds me when I'm lost.
  He gives me rest when I'm tired.
  He leads me when I don't know which way to go.
God is my Physician.
  He mends my heart when it is broken.
  He restores my peace of mind when I'm upset.
  He heals my body when I'm sick.
God is my Savior.
  He forgives me when I let Him down.
  He delivers me when I'm in danger.
  He saves me even from the trouble I bring on myself.
God is my Source.
  He is my bread when I'm hungry,
  My water fountain when I'm thirsty,
  My bank when I'm broke.
God is my Lord.
  He is the Ruler of my thoughts,
    the Inspiration of my words,
    the Initiator of my actions.
God is my Everything.
Who is He to you?

October 15

Promises, Promises

There's a difference between a promise and a commitment.
People are always making promises: "I promise I'll turn over a new
leaf. I promise I'll never drink again. I promise I won't fuss anymore. I promise I won't strike out in anger. I promise I'll clean up
my speech."

But what are promises? . . . promises, promises.

A commitment is something you start doing *now*. It's not something you say you're going to do sometime in the future. Jesus once said to some potential disciples, "Come, follow Me." And the Bible says, "*At once they left their nets and followed him*" (Mark 1:18 NIV). *Now that's commitment!*

I remember when I first surrendered my life to Christ. I was lying in bed with tuberculosis, unable to express myself because of stammering. But in my heart I made a commitment: "God, I'm going to serve You. I'm going to let You have my life. I'm going to trust You." For years I've trusted my God. I've fallen at times. I've made mistakes—lots of them. But I've kept that commitment. I can't tell you how much commitment means. But commit your life to God, and I promise you—no, *I make a commitment to you*—God will give you a brand-new life.

October 16

Every Man's World

When Oral Roberts University opened in 1965 and God said to me, "Raise up your students to hear My voice, to go where My light is dim, where My voice is heard small and My power is not known . . . to go even to the uttermost bounds of the earth," He also said: *Tell your students to go into every man's world.*

We usually think of Jesus' Great Commission to "go ye into all the world, and preach the gospel" (Mark 16:15) as getting on some big plane and flying overseas to do mission work. But it also means to go into every man's world where you are.

A freshman student once said, "President Roberts, I'm thinking about dropping my studies, because I've got to get out and go to the ends of the earth with the Gospel."

I said, "Look, the ends of the earth are right here. That's what they are saying over there—that the ends of the earth are over here where you and I are."

I explained, "Listen, the one you live nearest to doesn't always see God's light or hear His voice or know His power. While you are at ORU, you can go into the world of those eating with you, dating, studying, praying, laughing, or working with you, and tell them about Jesus Christ. You have a mission field right here where you are."

October 17

Clean Up Inside Out

Let us cleanse ourselves from all filthiness of the flesh and spirit.

2 Corinthians 7:1

Recently a person wrote: "Mr. Roberts, someone dumped trash near my house the other day, and it really upset me. Pollution is serious. Is God concerned about things like cleaning up litter?"

Yes, I believe God is concerned about our environment. Psalm 24:1 says, "The earth is the Lord's, and the fulness thereof." This earth we live on belongs to God, and He wants us to respect it. That means cleaning up our backyards and rooting out the infested holes that breed insects which carry disease. It means cleaning up our homes and our neighborhoods.

But cleaning up the environment goes deeper than picking up litter. I believe bad thoughts, foul language, and abuse of our bodies pollute our environment every bit as much as litter, or industrial wastes, or any other kind of filth.

Jesus once said, "What goes into a man . . . does not make him [polluted] but what comes out of [him]" (Matthew 15:11 NIV). So often we concentrate on cleaning up the outside. But Jesus taught, "Cleanse first that which is within . . . that the outside . . . may be clean also" (Matthew 23:26).

October 18

No One-Time Total Victory

If there is one word that characterizes the Christian life, it is *conflict.* Even our Lord faced conflict. Immediately after He was baptized at the River Jordan and the Holy Spirit came upon Him, He had a major confrontation with the devil. You see, the devil wasn't going to just stand by and let Jesus bring the Gospel to the world. He was going to challenge Him, tempt Him, do everything in his power to destroy Him.

Jesus won a great victory on this occasion, but that wasn't the end of His conflict. The Bible says the devil left Him "for a season" (Luke 4:13). This indicates he came right back, and he was right at Jesus' heels every step of His earthly ministry.

God never promised that the Christian life would be a bed of roses. Our Lord lived in conflict and we will live in conflict (*see* John 15:20). And there is no such thing as winning a one-time total victory over the devil in this life. He is going to tempt you as long as you have any breath or feeling left. But remember this—you don't belong to the devil, but to our God. And our God is mightier than the devil. Therefore, you can say, "I belong to God. Devil, take your hands off God's property—*me!*"

October 19

Jesus Is Person-Centered

Jesus is oriented toward the human being. You could say Jesus is oriented toward the human family and still be correct. But it's different when someone says, "God loves all the human family," than when he says, "God loves *you.*" Both statements are true. God does love all people. But when that love is crystallized and individualized for your life, it becomes infinitely more precious and desirable. It means . . .

God is in the midst of life . . . *your life!*

Do you recall the important incident in the life of our Savior when He was traveling with His disciples through a cornfield on the Sabbath? His disciples were hungry. Having nothing to eat, they plucked the ears of corn and ate them. The Pharisees said, "You are breaking the sabbath." But Jesus answered, "The sabbath was made for *man,* and not man for the sabbath" (Mark 2:27).

No greater statement was ever made by our Lord in connection with His concern and care about us as individuals. The hunger of these men was more important to Jesus than any special day. Jesus pointed out that *every day* is made for man, including the Sabbath. *Every day* God cares about you. *Every day* He is in the midst of your life—at the point of your need!

October 20

You Are Irreplaceable

. . . I have created you and cared for you since you were born. I will be your God through all your lifetime . . . . I will carry you along and be your Savior.

Isaiah 46:3, 4 LB

"I'm no good!" How often we hear that said by an elderly person who thinks he is no longer useful—by a student who has flunked an exam—by someone who can't keep a job.

But it's not true!

The Bible says that you have been purchased ". . . with the precious lifeblood of Christ . . ." (1 Peter 1:19 LB)—a cost paid by God Himself. How great is your value to our Lord, for Him to have paid such a price!

Merchandise purchased like this could not, by any stretch of the imagination, be considered "no good" or worthless. A Creator with the intelligence to fashion our universe, with its infinite variety of life, certainly would not use poor judgment in making investments. So before you start putting yourself down or giving up on yourself or anyone else, think of how meaningful your life is to God and the tremendous price that He paid for you.

You are God-bought—God-filled—God-owned—*unique and irreplaceable!*

October 21

"Mother, You Have to Let Me . . ."
by REBECCA ROBERTS NASH

When I was a child, my mother would say to me, "Rebecca, if you had done your chores earlier, you wouldn't be working while your friends are playing." Or, "If you had done your homework when you first got it, you wouldn't have to work so hard at the last minute." But I always seemed to wait until the last minute to do everything—including getting up in the morning.

I used to say to her, "Mother, you have to let me make my own mistakes. You have to let me suffer the consequences for my own actions." And I did suffer, too.

Now, I find myself saying the same things to my children that my mother said to me. And they say to me, "Mother, you have to let me do it myself."

That is so difficult to do. But it's so much better when I can guide them into finding answers to their problems for themselves. Some days are tougher than others, but my prayer is: "Lord, help me to keep quiet, and let my actions be a good example to my children."

> *. . . Don't keep on scolding and nagging your children, making them angry and resentful. Rather, bring them up with the loving discipline the Lord himself approves, with suggestions and godly advice.*
>
> Ephesians 6:4 LB

October 22

God's Upward Strokes

I was driving in the country one day, when I saw a cow having her calf. That little calf hit the ground, gave a hard kick, and tried to stand—but it couldn't do it alone. The mother cow began to lick the calf with her bristlelike tongue—*always with upward strokes.* She licked the calf with such force that she literally picked it up off the ground and caused it to stand. She licked upward again and the calf fell down. The cow kept this up until finally the calf was strong enough that it actually stood—trembling from head to foot—but able to stand. The whole process was for the purpose of getting the calf up on its feet, able to nurse and to become a healthy creature. Before long it started to run and jump. Soon it had its life, and mother and calf were together.

As I drove away, it came to me that I had seen a picture of how God works in our lives so that we can stand and be strong. God's every stroke is always upward—never downward. Even when it appears that someone or something knocks you down, it's still an upward stroke of God in your life. That divine invisible force is there, making all things work together for good to them who love God (Romans 8:28 PARAPHRASED).

How many times I've been like that little calf! Oral Roberts would never have amounted to anything without something knocking me down, then God picking me up again. When you get knocked down—and God picks you up again—that's when you begin to grow stronger and to know Jesus in a new dimension of understanding and trust.

October 23

Dependent in Spirit

It's when we become totally dependent upon God in our spirit that we start solving our problems and finding our life.

Dependency in spirit was something I did not know when I was a teenager. I wanted life the way I wanted it—that's why I ran away from home. I was brought back when I became ill with tuberculosis. For months I lay hurting, not knowing that the answer to life began in my spirit.

My family talked to me about God, and I gradually began to see that I had to become dependent upon God in my spirit. I couldn't be arrogant any longer and run my own life. One day my sister said to me, "Oral, God is going to heal you." With those words of hope, a flash of understanding came in me about God. And *God as God* became a real being to me. Out of the depths of my being I silently cried out, "God, You're all I have to look to." That's when I became dependent in my spirit. Suddenly I knew inside that God was making me alive and I was going to have life.

Jesus said He did nothing of Himself (John 5:30). In *everything* He did He was dependent on the power of the Holy Spirit. If Jesus, the Savior of man, had to depend on the Holy Spirit, how much more do we need to depend on the Holy Spirit!

October 24

Buy It and Don't Sell

"What do you do when someone turns against you and tells a lie about you?"

This is what one of my associates once asked me. He said, "Oral, when I came to work in this ministry I did it of my own free will. I resigned from my former position because I felt I could do more good by working with you. But now the man I used to work for is telling everybody that he let me go because I was inefficient."

"Is it true? Did he let you go?" I asked.

He said, "You know he didn't. He even offered me more money to try to get me to stay with him."

"Then don't worry about it," I said. "Anyone who sets himself up against the truth will not prosper. He cannot hurt you. The Bible says, 'Buy the truth, and sell it not' (Proverbs 23:23). Just be careful not to strike back at him. Every time someone tells you what he's saying about you, think of something good about him and say it. Pray for him. Some day that man may be the best friend you ever had.''

Three years passed. Then one day this associate said, ''Oral, remember the man who lied about me? Just the other day he did two things for me that were really wonderful. I wanted you to know that what you said is right. Truth *is* a powerful force!''

October 25

A Secret Place

> *But thou, when thou prayest, enter into thy closet, and when thou hast shut thy door, pray to thy Father which is in secret . . . .*
>
> Matthew 6:6

I have found that I can pray anywhere—at home or in my office or just driving down the street. But there's something very special to me about the room in the Prayer Tower on the Oral Roberts University campus where I often go to pray. It's a place where I can be completely alone with God. There is no outside distraction, and sometimes when I'm there, no one else knows about it. It's a secret place of prayer where many times I go to answer my partners' letters and to unburden by heart to God for their needs. I thank God for a place like that.

Everyone needs his own secret place. Yours may be your bedroom, or your favorite chair in the living room. Any place will do, if you can be alone to talk to God. Matthew 6:6 says that as you pour out your heart before Him in your secret place, . . . *thy Father which seeth in secret shall reward thee openly.*

October 26

''This Mean Ole World''
by EVELYN ROBERTS

When our youngest child, Roberta, was still small, we had a hard time explaining to her about the second coming of the Lord. I remember in particular one New Year's Day when the children and I were on the way to Sunday school. I told them, "Today is January one, the first day of the new year. And do you know what? Jesus may come before this year ends."

Roberta asked, "Why is Jesus coming?"

I said, "To take us all to heaven with Him."

"But why does He want to take us there?"

"He wants to get us out of this wicked, mean ole world," I explained.

Roberta said, "Oh, it isn't a mean ole world."

Just then Richard spoke up. "Oh, Roberta," he said, "you just haven't been downtown."

No matter how "mean" this world gets, we have the promise not only of God's presence with us now but also of that glorious day when "the Lord himself shall descend from heaven with a shout . . . and . . . we . . . shall be caught up together . . . in the clouds, to meet the Lord in the air: and so shall we ever be with the Lord" (1 Thessalonians 4:16, 17).

Jesus is coming soon—what a blessed hope!

October 27

Open Up!

Do you need a miracle of healing in your life?

Receiving a miracle can be a struggle. It's not something that just happens, like snapping your fingers. You lay a foundation for it. There's a preparation of your inner man—an opening of your heart.

James 5:16 says, "Confess your faults one to another, and pray one for another, that *ye* may be healed."

You see, healing is not the major problem. If it were, there would be much more healing among us. The real problem is *we* who are sick.

Our resentments, our confessions that we don't always make, our pulling back from people rather than praying one for another, the closing of ourselves to people and to God, refusing to open up our hearts for fear we will look bad or someone will look down on us—these need healing.

But our Lord says that to be healed we first need to . . .

Open Up!
Open Up!
Open Up!

October 28

Confess Your Faults One to Another . . .

The Bible tells us to "confess our faults," indicating that we have them.

And it's true!

We all have shortcomings and failures—places where we don't measure up like we ought. There are days when we sing and rejoice and feel close to God. On other days God seems to be a million miles away. It's hard on those days, and that's when we may say things we shouldn't say and do things we shouldn't do.

That is when God tells us to go to the person we have wronged and "confess our faults."

The Lord understands that there are occasions when you can't go and confess to the one you've wronged. The person may be dead or may live far away from you. Sometimes it's best not to say anything, because to do so might make the situation worse. And the Lord understands this.

But there is one thing you can do. And that is to open up and breathe God's love toward that person. It's a way of opening the door to a miracle of healing for *you!*

October 29

Pray One for Another . . .

Notice that in this phrase the emphasis is upon the *one doing the praying.*

Now I've had the privilege of traveling throughout the world. I've dealt with people en masse, in small groups, and face-to-face. I know from personal experience that this Scripture, *Pray one for another,* is possibly the most important thing that you and I can learn for our healing.

Often when I pray for someone I suggest a "two-way prayer." In other words, I ask the other person to pray for me first, before I begin my prayer for him. This is to help the sick person open up to a miracle by planting a seed of concern for someone else first.

So the Master is saying to us, "You pray for someone else so that *you* may also be healed. Put the seed in first, so that I can have something from your heart to work with."

This is another way of saying, "Give, and it shall be given unto you" (Luke 6:38)—another way of *seeding for a miracle.*

October 30

. . . That Ye May Be Healed

A man once said to me, "Brother Roberts, what does giving have to do with my healing?"

It has everything to do with it!

A closed hand or fist is symbolic of anger. An open hand shows interest, concern, and compassion. Remember, in healing you're dealing directly with the Healer—God. And He's saying, *"Open up! Open up!* Confess your faults one to another, and pray one for another, that ye may be healed." Anger, sarcasm, bitterness, and irritability work against your healing. So it's important to calm down and realize that obedience to God is better than sacrifice (*see* 1 Samuel 15:22).

You may go to church, but that is no substitute for doing what God tells you to do in His Word. You may listen to a fine sermon on Sunday, but that cannot take the place of hearing God's still, small voice in your own heart. You may give of your finances, but that cannot take the place of giving yourself to God.

Giving is important. However, for it to be a seed of faith it has to be a by-product of an obedient heart—one that is opening up to God and to others. Thus you're opening yourself up to miracles for healing for every area of your life.

October 31

Halloween Mask

Adam and Eve doubted God and believed the devil. And the moment they disobeyed God, their eyes were opened. *"They knew that they were naked; and they sewed fig leaves together, and made themselves aprons"* (Genesis 3:7).

Most people think of that as nudity, as though suddenly they realized that they had no clothes on. But it was far more than that. Suddenly *they knew* they were mortal. They knew that something had died within them. They knew they were separated from God. So they ran and hid and began to cover up, to put on a false image—a mask—like we do on Halloween to hide. Man has been phony ever since.

When God called to Adam, Adam said, "We were afraid . . . and we hid."

Do you see why we put on masks? *Fear. Guilt. Anxiety.* When we start doubting God, our security departs. We have nothing to lean on, and fear starts in the pit of our stomach and builds up. But, thank God, through Christ we can boldly say, "The Lord is my helper, and I will not fear" (Hebrews 13:6). When we know Christ and obey Him, we have nothing to fear—nothing to cover up. We become real people—genuine through and through!

NOVEMBER

November 1

A *Can-Do* Person

I can do *all things through Christ [who] strengtheneth me.*
Philippians 4:13

The Apostle Paul said, "I can do . . . ." He was God's *can-do* man. But he wasn't always like that. He was not one of the original twelve apostles of Christ. He came later. Yet, after his conversion, he traveled more missionary miles and reached more people for God than any apostle who had been with Christ. He said, "I can do it!"

Many of us have a can't-do attitude. Faced with a problem, we think, *I can't do it!* For a part of my life, I was a can't-do man. When I got up to preach, I could hardly believe that God would save even one soul. And I hated it like that.

There's a reason Paul was a can-do man, and it applies to us. He said, "I can do all things through Christ who strengthens me." A lot of people think they *can do* because they have an education or they have a friend somewhere or they get a particular opportunity. But these are only instruments. Our real Source of power is Jesus Christ, whose life can flow through us to the extent that we *can do* all things.

November 2

Can't Do It Alone

Notwithstanding ye have well done, that ye did communicate with my affliction [or necessities].
Philippians 4:14

Paul was a *can-do* man because of God *and* because of his partners. You see, Paul couldn't do it by himself. He had to have

224

help from God and from other people.

Paul had left Philippi, a great city in the province of Macedonia, to go out to establish churches in a region that was completely without the Gospel of Jesus Christ. He had no money, no transportation, no things with which to reach the people. Oh, he had the Lord, but he didn't have the physical things he needed to get the job done. So his partners, the Philippian Christians, communicated with Paul's need. That is, they contributed what they could to meet Paul's needs, and he commended them for it.

Without his partners, Paul's ministry would have been limited. He would have had God's Spirit flowing through him, but there would have been no other human instrumentality for the Spirit to work through.

None of us can do alone what God has asked us to do. It takes all of us working together to be *can-do* persons.

November 3

Giving and Receiving

Now ye Philippians know . . . that . . . no church communicated with me as concerning giving and receiving, but ye only.

Philippians 4:15

One reason the Philippians were such great givers was Paul's teaching. He made no apology for teaching them about giving and receiving.

So many times we're taught to give, but not to receive. Yet in many church services ministers take up the offering almost as an afterthought. They're so afraid someone's going to think they're asking for something that they hurry right through and don't put the proper emphasis upon giving.

I've pastored churches, and I've done the same thing. I was afraid I'd run someone off. But every time we do it like that, we do the people a disfavor. Paul was doing the people a favor, because he taught that giving and receiving go together, that receiving follows giving.

Giving is to be a major part not only of our church services, but also of our daily lives. We're to be givers—great givers. I'm not talking about giving some big amount of money but having the spirit of a great giver, which makes you a *can-do* person. And when you're a great giver, you make God a great Multiplier!

November 4

Getting or Receiving?

There's a difference between "getting" and "receiving." Getting comes from selfishness. Receiving comes from giving. Getting comes from trying to get something from someone without any regard for his needs. Receiving comes from giving as a seed; it's from what you've done for God and for others which reproduces itself. The seed multiplies and you get a return, and you know it's from God.

Some people ask, "Oral Roberts, you mean I'm to give so that I can receive? Isn't that wrong?" No, it's not wrong. It's scriptural. Jesus said, "Give, and it shall be given unto you" (Luke 6:38).

In other words, count it a joy to give and then count it a joy to receive. And be thankful to God when you receive from Him. I've heard people say, "I feel guilty because God's done so much for me." Not me! I say, "Lord, You can do a lot more for me any old day!" I'm always ready for more myself.

To become a *can-do* person, it's essential to learn that your giving and receiving are linked together. Your giving produces your receiving, and God wants you to receive, just as He wants you to give!

November 5

The *Can-Do* Way

For even in Thessalonica ye sent once and again unto my necessity.

Philippians 4:16

Here Paul was saying to the Philippians, "I've received from you *again and again.*" In other words, the Philippians hadn't given just one time. It wasn't, "Here, God, I'll give to You this one time because somebody has talked me into it." Rather, they had gotten into a rhythm of seed-faith. It was like water flowing constantly, giving and receiving. They gave and they received. They gave and they received—again and again, over and over—a rhythm in their lives.

Becoming a seed-faither—a disciple, a follower of Jesus Christ—is a day-by-day process. It's something you get into with your soul, your heart. It's a rhythmic operation of your inner self. Giving and receiving, putting in a seed and expecting the harvest, and receiving that harvest. It's a miraculous thing.

Seed-faith is not a one-time or a two-time thing. It's a life-style. I call it the *can-do* way, the miracle way of life where "the things which are impossible with men are possible with God" (Luke 18:27).

November 6

An Account With God

> *Not because I desire a gift: but I desire fruit that may abound to your account.*
>
> Philippians 4:17

I appreciate the Apostle Paul because he wasn't trying to get something from people for himself, but he wanted them to have an "account with God."

I serve on the board of a large bank and I've learned a little about banks. One thing is sure: You can't write checks on a bank if you don't have an account there. Also, if you write a check on an account that has no money in it, it will bounce. But if you write a check on an account in which you have money, it will be honored. So many people try to write checks on their account in heaven— they want God to bless them—but they haven't built up an account with Him.

It's important to have fruit abounding to your account with God, because you're dealing with God every day of your life. And you have needs every day of your life. You have problems every day of your life. Through giving and receiving, seed planting and harvesting, you are depositing to your account in heaven from which you can draw when you are in need.

November 7

A Big Thinker

But I have all, and abound: I am full, having received of
Epaphroditus the things which were sent from you.
Philippians 4:18

Some people think that to be a good Christian and serve God you have to be poor, drive a rattletrap car, wear worn-out hand-me-down clothes, and half starve. Yet here Paul is obviously enjoying his prosperity. He says over and over: "I have all. I abound. I am full. I have received everything I need—and more."

Why is it that when some person who hardly ever thinks of God drives a nice car and lives in a nice home, people think nothing of it? But let some person who loves God start doing well and people wonder about it. Tell me, what's wrong with having enough money to pay your bills? What's wrong with your prospering? What's wrong with your having health in your body? The Bible says Christ *became* poor (He wasn't poor!) for our sakes that we might be rich towards God (2 Corinthians 8:9).

I believe God wants you to prosper. He wants you to be able to say, "I have all and abound." He wants you to have your mind enlarged, to quit being a small thinker and start being a big thinker. He wants you to be a *can-do* person.

November 8

Sweet-Smelling Money

An odour of a sweet smell.
Philippians 4:18

Paul indicated to the Philippians that the money and gifts they had sent him had a "sweet smell." This is interesting, because in 1 Timothy 3:3 Paul referred to money as "filthy lucre." Of course money is filthy. It smells because it's handled by thousands of hands. But Paul wasn't talking about the physical odor of money. He was referring to the bad use to which money is often put, which makes it filthy in the sight of God. And that's why he called it filthy lucre.

There are a lot of people who have money that's dirty. They've made it dirty. They're getters, not givers, and their money smells bad. It has a bad odor to God. But here Paul says, "Your giving and receiving have given an odor to your money, and it smells sweet." It's a sweet-smelling gift to God.

In Romans 12:1, St. Paul goes beyond the giving of money, to the giving of our total selves by saying, "Present your bodies a living sacrifice, holy, acceptable unto God, which is your reasonable service." Our giving, which has love attached to it, is an acceptable sacrifice—a sweet-smelling gift!

November 9

Accepted or Rejected?

A sacrifice acceptable.
Philippians 4:18

The first murder was committed by a person whose sacrifice was not acceptable to God. Cain and Abel, who were brothers, each made a sacrifice to God. Abel's sacrifice was acceptable; Cain's wasn't. Cain's had no love in it; Abel's did. Because Cain was rejected, he flew into a rage and killed his brother.

It's terrible to feel unaccepted, rejected. Yet many people feel rejected by God. Their sacrifices are not acceptable to Him because their giving does not involve their love or faith. If you ever go to India, you'll see people lying on a bed of nails. They are sacrificing, trying to reach God, but it's an unacceptable sacrifice.

At one time I lived a life that was unacceptable to God. I never thought about giving to Him; I thought about getting from everybody I could. But that changed. I came into a new relationship with God, and today I know I'm accepted by Him. Sure, I make mistakes, but I don't make them from my heart. I've become a giver instead of a getter.

It is vital in becoming a *can-do* person to come into a new relationship with God, to get into giving and receiving, so that you no longer feel rejected, but accepted of God.

November 10

God Is a Rewarder

Wellpleasing to God.
Philippians 4:18

Hebrews 11:6 says that God "is a rewarder of them that diligently seek him."

God is a rewarder! Yet most people think of God as a punisher.
They think He'll slap them into hell if they don't watch what
they're doing. But that's wrong. God is a good God. There's a hell,
yes, and there's a heaven. But God isn't trying to put people into
hell. God wants to reward us.

Most of us are unacquainted with God's system of rewards. So
many times we have guilt feelings when something good happens to
us. Haven't you had problems with this? I have, but I'm overcoming them because I know God rewards those who have faith and
seek Him.

God wants us to feel good when good comes to us, so we can
accept that good and give God thanks. So don't feel guilty when
God blesses you. If you're a farmer and God gives you a good crop,
don't feel guilty. If God gives you a better job, don't feel guilty. If
God blesses your family, don't feel guilty. Somewhere you planted
a good seed. You've got an account in heaven. You've been making
sacrifices acceptable to God. And God rewards those who are
wellpleasing in His sight.

November 11

God's Riches in Glory

*But my God shall supply all your need according to his
riches in glory by Christ Jesus.*

Philippians 4:19

Philippians 4:19 cannot happen in your life until you've put verses 13–18 to work. All of us want God to meet our needs. And we
are to expect that. But there's no way God is going to meet them all
unless we do what He says, unless we get into giving and receiving.
And you notice I link them together.

With this in mind, let us say this affirmation together:

)

"I'll be a *can-do* person. Through my root system with God, who is the Source of my total supply, I will communicate by giving and receiving. And as I do this, I will be *wellpleasing* to God. My sacrifice will be acceptable. I will not be rejected. God will accept me. My giving will smell good to God. And because of it my God—*who is mine*—will supply all my need, not by human measurement, but by the measurement of God's riches in glory—not those limited to earth but by a breakthrough from *heaven*—for my life, for my loved ones, for the work I'm doing."

November 12

You Can Run Faster

The hand of the Lord was on Elijah; and he . . . ran before Ahab to . . . Jezreel.

1 Kings 18:46

There is a great lesson in the story of Elijah's outrunning the chariots of Ahab. Through this miracle God shows us that when His hand is upon us, we can do more than is humanly possible. That means: *You can run faster than you can run, when the hand of the Lord comes upon you.*

It's important to realize that first Elijah had to do what he could. He had to run. Second, he had to believe God would intervene—that the hand of God could come to him and a miracle could put him ahead of the swift horses of Ahab.

What does this mean to you and me? It means we can approach our careers, our jobs, or any other task in our own strength only—or we can go beyond that and expect God to do miracles through us. It starts with doing all we can, not asking God to do for us what we can do for ourselves. Then, as we sow that good seed, God will put His hand on us and help us to run faster than we can run!

November 13

Your Shining Moment

*Then said Jesus, Let her alone: against the day of my bury-
ing hath she kept this. For the poor always ye have with you;
but me ye have not always.*

John 12:7, 8

Jesus loved the poor. When he said, "The poor always ye have
with you," He was not saying that He didn't care or that we're not
to have deep social concerns. He was saying just the opposite: "A
day will never pass that you will not have the opportunity and
responsibility to share with the poor, because of the largeness of
their needs. The total need won't go away."

But He was saying, in effect, "There is one shining moment in
your life that will never come to you again. Mary has recognized
her shining moment. There is only one time that I can die for the
sins of the world. Mary has grasped that fact and has taken this
costly gift of perfume and anointed My feet for My burial. She has
poured all her love and faith and devotion into this act."

A shining moment comes to everyone—a moment when God
deals with you to put forth your hand and do something for Him
that nobody else can do. The important thing is to have your eyes
open and your heart alert, so that when your moment comes, you
will rise to the occasion and let God use you.

November 14

An Endurance Contest

In the fourteenth century Robert Bruce led the Scots in battle
against English domination. After failing miserably several times,
he fled in exile to a lonely island in the Irish Sea. There he found
shelter in a cave. One day, as he was looking toward the mouth of
the cave, he saw a spider spinning a web. The spider was trying to
span the entrance of the cave with its web of silk. But each time it
tried, it failed. Nevertheless, with quiet determination, it renewed
its efforts again—again—and again. At last, on its seventh attempt,
the spider made it.

This little incident inspired Robert Bruce to once again rally his people against the English, and this time he succeeded. He brought Scotland complete independence.

After we have struggled with a problem for a long time, it is easy to lose our perspective and give up. But God encourages us ". . . to keep on patiently doing God's will if you want him to do for you all that he has promised" (Hebrews 10:36 LB). It's something like an endurance contest—a case of do or die. There's no retreat. When you have this kind of spirit, victory is surely yours!

November 15

The Other Side of the Fence

Be ye stedfast . . . as ye know that your labour is not in vain in the Lord.

1 Corinthians 15:58

Often we are tempted to think our efforts are wasted, because we do not see results of our labors. We have passed a great milestone when we learn that nothing—absolutely nothing—is wasted if we do it in Jesus' name.

A lady who was a lover of flowers set out a rare vine beside her fence. It grew vigorously, but failed to produce blooms. Day after day she cultivated and watered the plant, hoping it would bloom. One day when she checked the plant for blossoms but found none, she was about to walk back into the house disappointed when her invalid neighbor called to her, "You can't imagine how much I have been enjoying the blooms of the vine you planted."

"But there are no blooms," the lady replied.

"Maybe not on your side of the fence," the invalid smiled, "but come over on my side and look."

Going over to the other side of the fence, the woman saw an array of blooms. The vine had flowered luxuriantly on the other side of the fence.

No prayer is wasted if offered in faith. No work is futile if we were moved by love to do it. No cross carried is too heavy if it brings us closer to the One who bore the cross for us.

November 16

Sink or Swim

John Adams, an articulate supporter of the Declaration of Independence, once avowed, "Sink or swim, live or die, survive or perish, I give my hand and my heart to this [declaration] . . . . It may cost treasure and it may cost blood, but . . . my whole heart is in it. All that I have and all that I am and all that I hope in this life I am now ready here to stake upon it . . . independence now and independence forever!"

Everyone reaches a point in his life where he has to make a stand for what he believes. Ruth, of the Old Testament, did when she told her mother-in-law, "Whither thou goest, I will go . . . thy people shall be my people, and thy God my God" (Ruth 1:16). Joshua did when he challenged the Israelites, "Choose you this day whom ye will serve . . . but as for me and my house, we will serve the Lord" (Joshua 24:15).

The only way you can live a successful Christian life is to reach a point where you decide that you are going to serve God—live or die, survive or perish—and where you decide you are going to have faith that if you do what is right, God will take care of you.

November 17

The Quaker's Son

A man once asked me, "Brother Roberts, how can I trust someone I've never seen? God will have to give me some kind of proof before I can trust Him."

This question reminds me of the old Quaker, whose son went off to college and came home with a know-it-all attitude. He said to his father, "I don't believe there is a God, because I don't believe in anything I can't see."

The father thought a moment and said, "Son, hast thee a brain?"

"Of course," answered the son.

His father asked, "Hast thee ever seen it?"

"No," was the reply.

"Then how dost thee know thou hast one?"

Who can see the wind? Or electricity? Or even love? But still we know they're real, because we see what they can do. To say, "I'll trust God after I have proof'' is like saying, ''I'll get into the water after I've learned to swim.''

The best way I know to prove God is to put Him to the test. As you ask and trust God, you will experience His love for yourself—and with it find the confidence you need to continue to trust Him. God won't let you down, for—

> *Blessed is the man that trusteth in him!*
> Psalm 34:8

November 18

Bless the Lord!
by EVELYN ROBERTS

We have to be reminded to be grateful sometimes. And I think one of the greatest chapters on thanksgiving is Psalm 103. You may want to read it in a different version, but I love the Amplified version:

Bless . . . the Lord, O my soul, and all that is [deepest] within me, bless His holy name!

Bless . . . the Lord, O my soul, and forget not [one of] all His benefits, who forgives [every one of] all your iniquities, who heals [each of] all your diseases; who redeems your life from the pit and corruption; who beautifies, dignifies, and crowns you with loving-kindness and tender mercies; who satisfies your mouth . . . with good; so that your youth, renewed, is like the eagle's [strong, over-coming, soaring]!

The Lord executes righteousness and justice . . . for all who are oppressed . . . The Lord is merciful and gracious, slow to anger, and plenteous in mercy and loving-kindness . . . .

He has not dealt with us after our sins, nor rewarded us according to our iniquities. For as the heavens are high above the earth, so great are His mercy and loving-kindness toward those who reverently and worshipfully fear Him. As far as the east is from the west, so far has He removed our transgressions from us.

Psalm 103:1–12 AMPLIFIED

November 19

Fringe Benefits
by EVELYN ROBERTS

Psalm 103 is such a beautiful passage because it tells the benefits of being a Christian. You know, when you get a job it usually has fringe benefits. Sometimes the company will furnish a car, sometimes they will have a pension fund or insurance, and those fringe benefits go along with the job. There are many wonderful benefits that go along with serving Jesus Christ, and in this psalm God says, "Don't forget a one of them."

The first of these benefits, of course, is God's love and forgiveness to us: "Who forgives [every one of] all your iniquities" (Psalm 103:3 AMPLIFIED). John 3:16 says that God loved us so much He gave His only Son to die for our sins that we might have eternal life. I don't think we can love, humanly speaking, like that. But God loves us when we're bad or when we're good. He takes us just as we are. God reads our hearts and He forgives us and loves us just the same.

How many times does the Bible say God will forgive us? Seventy times seven! Or an unlimited number of times. Oh, there's such blessed relief in forgiveness! It makes you feel so clean inside. One of God's healing miracles, really, is to be forgiven.

November 20

Healing in Forgiveness
by EVELYN ROBERTS

Who heals [each of] all your diseases.
Psalm 103:3 AMPLIFIED

There is healing in forgiveness. Sometimes I think we don't appreciate the benefit of God's forgiveness enough, because it has healing power. God said He would forgive all of our sins, which means all the bad things we've done and all the mistakes we make. Whatever it is, He forgives us. And He heals all of our diseases.

Of course, that means diseases in your body, but it doesn't mean just that. Sickness can be physical, mental, or spiritual. Whatever takes away from your peace of mind, your happiness, your general well-being is *dis*-ease. Sometimes you can be so worried about something it actually makes you sick. Anything that brings disharmony, discomfort, or distress physically, mentally, or spiritually is a form of illness. And God heals that.

Time and time again Jesus spoke the healing word by saying, "Thy faith hath made thee whole." The word *whole* means complete, well, sound, healthy. One of the benefits that God gives you is healing in every area of your life: your marriage, your finances, your home, your emotions, your relationships. Health and well-being in your total self!

November 21

God Redeems Your Life
by EVELYN ROBERTS

Who redeems your life from the pit and corruption.
Psalm 103:4 AMPLIFIED

You may say, "What pit? I've never been in a pit." But God says that before we accept Christ we're in one. The Psalmist wrote: "He drew me up out of a horrible pit . . . and set my feet upon a rock, steadying my steps and establishing my goings" (Psalm 40:2 AMPLIFIED). God lifts us out of the pit of despair and redeems us.

Now, in order to redeem or recover something, it has to be lost. As you know, Satan stole every one of us from God. Kidnapped us, really! We had to be rescued from the devil's clutches. So God sent His Son Jesus to redeem us.

When we accept Jesus in our hearts, He lives in us and helps us do the things we have to do in life, because we cannot do them alone. I've tried to run my own life, but I quickly discovered I can't run it. At one time I thought I could rear my children on my own. Did you ever try to do that? If so, you soon discovered you had some little independent human beings on your hands, didn't you? I finally had to say, "Lord, I can't do it by myself. I must have You." This is the beautiful thing about the Lord—it's one of His benefits. He's right there to help us when we call on Him.

November 22

A Gorgeous Crown
by EVELYN ROBERTS

Who beautifies, dignifies and crowns you with loving-kindness and tender mercies.
                                   Psalm 103:4 AMPLIFIED

The Lord has so many benefits that He literally loads us down with them!

When Britain celebrated the Silver Jubilee of Queen Elizabeth's reign, we all saw the queen on television, wearing her gorgeous crown with diamonds, rubies, and precious jewels. As a child you may have dreamed of being somebody great who could wear a crown like that. But do you know that when you belong to God, He beautifies and dignifies you? He crowns you with loving-kindness and tender mercies which, really, are worth more than diamonds or rubies. They really are, because there is one Scripture that says God's mercies are new every morning (Lamentations 3:23).

I think it's good, when you get up in the morning and you open your drapes, to look out the window, and just say out loud, "O God, thank You for today, because all Your mercies are new and at my doorstep today." It makes your day go so much better if you know that God has a special benefit for you for that particular day. And mercy is only one of them.

November 23

God Satisfies
by EVELYN ROBERTS

Who satisfies your mouth . . . with good.
                       Psalm 103:5 AMPLIFIED

This means that God wants to meet every need in our lives. If He satisfied our mouths with good things, that means He gives us the food that we need for our bodies. But God goes even further.

He also fills our mouths with words to help other people. He wants us to use our tongues to help people, not to condemn them. My husband had a friend who used vile language. Most all of us

know someone like that. They send everything and everybody to
hell.

One day, after the man had told someone to go to hell, Oral said,
"You don't really want him to go to hell, do you?" He said, "Well,
no, not really." And Oral said, "Well, then don't send him to hell.
Send him to heaven." Every time I see this man now he says, "I
want you to know your husband helped me clean up my language."

Hell is a terrible place. It wasn't even created for people. It was
created for Satan, who came and kidnapped us. So if we go there
with him, we choose to go there ourselves, because God will never
send us there. God wants us to take advantage of all of His benefits.

November 24

God Renews Our Youth
by EVELYN ROBERTS

. . . so that your youth, renewed, is like the eagle's!
Psalm 103:5 AMPLIFIED

Who is it among us who doesn't want to have our youth renewed
and to feel the vim, vigor, and vitality we felt when we were six-
teen? You know the story of the eagle. When she gets old she goes
off by herself and beats off her old feathers. New feathers grow and
her youth is renewed. Then she soars high above the clouds.

At times we let our problems get above us. But I believe our
spirits can be young and we can soar like the eagle above them until
we die.

I remember once when we were in Israel. We had some students
with us. Standing on the banks of the Sea of Galilee, my husband
said to them, "Tell me a Scripture that comes to your mind about
something Jesus did on this sea."

I shall never forget what Joyce Lampkin, one of the World Action Singers, said: "Brother Roberts, I'm reminded of the time
Jesus came to the disciples in the storm, walking on the water, and
He said, *It is I, be not afraid.*" She said, "That tells me that we
can't walk on the water like Jesus did, but we can walk on top of
our problems. With God's help, we don't have to let our problems
get on top of us."

November 25

Doesn't Do Us Wrong
by EVELYN ROBERTS

The Lord executes righteousness and justice . . . for all
who are oppressed . . . . The Lord is merciful and gracious,
slow to anger, and plenteous in . . . loving-kindness.
                                        Psalm 103:6, 8 AMPLIFIED

Do you feel oppressed? Is everything closing in on you? People
are mistreating you? Life itself is coming against you? There is no
justice in this world?

We are all prone to feel this way once in a while. But Jesus
doesn't do us wrong. One of the benefits of the Lord is that He
carries out righteousness and justice for all who are oppressed.

The Lord is merciful to us even when we don't deserve it. He is
slow to anger, and full of love and kindness. That's what I really
like, because sometimes I need to be reprimanded. Yet God's love
makes Him merciful to me. When I know I've made a mistake, the
Lord is right there to help me through it. It makes me cry to think of
such love, because even though I know my husband loves me,
Jesus loves me more. And that's beautiful.

You can do a lot to help yourself when you are oppressed if you
remember the benefits that are yours because you belong to the
Lord.

November 26

Doesn't Hold Grudges
by EVELYN ROBERTS

[God] has not dealt with us after our sins, nor rewarded us
according to our iniquities. For as the heavens are high
above the earth, so great are His mercy and loving-kindness
toward those who reverently and worshipfully fear Him.
                                        Psalm 103:10, 11 AMPLIFIED

There is a "fear of God" that makes you scared to death of
Him—afraid He is going to throw you into the lake of fire if you
make a mistake. That's not the kind of fear the Psalmist is talking
about, but fear that is reverential, worshipful, trusting—that causes

you to say in awe, "Lord, You're so great and I love You so much that I don't want to do anything to displease You."

The Psalmist continues to reassure us of the unspeakable benefits of our loving Heavenly Father by saying, "As far as the east is from the west, so far has He removed our transgressions from us" (Psalm 103:12 AMPLIFIED).

Did you ever have someone say to you, "Oh, I'll forgive you, but I'll never forget it"? We have a hard time forgetting wrongs, but God doesn't hold grudges. When we ask His forgiveness, He doesn't continually throw our past wrongs up to us. *He forgives and forgets!* I can't be grateful enough for this marvelous benefit.

November 27

Priceless Jewels

They shall be mine, saith the Lord of hosts, in that day when I make up my jewels.

Malachi 3:17

Hummingbirds are some of the most delicately beautiful of all birds. Yet when they hatch, they are ugly, blind, naked—no larger than insects. You'd think they'd never survive. But their mother cares for them as tenderly as she would priceless jewels. And within only two or three weeks the young birds are beautiful, fully feathered, bright-eyed, ready to fly.

When we are born into the family of God, many of us are like those baby hummingbirds. All our potential is hidden inside. To some of the people who know us—even to ourselves—we appear weak and helpless, unable to survive.

Yet, thank God, He sees the potential inside. And under His loving tender care we are slowly becoming all that He originally meant us to be. We are growing into beautiful people—whose eyes are opened to the Truth, Jesus Christ, and who are clothed in His goodness—equipped with His power—capable not just of surviving, but of living life to its fullest.

November 28

The Little Sailboat

One of the biggest concerns I've had lately is for the hurting that's going on in people's lives. Recently I came across a Scripture that lifted me up so much I want to share it with you. It says:

> *What? know ye not that your body is the temple of the Holy Ghost which is in you, which ye have of God, and ye are not your own? For ye are bought with a price: therefore glorify God in your body, and in your spirit, which are God's.*
> 1 Corinthians 6:19, 20

This Scripture tells you that you are somebody. And you belong to Somebody—Somebody who is stronger and more caring and compassionate than any human being could ever be. It tells you that your body is sacred and precious—a temple indwelt by the Holy Spirit. It tells you that you are bought with a price and that price is the shed blood of God's Son, Jesus Christ (1 Peter 1:18, 19). Therefore, you don't belong to yourself. You belong to God. *You are God's property!*

This reminds me of the story of the little boy who made a tiny sailboat, which he sailed up and down the stream that cut across his father's farm. One day a wind blew it downstream, and it was lost. Sometime later he went to town with his parents and they passed a secondhand store. There in the window the boy saw a sailboat that looked exactly like his. He ran inside the store, picked up the boat, and saw where he'd carved his initials on the bottom. He secured the money from his dad and bought the boat back.

On the way home, the little boy was hugging the sailboat to his chest and his parents heard him saying, "Little boat, you're twice mine."

"Son, why do you say that?" his father asked.

"Well, Dad," he said. "It's mine first because I made it with my own hands, and it's mine twice because I bought it back."

In a way that's what God meant when He said, "Ye are bought with a price." We are twice God's. First, because He created us and, second, because with the death of His Son Jesus on the cross, He bought us back. When you think of yourself as belonging to God, when you know you are His property, it puts you in a take-charge position. Any time the devil is coming against you and you are hurting, you're in a pôsition to tell the devil, "Take your hands off me. I belong to God." And the devil will have to do it, because you've joined your life to God and you have His power in you!

November 29

Just Ask

A man once said to me, "Mr. Roberts, I've never asked God for anything, and I never intend to."

"Have you ever read the Bible?" I asked.

"Not much."

"Well, you should," I said, "Particularly the story about the ten lepers. They were ten miserable, lonely men—outcasts of society, seemingly hopeless cases. But they came to Jesus and cried out to Him, 'Have mercy on us' [Luke 17:13]. They weren't afraid to come and ask. And if they could ask, why can't you?"

Many people think they shouldn't ask God to help them. I don't know why. They must think that God is aloof, that He is not in the midst of their concerns. They must think that He is vague and unreal and mystical—so far away that He has no relationship—

to their human existence

to their toils

to their torments

to the experience of their everyday lives.

But this is not so. God is in the *now*. He is in the midst of your concerns. He is at the point of your need. All you have to do is ask.

> *Ask, and ye shall receive, that your joy may be full.*
> John 16:24

November 30

The War Is Over!

Do you remember reading about the amazing discovery of a World War II Japanese soldier who was living in the jungles of the Philippines, not knowing the war was over? Just think, all those years the man had struggled for survival by his wits, when he could have been enjoying the blessings of peace: plenty of food to eat, good clothes to wear, and the love and companionship of his family and friends.

Are you fighting wars that have already been won? Most of us do, you know. Tight lips struggle to hold in the misery of some heartache. Sleepless nights are spent worrying about health problems, about bills piling up with no money to pay them, or about the need of some loved one. We constantly engage in such skirmishes, when the battle has already been won. Isaiah prophesied victory over these wars through Jesus Christ:

> *Surely he hath borne our griefs, and carried our sorrows . . . . he was wounded for our transgressions, he was bruised for our iniquities: the chastisement of our peace was upon him; and with his stripes we are healed!*
>
> Isaiah 53:4, 5

On the cross Jesus proclaimed, "It is finished" (John 19:30). By faith you can claim victory over any battle you face. The war is over!

DECEMBER

December 1

Expectancy Fights Discouragement

It is said that two very special invisible presences confront you and me every day. One is a demon and one is an angel. The story is told that one day the devil saw that he was not as effective as he wanted to be. So he said to his various demons, "What have you been doing?" The demon of lust said, "I've caused millions to lust." The demon of murder said, "I've caused people to hate and to kill each other." The devil said, "It is not enough," and he reached into the darkest recesses of his kingdom, opened the door, and let out a very special demon. His name was Discouragement. And he sent him to earth.

In a few weeks Discouragement returned and the devil said, "Tell me what happened."

He said, "Things are different now. People are feeling alone. Thousands are depressed and discouraged."

The devil replied, "Then I have succeeded, for when I can discourage a person, I can defeat him."

At that very same time, God called His angels in for their reports. The angel of joy reported how he had spread joy. The angel of peace said he had given peace to people. The angels of health and happiness also gave bright reports. But God said, "It's not enough." And He too opened a door and brought forth a very special creature. It was the angel of miracles. He said, "I want you to go throughout the earth."

When the angel returned, God could tell by the look on his face that things were better. And He said to the angel of miracles, "What did you do?" The angel said, "I gave the people hope. They're straightening up. They're holding their heads high. They're believing. And they're expecting something good to happen to them."

That is just a story, but I believe the principle of it to be true in every detail. I believe a breakthrough from *heaven* is coming. And I remind you that the devil will try to fight you with discouragement. I also remind you that God will try to lift you up by the angel of miracles. The thing I want you to do—and it is most important—is to fight your discouragements by expecting miracles. (Read Psalm 94:19 LB.) Look at every problem you have from the standpoint of breakthrough through Jesus Christ—from *heaven!* God is a miracle-working God, and you can have miracle-living. Expect it!

December 2

Just One String Left

There is a story of a world-famous concert violinist who was thrilling his audience with great selections, one after another. Suddenly one of the strings on his violin broke, and he didn't have another string. Without saying anything he calmly continued playing on the three remaining strings. Then a second string broke. And, would you believe it, almost immediately a third string broke!

There he stood, not knowing what to do. The orchestra accompanying him began to get nervous. The crowd grew silent. Then the violinist looked up toward heaven, lifted his violin, raised his bow, and finished playing the beautiful number on one string. When he finished, the crowd cheered and stood to their feet applauding.

Life has a way of leaving us with . . .

　　just one string to play on . . .

　　　　just one dollar left in our pocket . . .

　　　　　　just one ray of hope to cling to.

But sometimes this is good, for then we are more likely to call upon God, who is our Source for all help. No situation is too hard for God and you together.

> *Fear thou not; for I am with thee: be not dismayed; for I am thy God: I will strengthen thee; yea, I will help thee.*
>
> Isaiah 41:10

December 3

No Charge

Christ Jesus . . . gave himself as a ransom for all men.
1 Timothy 2:5, 6 NIV

A little ten-year-old boy left a note on the dining table. When his mother picked it up, she read:

Dear Mom: For mowing the lawn, you owe me $1.00; for going to the store, 25¢; and for cleaning my room, 50¢.
Johnny

The mother called Johnny in, pulled him up beside her on the divan, and said, "Son, for cooking your meals every day and washing your clothes, Mother makes no charge. For sitting up with you day and night when you were sick in the hospital, no charge. And, Son, for going down into the valley of the shadow of death to bring you into this world, no charge." Then she said, "You can go now."

That evening the mother found the same note, but it was marked: PAID IN FULL!

In like manner, for going down into the valley of human suffering for our sins, Christ makes no charge. For taking our infirmities and carrying our sicknesses in His own body so that we can be whole, no charge. All He asks is that we love Him and live for Him.

December 4

The Lord Is My Helper
by SALLY JO SHELTON

The Lord is my helper; I shall not fret.
He makes me to rest upon His promises:
He stills the murmurings of my heart.
He revitalizes my whole being:
He shows me the right way to go that I may
   bring honor to Him.
Yes, though bewildering problems press on me
   from every side,
I will not be afraid: for You are with me;

Your Word and Your still small Voice, they
   reassure me.
You supply all I need even when shortages
   are all around me:
You fill me with your Holy Spirit;
   my joy overflows.
I know from deep within me that
Your goodness and compassion will
   always be my close companions:
And I will abide in Your presence forever.
                  Psalm 23 PARAPHRASED

December 5

Church in Our Hearts

It is a common expression to say we go *to* church, whereas Jesus teaches us we *are* the church. We place emphasis on a church building for worship, while a building is just so much brick, mortar, steel, and wood. Christ is the Head of the Church. The Church is His body, and we are members of His body. Therefore, wherever we are, whatever we do, we are *in* church because we *are* the church.

It was Jesus' custom to go to the synagogue on the Sabbath, but He spent little time in sacred buildings. *Everything* was sacred to Him. Most of Jesus' ministry took place in the streets, in the marketplace, on the fishing docks, and in homes.

There is no question about it—we are instructed not to forsake "the assembling of ourselves together" for worship. But we are taught to come together with other believers for much the same purpose that we drive our car into a filling station. We don't park there. Once the car is filled up, we drive out and put it to use. We go to a church building to be filled with God's Spirit, edified, and inspired. Then with our hearts stirred, we go out where people with needs are—where the action is—to minister and to share Christ. *We worship in buildings, but the church is in our hearts.*

Read Luke 4:15; 1 Corinthians 12; 14:26; Ephesians 1:22, 23; Hebrews 10:25.

December 6

"Internalize" Jesus

As often as ye eat this bread, and drink this cup, ye do shew
the Lord's death till he come.

1 Corinthians 11:26

Jesus made His death and resurrection a communion through which you can receive both spiritual and physical healing. As you take the bread and wine, you are taking our Lord's health into your being.

I remember once in a Communion service I sat near a woman who was wheeled into the meeting in a wheelchair. She hadn't walked in months. As she ate and drank of our Lord's death and resurrection, she said a warmth went through her and a force struck her feet and legs. I saw her get up out of her wheelchair and walk. Then I saw her run. "What happened?" I asked.

"Oh, Brother Roberts," she said, "when I took the Communion, it seemed like Jesus exploded in me. I am healed!"

This woman grasped the full meaning of the Holy Communion— that just as you take the bread and the wine into your body and they eventually become a part of your body, in the same way you are taking Jesus into your being. You are "internalizing" Him—letting our resurrected Lord, who has no imperfections in His body and spirit, become a part of you—drawing upon His health, peace and joy—receiving all that He is for all that you need.

December 7

No Distance in Prayer

[Jesus said:] He [the Holy Spirit] dwelleth with you, and
shall be in you. I will not leave you comfortless: I will come
to you.

John 14:17, 18

When you have a need, you don't have to go anywhere for Christ to come to you. Through the Holy Spirit, Christ lives *in* you and there is no distance between you and Him.

The first understanding I had of this great truth was in the 1950s. I received a letter from a woman in Maryland. At the time, I was conducting a crusade in California, so her letter went from the East Coast to the West Coast. She wrote:

> *Brother Roberts, I am very ill. I wanted to come to your crusade and have you pray for me but I can't. So I am writing you instead and asking you to pray for me. I realize there is no distance in prayer . . . .*

A shock of comprehension swept through my being. It was an electrifying current of understanding. There I was some 2,000 miles from this woman, but suddenly she caught hold of a tremendous truth—*There is no distance in prayer!*

She wrote: "You pray there, and I'll pray here, and God will heal me." I prayed for her and wrote back to her. In a short time I received another letter from her, praising God for her healing!

December 8

Hold Jesus High

All men should honour the Son.
John 5:23

The greatest compliment I ever received was given to me years ago by a groom in the stables of a farm I was visiting. The owner had introduced me to the groom, who said:

> Brother Roberts, not long ago, one of the ladies from our church went to your crusade in Missouri. When she came back, the church people gathered around her and said, "We want you to tell us all about the crusade. What does Brother Roberts look like? What did he do?"
>
> She said, "Well, I didn't see Oral Roberts."
>
> "Didn't you go to the crusade?" they asked.
>
> "Yes, I was in every service. I saw the prayer line. I heard the sermons," she replied.
>
> "Well, what do you mean, you didn't see Oral Roberts?" they demanded.
>
> She smiled and said, "That man held Jesus so high, I couldn't see him for seeing Jesus."

I thanked the groom. But I went away with a thankfulness in my heart that I was doing what God had called me and all those who serve Him to do—to lift Jesus high. The world still says to us, as the visiting Greeks said to the disciples, "We would see Jesus." *Our business is to hold Him high.*

December 9

Love with No Strings Attached

Perfect love casteth out fear.
1 John 4:18

Everyone needs to feel loved for his own personal worth, not for how he acts or looks or for any other reason. But without realizing it most of us attach strings to our love. "I'll love you—*if* you love me, *if* you're good, *if* you live up to my expectations."

When being loved depends upon meeting conditions, you're always afraid. "What if I fail to please? Will I lose that person's love?" Somehow you realize you aren't loved just for yourself and, therefore, you feel you're not really loved at all.

Do you remember when Tevye in *Fiddler on the Roof* asked his wife, "Do you love me?" She enumerated all the years she had lived with him and all the things she had done for him. Even so, she had still not answered his question, "Do you love *me?*"

Something in you knows that true love is not something earned, but something freely given. The only love that works all the time is love with no strings attached. "I love you for yourself—just the way you are," are miraculous words. They free a person to be himself, to reach his full potential.

December 10

Open the Door to a Miracle

I once encountered a desperately ill woman who said to me, "Brother Roberts, I am reconciled now to the fact that my illness is the will of God." *She was shutting the door to a miracle in her life.* And that hurt me. I pulled a New Testament out of my coat pocket and read to her: "The Son can do nothing of himself, but what he seeth the Father do: for what things soever he doeth, these also doeth the Son likewise" (John 5:19).

I asked her, "What did Jesus do when He was on earth?"

"He helped people. He healed them."

"If Jesus walked into this room today, would you say what you have just said to me?"

I said, "In other words, in your mind God and Jesus are opposites. Jesus would heal you, but God won't."

She thought that over carefully. I reminded her that Jesus said, "The Father and I are one." Jesus came into the world to show us what God is like.

"Brother Roberts, are you saying that Jesus in me is God!"

I said, "Precisely. Jesus in you is God."

I will never forget what she said then. "Oh! Then will you pray for me that Jesus will heal me?"

I've often said that a miracle doesn't come from the outside in. A miracle starts inside you, with Jesus. And that's where I saw this woman's miracle start—in her attitude—in her understanding of God. I saw Jesus Christ become real to her in the now of her need and illness. Down deep inside she knew that God was going to raise her up.

Are you sick? There are all kinds of things that make people ill. You can be sick with fear, worry, and depression, or with the sinking feeling of being alone and unloved—because sickness is anything that brings disharmony in your spirit, mind, or body. If you give in to this sickness and accept it, you are shutting the door to a miracle. Jesus in you is God saying, *I want you to live.* Open the door to the possibility of a miracle in your life through your believing!

December 11

Treasures You Cannot Buy
by EVELYN ROBERTS

I had a woman tell me once that she thought everybody who was at church on Sunday morning was a Christian. Why else would they be there?

I said, "They are Christians if they have accepted Jesus Christ and have a personal relationship with Him."

I think this is what Jesus was saying to the young man who came to Him and asked, "Good Master, what shall I do that I may inherit eternal life?" Jesus said, "One thing thou lackest: go thy way, sell whatsoever thou hast, and give to the poor.''

Jesus didn't mean that everyone who has food and clothes and a place to live ought to sell them or give them away. He meant that, although this young man had kept the commandments, he lacked the most important thing, which was to put God first. His wealth and possessions were first. He lacked the love that Jesus Christ wants us to have and to share with other people. The Bible says the young man was sad ''and went away grieved: for he had great possessions'' (Mark 10:17–31).

We might think this story was put in the Bible just for rich people. But we're all rich in something. Maybe we don't have a lot of money, but many of us have something that we're tempted to put before a personal relationship with Jesus Christ. We can put a dollar before God. We can have a child that we put first. Sometimes we put our husband or wife, or our parents first. It can be a house, a car, or a job. But whoever or whatever takes the most of our time and is uppermost in our thoughts and affections is what we are putting first. Jesus was saying to this young man, ''Let Me be first in your affections, your thoughts, your actions, and start giving to the poor.''

Give! This is the seed-faith concept. And Jesus said it is one thing we lack. He was talking about more than money; He was talking about the giving of ourselves. It is often easier to give money than to give two hours of our time. Most of us say, ''I've got so many troubles I can't think of anybody else's problems.'' But when you minister to someone who has a need or a problem, you are giving ''to the poor.''

It's an exchange. You give whatever you have in exchange for treasures. Treasures are those things of a heavenly nature that you cannot buy: peace, personal fulfillment, healing, eternal life. Jesus said, *''Put Me first in your life, start giving, and you will have great treasure.''*

December 12

Nothing Is Too Hard

Is any thing too hard for the Lord?
Genesis 18:14

The other day, while driving through the desert, I looked over to the side of the road and I saw flowers growing out of bare rocks. I pulled over to get a better look, and I wondered how in the world flowers could come up out of rock. It occurred to me that at some time the winds had blown some seeds, and they had lodged in the cracks of the rocks and found a little bit of soil. A little rain came in and the seeds got connected to the soil and the water and started growing, and they burst through the rock and bloomed. Not even rock could keep the seeds from bursting forth.

I thought, *My, there must be a lot of God in a tiny seed, for it to be able to break through rock!*

Does your problem seem too hard, even for God? God can break through rock. God can break through impenetrable surfaces. God can break through impossible situations.

> *Ah Lord God! behold, thou hast made the heaven and the earth by thy great power and stretched out arm, and there is nothing too hard for thee.*
>
> Jeremiah 32:17

December 13

Babe Ruth's Philosophy

So let us never tire of doing good, for if we do not slacken our efforts we shall in due time reap our harvest.

Galatians 6:9 NEB

When we hear the name Babe Ruth, most of us think of the great home-run king. But did you know that he struck out more times than he made home runs? This man developed a philosophy. He said, "I have noticed that every time I strike out three times, I am due two home runs."

In one game, pitcher Lefty Grove struck the Babe out three times in succession. When Babe stepped up to bat the fourth time, the crowd was roaring for Lefty to strike him out again. Then it dawned on the Babe, *It's my time to get a home run!* He said, "Suddenly there was a surge of power that came up within me." Babe pointed the bat, and a breathless hush fell over the crowd. Lefty wound up and let go a ball with such blazing speed the eye could barely follow it. With a crack, the ball went sailing over the fence and out of the park.

You see, the Babe knew that he was due a home run. It's the same when you sow seeds of faith. There's a time for God to multiply it back to you. You may call it a harvest or a miracle. Whatever it is, it's wonderful, and it comes from God.

December 14

Commitment Is Discipleship

*Their giving surpassed our expectations; for they gave their
very selves . . . to the Lord.*

2 Corinthians 8:5 NEB

You may have heard the story about the chicken and the pig.
They were walking along together one morning when they came
upon some weary, hungry travelers. "Let's give them a breakfast
of ham and eggs," the chicken suggested.

"That's OK for you," the pig replied. "You'd only be making a
contribution, but for me that would mean total commitment!"

That's quite a difference! It's about the same as comparing conversion with commitment.

Salvation means giving your heart to Jesus.

Commitment means giving your whole self to Him—discipleship.

A disciple is a learner, a *now* follower of Christ. This involves a
continuous reaching out of the soul, a burning desire to know Jesus
better, so that you become more like Him. You can sum it up in one
key statement: *Commitment is opening up yourself to the living
Christ and giving of your whole self to Him—in joy—daily!*

December 15

Thank You, Lord

Be thankful unto him and bless his name.
Psalm 100:4

When Jesus healed the ten lepers, only one returned to give Him
thanks, and His wistful question has been echoing ever since:
"Where are the nine?"

Perhaps it is not that we are ungrateful at heart. It is more that we
are not thoughtful enough to speak out. A little girl expressed what
really happens many times. Her uncle brought her a beautiful doll
when he returned from a trip. "Did you thank him for it?" her
mother asked.

"Oh, yes, Mamma," the child replied, "but I didn't tell him so."

In our hearts we are thankful for God's blessings—for health, for
salvation, for sound minds, and the joy of living—but have we told
Him so?

December 16

Remove the Stone

When Jesus raised Lazarus from the dead, He said five words that have tremendous personal meaning to us: *Take ye away the stone* (John 11:39).

Even though Mary and Martha had sent for Jesus to come, they weren't expecting Him to do anything. A stone stood between them and a miracle. Sometimes it is the same with us. Our faith is blocked by a stone. A stone of fear. A stone of doubt. A stone of hopelessness.

Out of fear and doubt, Martha began to argue, "Lord, by this time his body is deteriorating." Jesus said, *Take ye away the stone.*

"But, Lord, he's been dead four days!" *Take ye away the stone.*

You too may be arguing, "Lord, I cannot get well. The doctor says my case is hopeless." *Take ye away the stone.*

"Lord, my finances are so messed up, I know I'll go bankrupt." *Take ye away the stone.*

"My marriage—there's nothing left to build on." *Take ye away the stone.*

You can argue with the Lord until you completely talk yourself out of your miracle. When the people finally removed the stone, Jesus performed the miracle. The dead man—Lazarus—came forth. The problem was solved and their need was met. Find your stone, move it out of the way with your faith, and make room for the miracle God wants to give you.

December 17

Somebody Really Special

When the angel of God appeared to Mary and told her that she, of all the young Jewish women, was chosen to bear the baby Jesus, she said, "How? I'm a virgin." And the angel answered, "The Holy Spirit is going to mysteriously overshadow you. The seed for this child will be put in your womb by the Spirit."

Now this is beyond human comprehension, even today. But this was Mary's response: "Behold the handmaid of the Lord; be it unto me according to thy word" (Luke 1:38).

Mary was asked to do a hard thing, and sometimes God asks us to do hard things. But we can go ahead and do them if we know we don't have to do them by ourselves. We can depend on the Spirit of God to do them through us. And this is what Mary did. She simply yielded herself to the Holy Spirit and said, "Lord, work through me. I want whatever You want to happen, just as You say."

Mary gave herself to God as a vessel. And today we look on her as somebody really special because she did that. But when we give ourselves as vessels in whom the Holy Spirit can dwell and through whom He can work, then we are special, too.

December 18

A Confirmation

After Mary was told she was to have a child, she went to the home of her cousin Elisabeth. Mary needed to talk things over with someone, and Elisabeth would understand, because God was miraculously enabling her to have a child as well. And her child was to be John the Baptist, the forerunner of Christ.

As Mary entered her cousin's home, the baby in Elisabeth's womb leaped for joy. And Elisabeth prophesied, "Blessed is the fruit of thy womb . . . . And blessed is she that believed: for there shall be a performance of those things which were told her from the Lord" (Luke 1:42, 45).

No doubt Mary wondered if perhaps she had just imagined the angel and what he had told her. But through Elisabeth, God's message was confirmed to Mary, and she was able to return to Nazareth with assurance that things were going as the angel had said they would.

When God begins working in our lives in a new way, it's good for us to talk things over with a fellow believer—someone who understands God and His ways. And often God will speak to us through that person, to give us the encouragement and confirmation we need to carry out what He has asked us to do.

December 19

Man on the Spot

When the angel told Mary she was to be the mother of Jesus, she was already engaged to be married to Joseph. In those days engagement or betrothal was as legally binding as marriage. Unfaithfulness during the year of betrothal was considered equivalent to adultery.

So when Joseph found out Mary was going to have a baby, the only solution he knew was divorce. But then God spoke to him through an angel and said, "Joseph . . . fear not to take unto thee Mary thy wife: for that which is conceived in her is of the Holy Ghost" (Matthew 1:20).

Joseph was really put on the spot. How many men would marry a woman who was carrying a baby that wasn't their own, then raise the child as well? Yet this is what Joseph did. He believed God and obeyed Him, even though he knew people would ridicule him for it. But because he did, Joseph had the privilege of becoming Jesus' earthly guardian and saving the Child's life by taking Him to Egypt, away from Herod's wrath.

Joseph shows us what to do when we're put on the spot—when God asks us to do something others might not understand. And that's simply to obey, knowing God will reward us richly for any sacrifice we have to make.

December 20

A Touch of Greatness

Bethlehem is a little town just south of Jerusalem. If you visited there today you would see that it hasn't changed much in the last two thousand years. Camels still carry their loads in caravans, shepherds still watch over their flocks, and turbaned and robed townspeople still trudge along the roads.

But that little town is the biggest town in the world at least once a year—at Christmastime. And in God's eyes it will always have a special significance, a touch of greatness, because there in that little town His Son Jesus Christ was born. There was fulfilled one of the great prophecies of the Bible: "And thou Bethlehem, in the land of Juda, art not the least among the princes of Juda: for out of thee shall come a Governor, that shall rule my people Israel" (Matthew 2:6).

Now it's significant that Jesus was not born in Jerusalem or Babylon or Rome or any of the other great cities of that time—that He was born in a town of a few hundred people. It's significant because it tells us the important thing in life isn't to be considered big by the *world's* standards. Rather, the important thing is to have a "touch of greatness" in *God's* eyes because we have allowed His will to be done in our lives.

December 21

A Divine Destiny

It has been said that when God gets ready to lift an empire off its hinges, to change the course of human history, or to save the world, He has a baby born somewhere. And He gives that baby some of His own attributes with which to do the job.

When God was ready to come to earth, He had a child born in Bethlehem. He gave to that child all of His attributes and sent Him into the world to save it (Matthew 1:21).

Whoever would have thought that the baby in the manger—so little, so helpless, so vulnerable—was destined to become great? Yet the angel foretold, "He . . . shall be called the Son of the Highest: and the Lord God shall give unto him the throne of his father David: and he shall reign over the house of Jacob for ever; and of his kingdom there shall be no end" (Luke 1:32, 33).

I believe that for every baby born, God has a divine destiny. Oh, you may shrink from what God has called you to do and ask, "How can I do that?" But God knew what He was doing when He had you born. And you are not to berate yourself by wishing you were someone else or that you were made in some different way. God made you the way you are, and He has a special purpose for your life.

December 22

Put First Things First

Think a moment about the shepherds and how the angel appeared to them and told them that the baby Jesus was born. Afterwards they said to one another, "Let us now go even unto Bethlehem, and see this thing which is come to pass" (Luke 2:15).

Shepherds never leave their flocks—especially not at night—because of the danger of wild animals and thieves. But these shepherds believed the angel's message and left their most precious earthly possessions—the sheep that had been committed to their care. They put aside their sense of duty and responsibility to do their job. Why? Because they felt a dream: the dream of becoming a part of something so important it overshadowed any of their private plans.

The shepherds saw something far greater than tending sheep— the opportunity to look with their own eyes upon the Lord's Christ. Of course they hurried back to their sheep as soon as they could, but they put first things first. And that's what God is always urging us to do: to put Him first, to be willing to put aside our personal plans so that we can become part of something far greater than ourselves.

December 23

The Star Disappeared

Has God told you to do something, but now that you've been doing it for a while, you've begun to doubt that God really told you to do it in the first place? This may have happened to the wise men.

You see, according to many Bible scholars, the wise men didn't follow the star from the East to Bethlehem, as many of us learned in Sunday school. Rather, when they saw the star in the East, they simply recognized it as a star of royalty and went out in search of the newborn King.

Arriving in Jerusalem, they were told that prophecy said a King would be born in Bethlehem, and so they started that way. And as they went, the star reappeared and went before them into Bethlehem. Apparently the wise men hadn't seen the star for quite a while, perhaps since the beginning of their journey, for when they saw it, "they rejoiced with exceeding great joy" (Matthew 2:10).

Often God gives us a "star," a clear indication of something He wants us to do. But then the star disappears. For a time there is no outward evidence that we're on the right track. But just as God allowed the star to reappear to the wise men, so He will confirm that we are going in the right direction if we keep on doing what God has said—if we don't turn back.

December 24

"Fear Not"

Have you ever noticed how the angels in the Christmas story were always telling people not to be afraid? First, the angel Gabriel appeared to Zacharias. His first words were: *Fear not* (Luke 1:13). Then Gabriel came to Mary. Again he said: *Fear not* (Luke 1:30). Later the angel said those same words to Joseph in a dream (Matthew 1:20).

When the angel appeared to the shepherds in the field, "They were sore afraid." And once more the angel said: *"Fear not"* (Luke 2:9, 10).

There must be something awe-inspiring about angels, for them to have to always reassure people that everything is all right, that we are not to be afraid, when they appear. And if people are that afraid of angels, how much more afraid they must be of God Himself!

Through the angels, God is saying to us over and over, "You don't have to be afraid of Me. I love you." God wants us to fear Him, in the sense of our obeying Him and reverencing Him. But He doesn't want us to be terrified of Him or afraid to ask for His help when we need it.

This Christmas, God is inviting us to "come boldly [without fear or hesitation] unto the throne of grace, that we may obtain mercy, and find grace to help in time of need" (Hebrews 4:16).

December 25

Don't Throw It Away

Forty days after the birth of Jesus, Mary and Joseph took Him to Jerusalem to present Him to the Lord.

Simeon, a righteous and devout man, had come to the temple that day by the leading of the Holy Spirit. He had been waiting for the coming of the Messiah, and God had revealed to him that he would not die until he had seen the Lord's Christ. "And when the parents brought in the child Jesus, to do for him after the custom of the law, Then [Simeon] took . . . him up in his arms, and blessed God, and said, Lord, now lettest thou thy servant depart in peace, according to thy word: For mine eyes have seen thy salvation" (Luke 2:27–30).

Tradition says Simeon was an extremely old man, but he had not given up on God's promise that he would see the Messiah. Hundreds of years had passed since the prophets had foretold the Messiah's coming, and many of Simeon's contemporaries had given up on the idea, but Simeon never did. He clung to God's promise, and God honored his heart's desire.

> *Do not throw away your confidence; it will be richly rewarded. You need to persevere so that when you have done the will of God, you will receive what [God] has promised.*
> Hebrews 10:35, 36 NIV

December 26

Know-It-All

Following the tragic death of a young woman in the community, fifteen-year-old Rusty turned to his mother. "Why did God let this happen?" he asked.

It was a hard question to answer. "Well, Rusty, sometimes we do rash things and then we have to bear the consequences. And sometimes Satan steps in and tries to destroy us . . . ." She hesitated a moment, then continued, "But sometimes, Rusty, I just don't know why."

To hear someone say, "I don't know," is refreshing these days. Many of us seem to have the idea there's something wrong about not knowing. But there are some things God doesn't intend for us to understand completely.

When Job was struggling with why tragedy had struck him, he had some know-it-all friends who said things like: "Job, you're suffering because you've sinned. You should repent." But Job didn't let them get him down. He said: *There is only One who knows it all.* "Only with God is [perfect] wisdom and might; He alone has [true] counsel and understanding" (Job 12:13 AMPLIFIED).

Perhaps the best way to deal with the whys that crop up when bad things happen is to admit, "I don't know why this happened. But I do know that no matter how bad things seem, God is in control and *He hath done all things well*" (Mark 7:37).

December 27

Why Obedience Is Better Than Sacrifice
by EVELYN ROBERTS

*Behold, to obey is better than sacrifice . . . for rebellion is
. . . sin.*

1 Samuel 15:22, 23

I used to read the Scripture, "Obedience is better than sacrifice," and I wondered, *How can obedience be better than sacrifice?*

Then one day, during the years of the riots, I heard about a young man who stood in front of a government building in Washington, D.C., poured gasoline on himself, and set himself on fire.

That young man sacrificed his life. But it didn't help him, and it didn't help anybody else. However, it did cause me to understand why being obedient to God is far better than sacrifice. It brought home to me the Scripture that says, "Though I give my body to be burned, and have not [love], it profiteth me nothing" (1 Corinthians 13:3).

Sacrifice, as noble as it sounds, can have an element of self-will, a seed of rebellion. Obedience is better, because it sets aside all self-will in order to do God's will.

December 28

Unplanted Seed

When the ancient Egyptians died, many of their possessions were put into the tomb with them. Recently one of the tombs was unearthed where the person had been dead about 2,500 years, and buried with him was a big sack of wheat. The discoverers were curious to know what would happen if the wheat were planted after so many years. So they planted it. Lo and behold, it grew and produced a harvest! But this poor guy died and left unplanted seed—a wasted harvest.

Think about your life. Do you feel it is messed up and nothing is going right? Maybe you're not expecting miracles because you have no aim in life. And yet within you, you have these seeds of faith you could plant. Seeds of your love, seeds of your concern, seeds of your forgiveness. It may be that's the very seed God wants you to plant for the most wonderful harvest your life has ever known. Unplanted seed can never produce a harvest, but when you plant it with God, you have the promise of a miracle in your life.

> *And [God] who provides seed for the sower . . . will also provide and multiply your [resources for] sowing, and increase the fruits of your righteousness [which manifests itself in active goodness, kindness and charity]. Thus you will be enriched in all things and in every way.*
>   2 Corinthians 9:10, 11 AMPLIFIED

December 29

Special-Delivery Letter

Has anyone ever sent you a special-delivery letter? One time someone sent me one (I wasn't expecting it) and I wasn't at home to receive it when the postman brought it. Do you know what he did with it? He took it back. The next day, when the postman brought it back, I was home and I received it. Now suppose I had kept on being "gone." Where do you think that special delivery letter would have ended up? In the dead-letter office in Washington, D.C.

Do you know that when you plant your seed, trusting in God your Source, that God will multiply it? God will send you a miracle. But if you're not expecting it, you can miss it.

When people say, "I'm not getting miracles," there is usually one of two reasons. Either they've not put in the seed, or if they have planted seed, they're not expecting any return, any harvest. When their miracle comes, they miss it, and they think God has forgotten them and they ask, "Where are You, God?" (*See* Judges 6:13.)

You have a miracle coming toward you or going past you every day; therefore expect it. *Reach out and receive your miracle today!*

December 30

The Holy Spirit Is God Himself Living in You

Have you ever wondered who the Holy Spirit is and what His work is? I think the way to understand is to think of God coming down in the likeness of a human being—Jesus Christ—and Christ being here on earth, feeling what we feel and going through what we go through. Therefore, He knows how to take us through it.

Then think of Jesus saying, "I've got to go away. I can't remain here in this limited human body, because I have to deal with time, space, and death just like any other human does. When I go away, however, I will not leave you alone. I will send you the Holy Spirit—another Comforter, another One like Me." (*See* John 14:16–26; 16:7.)

That means God was going to replace the physical presence of Jesus with Himself in the form of His own Spirit. God is a Spirit—*holy* Spirit. Jesus said, "The Holy Spirit dwells *with* you, but He shall be *in* you."

There's a lot of difference in having food on your plate beside you and having that food inside your stomach. There's a lot of difference in having God here in the flesh beside you, walking with you, and having God and the Holy Spirit inside you.

So the Holy Spirit is God, in His unlimited form, living inside you in your spirit. Your spirit is the only unlimited part of you. Your mind is limited and your body is limited. But your spirit is unlimited, and that's where the unlimited Holy Spirit is, making you unlimited inwardly.

You can do everything God said you can do, and you can be everything He said you can be, because God Himself is living *in* you!

December 31

Make Next Year More Exciting
by EVELYN ROBERTS

At the end of each year I like to get rid of all the things that are pulling me down spiritually and mentally—things like mistakes, failures, disappointments, frustrations, and hurts.

Here's how I do it. I write each of them down separately on a slip of paper. Then I get a wastebasket, read them off one at a time, wad them up, and throw them into the wastebasket. By doing this I get my mind and spirit cleaned out and start the new year with nothing weighing me down. This new year I challenge you to do this with me. And here's the biblical basis for it:

> *Let us lay aside every weight . . . and let us run with patience the race that is set before us, looking unto Jesus.*
>
> Hebrews 12:1, 2

After I've thrown out the bad things of last year, I do something positive. I don't want to leave myself empty. Emptiness creates a vacuum. So I fill that vacuum with a goal or a purpose.

You can't achieve goals if you don't have any. Sometimes this idea is so simple that many people pass it by. In order to accomplish anything, we've got to first purpose in our hearts to do it. We've got to make up our minds. If we don't, we just waste our time and energy and find ourselves going around in circles, looking back at the past and wondering where it went.

There is one ultimate goal that all of us can strive for—"the goal to win the [supreme . . .] prize to which God in Christ Jesus is calling us" (Philippians 3:14 AMPLIFIED).

Life is exciting with Jesus in it! You're always looking ahead and wondering what good thing the Lord has for you around the next corner. Purpose to lay aside every weight and keep Jesus Christ uppermost in your heart and life, and next year can be the most exciting year of your life!

INDEX

Although it is my prayer that the strengthening power of God's Word combined with a devotional reading may provide a fresh new start for each day, the following topical index may be a helpful reference for those of you who face a specific need which God will answer—on *any* day. *O. R.*

Dear Friend,

My prayer for you is that DAILY BLESSING will help you learn that God is greater than any problem you have. But, I want to go beyond that. I want to pray for you personally. So, I invite you to write me and tell me your prayer request. I promise I'll pray and I'll write you back. Simply address your letter:

Oral Roberts
Tulsa, Oklahoma 74171

If you have a special prayer request, I also invite you to call the Abundant Life Prayer Group at (918)492-7777. Call anytime, day or night, and a trained prayer partner will answer your call and pray with you.

Oral Roberts